Eleventh Hour CISSP®

Eleventh Hour CISSP®
Study Guide
Third Edition

Eric Conrad

Seth Misenar

Joshua Feldman

Bryan Simon, Technical Editor

ELSEVIER

AMSTERDAM • BOSTON • HEIDELBERG • LONDON
NEW YORK • OXFORD • PARIS • SAN DIEGO
SAN FRANCISCO • SINGAPORE • SYDNEY • TOKYO

SYNGRESS.

Syngress is an Imprint of Elsevier

Syngress is an imprint of Elsevier
50 Hampshire Street, 5th Floor, Cambridge, MA 02139, United States

Notices

Knowledge and best practice in this field are constantly changing. As new research and experience
broaden our understanding, changes in research methods, professional practices, or medical treatment
may become necessary.

Practitioners and researchers must always rely on their own experience and knowledge in evaluating and
using any information, methods, compounds, or experiments described herein. In using such information
or methods they should be mindful of their own safety and the safety of others, including parties for
whom they have a professional responsibility.

To the fullest extent of the law, neither the Publisher nor the authors, contributors, or editors, assume any
liability for any injury and/or damage to persons or property as a matter of products liability, negligence
or otherwise, or from any use or operation of any methods, products, instructions, or ideas contained in
the material herein.

Library of Congress Cataloging-in-Publication Data
A catalog record for this book is available from the Library of Congress

British Library Cataloguing-in-Publication Data
A catalogue record for this book is available from the British Library

ISBN: 978-0-12-811248-9

For information on all Syngress publications visit our
website at https://www.elsevier.com/

Working together
to grow libraries in
developing countries

www.elsevier.com   www.bookaid.org

Acquisition Editor: Todd Green
Editorial Project Manager: Anna Valutkevich
Production Project Manager: Mohana Natarajan
Cover Designer: Alan Studholme

Typeset by SPi Global, India

Contents

Author biography

Eric Conrad (CISSP, GIAC GSE, GPEN, GCIH, GCIA, GCFA, GAWN, GSEC, GISP, GCED), is a senior SANS instructor and CTO of Backshore Communications, which provides information warfare, hunt teaming, penetration testing, incident handling, and intrusion detection consulting services. He started his professional career in 1991 as a UNIX systems administrator for a small oceanographic communications company. He gained information security experience in a variety of industries, including research, education, power, Internet, and health care, in positions ranging from systems programmer to security engineer to HIPAA security officer and ISSO. He is lead author of *MGT414: SANS Training Program for CISSP® Certification*, and co-author of both *SANS SEC511: Continuous Monitoring and Security Operations* and *SANS SEC542: Web App Penetration Testing and Ethical Hacking*. He graduated from the SANS Technology Institute with a master of science degree in information security engineering, and he earned his bachelor of arts in English from Bridgewater State College. He lives in Peaks Island, Maine, with his family, Melissa, Eric, and Emma. His website is http://ericconrad.com.

Joshua Feldman (CISSP) is a vice president at Moody's, a bond ratings agency critical to the security, health, and welfare of the global commerce sector. He drives M&A, security architecture, design, and integration efforts for IT Risk and InfoSec. Before taking on this promotion, Feldman was the Enterprise Security Architect for Corning, Inc., where he helped to deliver numerous security transformations for Corning and was a key team member focused on maturing the security function. From 2002 to 2012, he worked as the technical director of a US DoD cybersecurity services contract. Supporting the DoD, he helped create the current standard used for assessing cyberthreats and analyzing potential adversaries for impact. During his tenure, he supported many DoD organizations including the Office of the Secretary of Defense, DISA, and the Combatant Commands. He got his start in the cybersecurity field when he left his high school science teaching position in 1997 and began working for Network Flight Recorder (NFR, Inc.), a small Washington, DC-based startup, making the first generation of network intrusion detection systems (NIDS). He earned a master of science in cyber operations from National Defense University and a bachelor of science degree from the University of Maryland. He currently resides in New York, with his two dogs, Jacky and Lily.

Seth Misenar (CISSP, GIAC GSE, GSEC, GPPA, GCIA, GCIH, GCWN, GCFA, GWAPT, GPEN) is a cybersecurity expert who serves as a senior instructor with the SANS Institute and as a principal consultant at Context Security, LLC. He is numbered among the few security experts worldwide to have achieved the GIAC GSE (#28) credential. He teaches a variety of cybersecurity courses for the SANS Institute including two very popular courses for which he is lead author: the bestselling

SEC511: Continuous Monitoring and Security Operations and SEC542: Web Application Penetration Testing and Ethical Hacking. He also serves as coauthor for MGT414: SANS Training Program for CISSP® Certification. His background includes security research, intrusion analysis, incident response, security architecture design, and network and web application penetration testing. He has previously served as a security consultant for Fortune 100 companies and as the HIPAA security officer for a state government agency. He has a bachelor of science degree in philosophy from Millsaps College and resides in Jackson, Mississippi, with his wife, Rachel, and children, Jude, Hazel, and Shepherd.

Bryan Simon, CISSP is an internationally recognized expert in cybersecurity and has been working in the information technology and security field since 1991. Over the course of his career, Bryan has held various technical and managerial positions in the education, environmental, accounting, and financial services sectors. Bryan speaks on a regular basis at international conferences and with the press on matters of cybersecurity. He has instructed individuals from organizations such as the FBI, NATO, and the UN in matters of cybersecurity, on three continents. Bryan has specialized expertise in defensive and offensive capabilities. He has received recognition for his work in IT Security and was most recently profiled by McAfee (part of Intel Security) as an IT Hero. Bryan holds 11 GIAC Certifications including GSEC, GCWN, GCIH, GCFA, GPEN, GWAPT, GAWN, GISP, GCIA, GCED, and GCUX. Bryan's scholastic achievements have resulted in the honor of him sitting as a current member of the Advisory Board for the SANS Institute and his acceptance into the prestigious SANS Cyber Guardian Program. Bryan is a SANS Certified Instructor for SEC401: Security Essentials Bootcamp Style, SEC501: Advanced Security Essentials - Enterprise Defender, SEC505: Securing Windows with PowerShell and the Critical Security Controls, and SEC511: Continuous Monitoring and Security Operations.

Bryan dedicates this book to his little boy, Jesse. Daddy loves you!!!

Domain 1: Security risk management

1

CHAPTER OUTLINE

Eleventh Hour CISSP®. http://dx.doi.org/10.1016/B978-0-12-811248-9.00001-2

INTRODUCTION

Our job as information security professionals is to evaluate *risks* against our critical *assets* and deploy *safeguards* to mitigate those risks. We work in various roles: firewall engineers, penetration testers, auditors, management, etc. The common thread is risk, which is part of our job description.

The Security and Risk Management domain focuses on risk analysis and mitigation. This domain also details security governance, or the organizational structure required for a successful information security program. The difference between organizations that are successful versus those that fail in this realm is usually not tied to budget or staff size; rather, it is tied to the right people in the right roles. Knowledgeable and experienced information security staff with supportive and vested leadership is the key to success.

Speaking of leadership, learning to speak the language of your leadership is another key to personal success in this industry. The ability to effectively communicate information security concepts with C-level executives is a rare and needed skill. This domain will also help you to speak their language by discussing risk in terms such as *total cost of ownership (TCO)* and *return on investment (ROI)*.

CORNERSTONE INFORMATION SECURITY CONCEPTS

Before we can explain access control, we must define cornerstone information security concepts. These concepts provide the foundation upon which the eight domains of the Common Body of Knowledge are built.

CONFIDENTIALITY, INTEGRITY, AND AVAILABILITY

Confidentiality, *integrity*, and *availability* are referred to as the CIA triad, which is the cornerstone concept of information security. The triad, shown in Fig. 1.1, forms the three-legged stool upon which information security is built. The order of the acronym may change (some prefer AIC, perhaps to avoid association with a certain intelligence agency), but that is not important; what is critical is understanding each concept. This book will use the CIA acronym.

Confidentiality
Confidentiality seeks to prevent the unauthorized disclosure of information; it keeps data secret. In other words, confidentiality seeks to prevent unauthorized read access to data. An example of a confidentiality attack would be the theft of *personally identifiable information* (PII), such as credit card information.

Integrity
Integrity seeks to prevent unauthorized modification of information. In other words, integrity seeks to prevent unauthorized write access to data.

FIG. 1.1

The CIA triad.

CRUNCH TIME

There are two types of integrity: data integrity and system integrity. Data integrity seeks to protect information from unauthorized modification, while system integrity seeks to protect a system, such as a Windows 2012 server operating system, from unauthorized modification.

Availability

Availability ensures that information is available when needed. Systems need to be usable (available) for normal business use. An example of attack on availability would be a *denial of service* (DoS) attack, which seeks to deny service (or availability) of a system.

Disclosure, alteration, and destruction

The CIA triad may also be described by its opposite: *disclosure, alteration, and destruction* (DAD). Disclosure is the unauthorized release of information, alteration is the unauthorized modification of data, and destruction is making systems or data unavailable. While the order of the individual components of the CIA acronym sometimes changes, the DAD acronym is shown in that order.

IDENTITY AND AUTHENTICATION, AUTHORIZATION, AND ACCOUNTABILITY

The term AAA is often used to describe the cornerstone concepts *authentication, authorization, and accountability*. Left out of the AAA acronym is *identification*, which is required before the remaining three As can be achieved.

Identity and authentication

Identity is a claim: If your name is "Person X," you identify yourself by saying, "I am Person X." Identity alone is weak because there is no proof. You can also identify yourself by saying, "I am Person Y." Proving an identity claim is called authentication. You authenticate the identity claim, usually by supplying a piece of information or an object that only you possess, such as a password or your passport.

Authorization

Authorization describes the actions you can perform on a system once you have been identified and authenticated. Actions may include reading, writing, or executing files or programs.

Accountability

Accountability holds users accountable for their actions. This is typically done by logging and analyzing audit data. Enforcing accountability helps keep honest people honest. For some users, knowing that data is logged is not enough to provide accountability; they must know that the data is logged and audited, and that *sanctions* may result from violation of *policy*.

NONREPUDIATION

Nonrepudiation means a user cannot deny (repudiate) having performed a transaction. It combines authentication and integrity; nonrepudiation authenticates the identity of a user who performs a transaction and ensures the integrity of that transaction. You must have both authentication and integrity to have nonrepudiation; for example, proving you signed a contract to buy a car (authenticating your identity as the purchaser) is not useful if the car dealer can change the price from $20,000 to $40,000 (violate the integrity of the contract).

LEAST PRIVILEGE AND NEED TO KNOW

Least privilege means users should be granted the minimum amount of access (authorization) required to do their jobs, but no more. Need to know is more granular than least privilege; the user must need to know that specific piece of information before accessing it.

SUBJECTS AND OBJECTS

A *subject* is an active entity on a data system. Most examples of subjects involve people accessing data files. However, computer programs can be subjects as well. A dynamic link library file or a Perl script that updates database files with new information is also a subject.

An *object* is any passive data within the system. Objects can range from documents on physical paper to database tables to text files. The important thing to remember about objects is that they are passive within the system; they do not manipulate other objects.

DEFENSE IN DEPTH

Defense in depth (also called layered defense) applies multiple safeguards (also called controls, which are measures taken to reduce risk) to protect an asset. Any single security control may fail; by deploying multiple controls, you improve the confidentiality, integrity, and availability of your data.

LEGAL AND REGULATORY ISSUES

Though general understanding of major legal systems and types of law is important, it is critical that information security professionals understand the concepts described in the next section. With the ubiquity of information systems, data, and applications comes a host of legal issues that require attention.

COMPLIANCE WITH LAWS AND REGULATIONS

Complying with laws and regulations is a priority for top information security management, both in the real world and on the exam. An organization must be in compliance with all laws and regulations that apply to it. Ignorance of the law is never a valid excuse for breaking the law.

MAJOR LEGAL SYSTEMS

In order to begin to appreciate common legal concepts at work in today's global economy, an understanding of the major legal systems is required. These legal systems provide the framework that determines how a country develops laws pertaining to information systems in the first place. The three major systems of law are civil, common, and religious law.

Civil law (legal system)

The most common of the major legal systems is that of *civil law*, which is employed by many countries throughout the world. The system of civil law leverages codified laws or statutes to determine what is considered to be within the bounds of law. Though a legislative branch typically wields the power to create laws, there will still exist a judicial branch that is tasked with interpretation of the existing laws. The most significant difference between civil and common law is that under civil law judicial precedents and particular case rulings do not carry the weight they would have under common law.

Common law

Common law is the legal system used in the United States, Canada, the United Kingdom, and most former British colonies, amongst others. As we can see by the short list above, English influence has historically been the main indicator of common law being used in a country. The primary distinguishing feature of common law is the significant emphasis on particular cases and judicial precedents as determinants of laws. Though there is typically also a legislative body tasked with the creation of new statutes and laws, judicial rulings can at times supersede those laws. Because of the emphasis on judges' interpretations, there is significant possibility that as society changes over time, so can judicial interpretations.

Religious and customary law

Religious law serves as the third of the major legal systems. Religious doctrine or interpretation serves as the primary source of legal understanding and statutes. While Christianity, Judaism, and Hinduism have all had significant influence on national legal systems, Islam serves as the most common source for religious legal systems. Sharia is an example of Islamic law that uses the Qur'an and Hadith as its foundation.

Customary law refers to those customs or practices that are so commonly accepted by a group that the custom is treated as a law. These practices can be later codified as laws in the more traditional sense, but the emphasis on the prevailing acceptance of a group is quite important.

CRIMINAL, CIVIL, AND ADMINISTRATIVE LAW

Within common law there are various branches of laws, including criminal, civil, and administrative law.

Criminal law

Criminal law pertains to those laws where the victim can be seen as society itself. While it might seem odd to consider society the victim when an individual is murdered, the goal of criminal law is to promote and maintain an orderly and law-abiding citizenry. Criminal law can include penalties that remove an individual from society by incarceration or, in some extreme cases in some regions, death. The goals of criminal law are to deter crime and to punish offenders.

Due to the severity of depriving criminals of either freedom or their lives, the burden of proof in criminal cases is beyond any reasonable doubt.

Civil law

In addition to *civil law* being a major legal system in the world, it also serves as a type of law within the common law legal system. Another term associated with civil law is tort law, which deals with injury (loosely defined), resulting from someone violating their responsibility to provide a duty of care. Tort law is the primary component of civil law, and it is the most significant source of lawsuits that seek damages.

In the United States, the burden of proof in a criminal court is beyond a reasonable doubt, while the burden of proof in civil proceedings is the preponderance of the evidence. "Preponderance" means more likely than not. Satisfying the burden of proof requirement regarding the preponderance of the evidence in a civil matter is much easier than meeting the burden of proof requirement in criminal proceedings. The most common types of financial damages are presented in Table 1.1.

Administrative law

Administrative law or *regulatory law* is law enacted by government agencies. The executive branch (deriving from the Office of the President) enacts administrative law in the United States. Government-mandated compliance measures are administrative laws. Some examples of administrative law are FCC regulations, Health Insurance Portability and Accountability Act (HIPAA) security mandates, FDA regulations, and FAA regulations.

LIABILITY

Legal liability is another important legal concept for information security professionals and their employers. Society has grown quite litigious over the years, and the question of whether an organization is legally liable for specific actions or inactions can prove costly. Questions of liability often turn into questions regarding potential negligence. When attempting to determine whether certain actions or inactions constitute negligence, the *Prudent Man Rule*, which we will define shortly, is often applied.

Table 1.1 Common Types of Financial Damages

Financial Damages	Description
Statutory	Statutory damages are those prescribed by law, which can be awarded to the victim even if the victim incurred no actual loss or injury
Compensatory	The purpose of compensatory damages is to provide the victim with a financial award in effort to compensate for the loss or injury incurred as a direct result of the wrongdoing
Punitive	The intent of punitive damages is to punish an individual or organization. These damages are typically awarded to attempt to discourage a particularly egregious violation where the compensatory or statutory damages alone would not act as a deterrent

Two important terms to understand are due care and due diligence, which have become common standards that are used in determining corporate liability in courts of law.

DUE CARE AND DUE DILIGENCE

Due care is doing what a reasonable person would do in a given situation. It is sometimes called the "prudent man" rule. The term is derived from "duty of care"; for example, parents have a duty to care for their children. *Due diligence* is the management of due care.

Due care and due diligence are often confused; they are related, but there is a difference between them. Due care is informal, while due diligence follows a process. Think of due diligence as a step beyond due care. For example, expecting your staff to keep their systems patched means that you expect them to exercise due care, while verifying that your staff has patched their systems is an example of due diligence.

Gross negligence

Gross negligence is the opposite of due care. It is a legally important concept. For example, if you suffer loss of PII, but can demonstrate due care in protecting the PII, you are on stronger ground in a legal proceeding. If you cannot demonstrate due care (ie, you acted with gross negligence), you are in a much worse legal position.

LEGAL ASPECTS OF INVESTIGATIONS

Investigations are a critical way in which information security professionals come into contact with the law. Forensic and incident response personnel often conduct investigations, therefore both need to have a basic understanding of legal matters to ensure that the legal merits of the investigation are not unintentionally tarnished.

Evidence

Evidence is one of the most important legal concepts for information security professionals to understand. Information security professionals are commonly involved in investigations, and they often have to obtain or handle evidence during the investigation.

CRUNCH TIME

Real evidence consists of tangible or physical objects. A knife or bloody glove might constitute real evidence in some traditional criminal proceedings. *Direct evidence* is testimony provided by witnesses regarding what they actually experienced through their five senses. *Circumstantial evidence* serves to establish the circumstances related to particular points or other evidence. *Corroborative evidence* provides additional support for a fact that might have been called into question. *Hearsay evidence* constitutes second-hand evidence. As opposed to direct evidence, which is witnessed using any of the five senses, hearsay evidence involves indirect information. *Secondary evidence* consists of copies of original documents and oral descriptions. Computer-generated logs and documents might also constitute secondary rather than best evidence, which we will define shortly.

Best evidence rule

Courts prefer the best evidence possible. Original documents are preferred over copies, and conclusive tangible objects are preferred over oral testimony. The *best evidence rule* prefers evidence that meets these criteria.

Evidence integrity

Evidence must be reliable. It is common during forensic and incident response investigations to analyze digital media. It is critical to maintain the integrity of the data during the course of its acquisition and analysis. Checksums can ensure that no data changes occurred as a result of the acquisition and analysis. One-way hash functions such as MD5 or SHA-1 are commonly used for this purpose. *Chain of custody* requires that once evidence is acquired, full documentation must be maintained regarding who or what handled the evidence and when and where it was handled.

Entrapment and enticement

Entrapment is when law enforcement, or an agent of law enforcement, persuades someone to commit a crime when the person otherwise had no intention to commit a crime. Enticement could still involve agents of law enforcement making the conditions for commission of a crime favorable, but the difference is that the person is determined to have already broken a law or is intent on doing so.

COMPUTER CRIME

One aspect of the interaction of information security and the legal system is that of *computer crimes*. Applicable computer crime laws vary throughout the world, according to jurisdiction. However, regardless of region, some generalities exist.

FAST FACTS

Computer crimes can be based upon the way in which computer systems relate to the wrongdoing. For example, computer systems can be used as targets, or they can be used as the tools used in perpetrating the crime.

Computer systems as target of crime—Examples include disrupting online commerce by means of distributed DoS attacks, installing malware on systems for the distribution of spam, or exploiting vulnerability of a system to store illegal content.

Computer as a tool used to perpetrate crime—Examples include leveraging computers to steal cardholder data from payment systems, conducting computer based reconnaissance to target an individual for information disclosure or espionage, and using computer systems for the purposes of harassment.

INTELLECTUAL PROPERTY

As opposed to physical or tangible property, *intellectual property* refers to intangible property that is created as the result of a creative act. The following intellectual property concepts effectively create an exclusive monopoly on their use.

Trademark

Trademarks are associated with marketing. A trademark allows for the creation of a brand in order to distinguish the source of products or services. A name, logo, symbol, or image represents the most commonly trademarked items. In the United States, there are two different symbols that are used by an individual or organization in order to protect distinctive marks. The superscript TM symbol, as seen in Fig. 1.2, can be used freely to indicate an unregistered mark. The circle R symbol, as seen in Fig. 1.3, is used with marks that have been formally registered as a trademark with the US Patent and Trademark Office.

Patent

Patents provide a monopoly to the patent holder regarding the right to use, make, or sell an invention for a period of time in exchange for the patent holder's promise to make the invention public. During the life of the patent, the patent holder can, through the use of civil litigation, exclude others from leveraging the patented invention. Obviously, in order for an invention to be patented, it should be novel and unique. The patent term, which is the length that a patent is valid, varies by region

Syngress™

FIG. 1.2

Trademark symbol.

Syngress®

FIG. 1.3

Registered trademark symbol.

FIG. 1.4

Copyright symbol.

and also by the type of invention being patented. Generally, in both Europe and the United States, the patent term is 20 years from the initial filing date.

Copyright

Copyright represents a type of intellectual property that protects the form of expression in artistic, musical, or literary works and is typically denoted by the circled c symbol, as shown in Fig. 1.4. The purpose of a copyright is to preclude unauthorized duplication, distribution, or modification of a creative work. Note that it is the form of expression that is protected, not the subject matter or ideas represented.

Licenses

Software licenses are a contract between a provider of software and the consumer. Though there are licenses that provide explicit permission for the consumer to do virtually anything with the software, including modifying it for use in another commercial product, most commercial software licensing provides explicit limits on the use and distribution of the software. Software licenses, such as end-user license agreements (EULAs), are an unusual form of contract because using the software typically constitutes contractual agreement, even though a small minority of users read the lengthy EULA.

Trade secrets

Trade secrets are business-proprietary information that is important to an organization's ability to compete. The organization must exercise due care and due diligence in the protection of their trade secrets. Noncompete and nondisclosure agreements are two of the most common protection methods used.

PRIVACY

Privacy is the protection of the confidentiality of personal information. Many organizations host users' PII such as Social Security numbers, financial information (eg, annual salary and bank account information required for payroll deposits), and health care information for insurance purposes. The confidentiality of this information must be assured.

European union privacy

The European Union has taken an aggressive proprivacy stance while balancing the needs of business. Commerce would be impacted if member nations had different regulations regarding the collection and use of PII. The *EU Data Protection Directive* allows for the free flow of information while still maintaining consistent protection of citizen data in each member nation.

> **FAST FACTS**
>
> The principles of the EU Data Protection Directive are:
>
> - Notifying individuals how their personal data is collected and used
> - Allowing individuals to opt out of sharing their personal data with third parties
> - Granting individuals the right to choose to opt into sharing the most sensitive personal data, as opposed to being opted in automatically.
> - Providing reasonable protections for personal data

OECD privacy guidelines

The Organisation for Economic Co-operation and Development (OECD), though often considered exclusively European, consists of 30 member nations from around the world. The members include such countries as the United States, Mexico, Australia, Japan, and the Czech Republic, as well as prominent European countries. The OECD provides a forum in which countries can focus on issues that impact the global economy. The OECD will routinely issue consensus recommendations that can serve as an impetus to change current policies and legislation in the OECD member countries and beyond.

EU-US safe harbor

An interesting aspect of the EU Data Protection Directive is that the personal data of EU citizens may not be transmitted, even when permitted by the individual, to countries outside of the EU unless the receiving country is perceived by the EU to adequately protect their data. This presents a challenge regarding the sharing of the data with the United States, which is perceived to have less stringent privacy protections. To help resolve this issue, the United States and the European Union created the Safe Harbor framework that will give US-based organizations the benefit of authorized data sharing. In order to participate, US organizations must voluntarily consent to data privacy principles that are consistent with the EU Data Protection Directive.

INTERNATIONAL COOPERATION

To date, the most significant progress toward international cooperation in computer crime policy is the Council of Europe Convention on Cybercrime. In addition to the treaty being signed and subsequently ratified by a majority of the 47 European member countries, the United States has also signed and ratified the treaty. The primary focus of the Convention on Cybercrime is to establish standards in cybercrime policy in order to promote international cooperation during the investigation and prosecution of cybercrime. Additional information on the Council of Europe Convention on Cybercrime can be found here: http://www.coe.int/en/web/conventions/full-list/-/conventions/treaty/185.

IMPORT/EXPORT RESTRICTIONS

Due to the successes of cryptography, many nations have limited the import and/ or export of cryptosystems and associated cryptographic hardware. In some cases, countries would prefer that their citizens be denied the use of any cryptosystems that their intelligence agencies cannot crack, and therefore those countries attempt to impose import restrictions on cryptographic technologies.

During the Cold War, CoCom, the Coordinating Committee for Multilateral Export Controls, was a multinational agreement restricting the export of certain technologies, which included encryption, to many Communist countries. After the Cold War, the Wassenaar Arrangement became the standard for export controls. This multinational agreement was far less restrictive than the former CoCom, but did still suggest significant limitations on the export of cryptographic algorithms and technologies to countries not included in the Wassenaar Arrangement.

SECURITY AND THIRD PARTIES

Organizations are increasingly reliant upon third parties to provide significant and sometimes business-critical services. While leveraging external organizations is by no means a recent phenomenon, the critical nature of their roles and the volume of services and products now typically warrant specific attention toward an organization's information security department.

SERVICE PROVIDER CONTRACTUAL SECURITY

Contracts are the primary control for ensuring security when dealing with services provided by third-party organizations. The tremendous surge in outsourcing, especially the ongoing shift toward cloud services, has made contractual security measures much more prominent.

Service level agreements

Service level agreements (SLA) identify key expectations that the vendor is contractually required to meet. SLAs are widely used for general performance expectations, but are increasingly leveraged for security purposes as well. SLAs primarily address availability.

Attestation

Information security attestation involves having a third-party organization review the practices of the service provider and make a statement about the security posture of the organization. The goal of the service provider is to provide evidence that they can and should be trusted. Typically, a third party provides attestation after performing an audit of the service provider against a known baseline.

Right to penetration test/right to audit

The right to penetration test and right to audit documents provide the originating organization with written approval to perform their own testing or have a trusted provider perform the assessment on their behalf.

An alternative to the right to penetration test/right to audit documents is for the service provider to present the originating organization with a third-party audit or penetration test that the service provider had performed.

PROCUREMENT

Procurement is the process of acquiring products or services from a third party. Leveraging the security department early and often can serve as a preventive control that can allow the organization to make risk-based decisions even prior to vendor or solution acceptance.

VENDOR GOVERNANCE

The goal of vendor governance is to ensure that the business is continually getting sufficient quality from its third-party providers. Professionals performing this function will often be employed at both the originating organization as well as the third-party provider.

ACQUISITIONS

Acquisitions can be disruptive to business and may impact aspects of both organizations. This is doubly true for information security.

Due diligence requires a thorough risk assessment of any acquired company's information security program, including an effective assessment of the current state of network security. This includes performing vulnerability assessment and penetration testing of the acquired company before any merger of networks.

DIVESTITURES

Divestitures (also known as demergers and deacquisitions) represent the flip side of acquisitions in that one company becomes two or more. Divestitures can represent more risk than acquisitions and pose important questions like how will sensitive data be split up? how will IT systems be split?

It is quite common for formerly unified companies to split off and inadvertently maintain duplicate accounts and passwords within the two newly spun-off companies. This allows (former) insider attacks, in which an employee of the formerly unified company hacks into a divested company by reusing old credentials. Similar risks exist with the reuse of physical security controls, including keys and badges. All forms of access for former employees must be revoked.

ETHICS

Ethics is the practice of doing what is morally right. The Hippocratic Oath, taken by doctors, is an example of a code of ethics. Ethics are of paramount concern for information security professionals: because we are often trusted with highly sensitive information, and our employers, clients, and customers must know that we will treat their information with the utmost integrity.

THE (ISC)²® CODE OF ETHICS

The (ISC)²® code of ethics is the most testable code of ethics on the exam. That's fair; you cannot become a CISSP® without agreeing to the code of ethics, among other steps, so it is reasonable to expect new CISSPs® to understand what they are agreeing to do or not do. The (ISC)²© Code of Ethics is available at the following website: http://www.isc2.org/ethics/default.aspx.

The (ISC)²® code of ethics include the preamble, canons, and guidance. The preamble is the introduction to the code. The canons are mandatory; you must follow them to become and remain a CISSP®. The guidance is "advisory," not mandatory, and it provides supporting information for the canons.

The code of ethics preamble and canons is quoted here: "Safety of the commonwealth, duty to our principals, and to each other requires that we adhere, and be seen to adhere, to the highest ethical standards of behavior. Therefore, strict adherence to this Code is a condition of certification."[1]

The (ISC)²® code of ethics canons in detail

The first and therefore most important canon of the (ISC)²® Code of Ethics requires the information security professional to "*protect society, the commonwealth, and the infrastructure.*"[1] The focus of the first canon is on the public and their understanding and faith in information systems. Security professionals are charged with the promotion of safe security practices and the improvement of the security of systems and infrastructure for the public good.

The second canon in the (ISC)²® Code of Ethics charges information security professionals to "*act honorably, honestly, justly, responsibly, and legally.*"[1] This canon is fairly straightforward, but there are a few points worth emphasizing here. One point that is detailed within this canon is related to laws from different jurisdictions found to be in conflict. The (ISC)²® Code of Ethics suggests that priority be given to the jurisdiction in which services are being provided. Another point made by this canon is in regard to providing prudent advice and cautioning the security professional against unnecessarily promoting fear, uncertainty, and doubt.

The (ISC)²® Code of Ethics' third canon requires that security professionals "*provide diligent and competent service to principals.*"[1] The primary focus of this canon is ensuring that the security professional provides competent service for which he or she is qualified and which maintains the value and confidentiality of information and the associated systems. An additional important consideration is to ensure that the professional does not have a conflict of interest in providing quality services.

The fourth and final canon in the (ISC)²® Code of Ethics mandates that information security professionals *"advance and protect the profession."*[1] This canon requires that the security professionals maintain their skills and advance the skills and knowledge of others. Additionally, this canon requires that individuals protect the integrity of the security profession by avoiding any association with those who might harm the profession.

DID YOU KNOW?

The (ISC)²® Code of Ethics is highly testable, including applying the canons in order. You may be asked for the "best" ethical answer, even though all answers are ethical, per the canons. In that case, choose the answer that is mentioned first in the canons. Also, the most ethical answer is usually the best, so hold yourself to a very high level of ethics for questions posed during the exam.

COMPUTER ETHICS INSTITUTE

The Computer Ethics Institute provides their *Ten Commandments of Computer Ethics* as a code of computer ethics. The code is both short and fairly straightforward. Both the name and format are reminiscent of the Ten Commandments of Judaism, Christianity, and Islam, but there is nothing overtly religious in nature about the Computer Ethics Institute's Ten Commandments. The Computer Ethics Institute's Ten Commandments of Computer Ethics are:

1. Thou shalt not use a computer to harm other people.
2. Thou shalt not interfere with other people's computer work.
3. Thou shalt not snoop around in other people's computer files.
4. Thou shalt not use a computer to steal.
5. Thou shalt not use a computer to bear false witness.
6. Thou shalt not copy or use proprietary software for which you have not paid.
7. Thou shalt not use other people's computer resources without authorization or proper compensation.
8. Thou shalt not appropriate other people's intellectual output.
9. Thou shalt think about the social consequences of the program you are writing or the system you are designing.
10. Thou shalt always use a computer in ways that ensure consideration and respect for your fellow humans.[2]

IAB'S ETHICS AND THE INTERNET

Much like the fundamental protocols of the Internet, the Internet Activities Board's (IAB) code of ethics is defined in an RFC document. RFC 1087, *Ethics and the Internet*, was published in 1987 to present a policy relating to ethical behavior associated with the Internet. The RFC is short and easy to read, and it provides five basic ethical principles. According to the IAB, the following practices would be considered unethical behavior if someone purposely:

- Seeks to gain unauthorized access to the resources of the Internet
- Disrupts the intended use of the Internet
- Wastes resources (people, capacity, computer) through such actions
- Destroys the integrity of computer-based information
- Compromises the privacy of users.[3]

INFORMATION SECURITY GOVERNANCE

Information security governance is information security at the organizational level, which includes senior management, policies, processes, and staffing. It is also the organizational priority provided by senior leadership, which is required for a successful information security program.

SECURITY POLICY AND RELATED DOCUMENTS

Documents such as policies and procedures are a required part of any successful information security program. These documents should be grounded in reality; they are not idealistic documents that sit on shelves collecting dust. They should mirror the real world and provide guidance on the correct (and sometimes required) way of doing things.

Policy

Policies are high-level management directives. Policy is mandatory; for example, even if you do not agree with your company's sexual harassment policy, you still must follow it.

Policy is high level, and it does not delve into specifics. A server security policy would discuss protecting the confidentiality, integrity, and availability of the system, usually in those terms. It may discuss software updates and patching. The policy would not use low-level terms like "Linux" or "Windows." In fact, if you converted your servers from Windows to Linux, your server policy would not change. However, other documents, like procedures, would change.

Procedures

A procedure is a step-by-step guide for accomplishing a task. Procedures are low level and specific. Like policies, procedures are mandatory.

Here is a simple example procedure for creating a new user:

1. Receive a new-user request form and verify its completeness.
2. Verify that the user's manager has signed the form.
3. Verify that the user has read and agreed to the user account security policy.
4. Classify the user's role by following role-assignment procedure NX-103.

5. Verify that the user has selected a secret word, such as his or her mother's maiden name, and enter it into the help desk account profile.
6. Create the account and assign the proper role.
7. Assign the secret word as the initial password, and set "Force user to change password on next login to 'True.'"
8. Email the new account document to the user and their manager.

The steps of this procedure are mandatory. Security administrators do not have the option of skipping Step 1, for example, and create an account without a form.

Other safeguards depend on this procedure. For example, when a user calls the help desk as a result of a forgotten password, the help desk will follow their "forgotten password" procedure, which includes asking for the user's secret word. The help desk cannot do that unless Step 5 was completed; without that word, the help desk cannot securely reset the password. This mitigates the risks of social engineering attacks, during which an imposter tries to trick the help desk into resetting a password for an account he or she is not authorized to access.

Standards

A standard describes the specific use of technology, often applied to hardware and software. "All employees will receive an ACME Nexus-6 laptop with 8 GB of memory, a 3.3 GHZ quad core central processing unit (CPU), and 500-gigabyte disk" is an example of a hardware standard. "The laptops will run Windows 10 Enterprise, 64-bit version" is an example of a software (operating system) standard.

Standards are mandatory. Not only do they lower the TCO of a safeguard, but they also support disaster recovery.

Guidelines

Guidelines are discretionary recommendations. A guideline can be a useful piece of advice, such as "To create a strong password, take the first letter of every word in a sentence, and mix in some numbers and symbols. 'I will pass the CISSP® exam in six months!' becomes 'Iwptcei6m!'"

Baselines

Baselines are uniform ways of implementing a standard. "Harden the system by applying the Center for Internet Security Linux benchmarks" is an example of a baseline (see https://benchmarks.cisecurity.org for the Security Benchmarks division of the Center for Internet Security, a great resource). The system must meet the baseline described by those benchmarks.

Baselines are discretionary. It is acceptable to harden the system without following the aforementioned benchmarks, as long as it is at least as secure as a system hardened using the benchmarks. Formal exceptions to baselines will require senior management sign-off.

Table 1.2 summarizes the types of security documentation.

Table 1.2 Summary of Security Documentation

Document	Example	Mandatory or Discretionary?
Policy	Protect the CIA of PII by hardening the operating system	Mandatory
Procedure	Step 1: Install prehardened OS Image. Step 2: Download patches from update server. Step 3: ...	Mandatory
Standard	Use Nexus-6 laptop hardware	Mandatory
Guideline	Patch installation may be automated via the use of an installer script	Discretionary
Baselines	Use the CIS Security Benchmarks Windows Benchmark	Discretionary

PERSONNEL SECURITY

Users can pose the biggest security risk to an organization. Background checks should be performed, contractors need to be securely managed, and users must be properly trained and made aware of security risks, as we will discuss next.

Security awareness and training

Security awareness and training are often confused. Awareness changes user behavior, while training provides a skill set.

Reminding users to never share accounts or write their passwords down is an example of awareness. It is assumed that some users are doing the wrong thing, and awareness is designed to change that behavior.

Security training teaches a user how to do something. Examples include training new help desk personnel to open, modify, and close service tickets; training network engineers to configure a router, or training a security administrator to create a new account.

Background checks

Organizations should conduct a thorough background check before hiring an individual. This includes a check of criminal records and verification of all experience, education, and certifications. Lying or exaggerating about education, certifications, and related credentials is one of the most common examples of dishonesty in regards to the hiring process.

Employee termination

Termination should result in immediate revocation of all employee access. Beyond account revocation, termination should be a fair process. There are ethical and legal reasons for employing fair termination, but there is also an additional information security advantage. An organization's worst enemy can be a disgruntled former employee, who, even without legitimate account access, knows where the weak spots are. This is especially true for IT personnel.

Vendor, consultant, and contractor security

Vendors, consultants, and contractors can introduce risks to an organization. They are not direct employees, and sometimes have access to systems at multiple organizations. If allowed to, they may place an organization's sensitive data on devices not controlled (or secured) by the organization.

Third-party personnel with access to sensitive data must be trained and made aware of risks, just as employees are. Background checks may also be required, depending on the level of access required. Information security policies, procedures, and other guidance should apply as well. Additional policies regarding ownership of data and intellectual property should be developed. Clear rules dictating where and when a third party may access or store data must be developed.

Outsourcing and offshoring

Outsourcing is the use of a third party to provide information technology (IT) support services that were previously performed in-house. *Offshoring* is outsourcing to another country.

Both can lower TCO by providing IT services at a reduced cost. They may also enhance the IT resources available to a company (especially a small company), which can improve confidentiality, integrity, and availability of data.

Offshoring can raise privacy and regulatory issues. For example, for a US company that offshores data to Australia, there is no HIPAA, the primary regulation covering health care data in the United States in Australia. There is no SOX (Sarbanes-Oxley, protecting publicly traded data in the United States), no Gramm-Leach-Bliley Act (GLBA, which protects financial information in the United States), etc. Always consult with legal staff before offshoring data. Contracts must ensure that data is protected, regardless of where it is located.

ACCESS CONTROL DEFENSIVE CATEGORIES AND TYPES

In order to understand and appropriately implement access controls, it is vital to understand what benefits each control can add to security. In this section, each type of access control will be defined on the basis of how it adds to the security of the system.

There are six access control types:

- Preventive
- Detective
- Corrective
- Recovery
- Deterrent
- Compensating

FAST FACTS

These access control types can fall into one of three categories: administrative, technical, or physical.

1. *Administrative* (also called directive) controls are implemented by creating and following organizational policy, procedure, or regulation. User training and awareness also fall into this category.
2. *Technical* controls are implemented using software, hardware, or firmware that restricts logical access on an IT system. Examples include firewalls, routers, encryption, etc.
3. *Physical* controls are implemented with physical devices, such as locks, fences, gates, and security guards.

PREVENTIVE

Preventive controls prevent actions from occurring. It applies restrictions to what a potential user, either authorized or unauthorized, can do. An example of an administrative preventive control is a preemployment drug screening. It is designed to prevent an organization from hiring an employee who is using illegal drugs.

DETECTIVE

Detective controls are controls that send alerts during or after a successful attack. Examples of detective controls are intrusion detection systems that send alerts after a successful attack, closed-circuit television cameras that alert guards to an intruder, and a building alarm system that is triggered by an intruder.

CORRECTIVE

Corrective controls work by "correcting" a damaged system or process. The corrective access control typically works hand in hand with detective access controls. Antivirus software has both components. First, the antivirus software runs a scan and uses its definition file to detect whether there is any software that matches its virus list. If it detects a virus, the corrective controls take over and either places the suspicious software in quarantine or deletes it from the system.

RECOVERY

After a security incident has occurred, *recovery controls* may need to be taken in order to restore the functionality of the system and organization. Recovery means that the system must be restored, which involves reinstallation from OS media or image, data restored from backups, etc.

DETERRENT

Deterrent controls deter users from performing certain actions on a system. One example is a "Beware of Dog" sign; a thief encountering two buildings, one with guard dogs and one without, is more likely to attack the building without guard dogs. Another example is large fines for drivers who speed. A deterrent control is a sanction policy that makes users understand that they will be fired if they are caught surfing illicit or illegal websites.

COMPENSATING

A *compensating* control is an additional security control put in place to compensate for weaknesses in other controls.

RISK ANALYSIS

Accurate risk analysis is a critical skill for an information security professional. We must hold ourselves to a higher standard when judging risk. Our risk decisions will dictate which safeguards we should deploy in order to protect our assets, and the amount of money and resources we will spend doing so. Poor decisions will result in wasted money, or even worse, compromised data.

ASSETS

Assets are valuable resources that need protection. Assets can be data, systems, people, buildings, property, and so forth. The value or critical nature of the asset will dictate what safeguards you deploy.

THREATS AND VULNERABILITIES

A *threat* is a potentially harmful occurrence, like an earthquake, a power outage, or a network-based worm.

A *vulnerability* is a weakness that can allow a threat to cause harm. Examples of vulnerabilities are buildings that are not built to withstand earthquakes, a data center without proper backup power, or a Microsoft Windows 10 system that has not been patched in a long time.

RISK = THREAT × VULNERABILITY

To have risk, a threat must connect to a vulnerability. This relationship is stated by the formula:

$$\text{Risk} = \text{Threat} \times \text{Vulnerability}$$

You can assign a value to specific risks using this formula. Assign a number to both threats and vulnerabilities. We will use a range of 1–5 (the range is arbitrary; whatever range you choose to use, keep it consistent when comparing different risks).

IMPACT

The Risk = Threat × Vulnerability equation sometimes uses an added variable called *impact*: Risk = Threat × Vulnerability × Impact. Impact, or consequences, is the severity of the damage, sometimes expressed in dollars. Risk = Threat × Vulnerability × Cost is sometimes used for that reason.

EXAM WARNING

Loss of human life has a near-infinite impact on the exam. When calculating risk using the Risk = Threat × Vulnerability × Impact formula, any risk involving loss of human life is extremely high and must be mitigated.

RISK ANALYSIS MATRIX

A *risk analysis matrix*, as seen in Table 1.3,[4] uses a quadrant to map the likelihood of a risk occurring against the consequences (or impact) that risk would have.

A risk analysis matrix allows you to perform qualitative risk analysis (see section "Qualitative and Quantitative Risk Analysis") based on likelihood (from "rare" to "almost certain") and consequences or impact, from "insignificant" to "catastrophic." The resulting scores are low (L), medium (M), high (H), and extreme risk (E). Low risks are handled via normal processes; moderate risks require management notification; high risks require senior management notification; and extreme risks require immediate action including a detailed mitigation plan and senior management notification.

The goal of the matrix is to identify high likelihood/high consequence risks (upper right quadrant of Table 1.3), and drive them down to low likelihood/low consequence risks (lower left quadrant of Table 1.3).

Table 1.3 Risk Analysis Matrix

		Consequences				
		Insignificant 1	Minor 2	Moderate 3	Major 4	Catastrophic 5
Likelihood	5. Almost Certain	H	H	E	E	E
	4. Likely	M	H	H	E	E
	3. Possible	L	M	H	E	E
	2. Unlikely	L	L	M	H	E
	1. Rare	L	L	M	H	H

CALCULATING ANNUALIZED LOSS EXPECTANCY

The *annualized loss expectancy* (ALE) calculation allows you to determine the annual cost of a loss due to a risk. Once calculated, ALE allows you to make informed decisions to mitigate the risk.

This section will use an example of risk due to lost or stolen unencrypted laptops. Assume your company has 1000 laptops that contain PII. You are the security officer, and you are concerned about the risk of exposure of PII due to lost or stolen laptops. You would like to purchase and deploy a laptop encryption solution. The solution is expensive, so you need to convince management that the solution is worthwhile.

Asset value

The *asset value* (AV) is the value of the asset you are trying to protect. In this example, each laptop costs $2500, but the real value is the PII. Theft of unencrypted PII has occurred previously and has cost the company many times the value of the laptop in regulatory fines, bad publicity, legal fees, staff hours spent investigating, etc. The true average AV of a laptop with PII for this example is $25,000 ($2500 for the hardware, and $22,500 for the exposed PII).

Tangible assets, such as computers or buildings, are straightforward to calculate. Intangible assets are more challenging. For example, what is the value of brand loyalty? According to Deloitte, there are three methods for calculating the value of intangible assets: market approach, income approach, and cost approach:

- *Market approach*: This approach assumes that the fair value of an asset reflects the price at which comparable assets have been purchased in transactions under similar circumstances.
- *Income approach*: This approach is based on the premise that the value of an ... asset is the present value of the future earning capacity that an asset will generate over its remaining useful life.
- *Cost approach*: This approach estimates the fair value of the asset by reference to the costs that would be incurred in order to recreate or replace the asset.[5]

Exposure factor

The *exposure factor* (EF) is the percentage of value an asset loses due to an incident. In the case of a stolen laptop with unencrypted PII, the EF is 100%, because the laptop and all of the data are gone.

Single-loss expectancy

The *single-loss expectancy* (SLE) is the cost of a single loss. SLE is the AV multiplied by the EF. In our case, SLE is $25,000 (AV) times 100% (EF), or $25,000.

Annual rate of occurrence

The *annual rate of occurrence* (ARO) is the number of losses suffered per year. For example, when looking through past events, you discover that you have suffered 11 lost or stolen laptops per year on average. Your ARO is 11.

Table 1.4 Summary of Risk Equations

	Formula	Description
Asset value (AV)	AV	Value of the asset
Exposure factor (EF)	EF	Percentage of asset value lost
Single-loss expectancy (SLE)	AV×EF	Cost of one loss
Annual rate of occurrence (ARO)	ARO	Number of losses per year
Annualized loss expectancy (ALE)	SLE×ARO	Cost of losses per year

Annualized loss expectancy

The ALE is the yearly cost due to a risk. It is calculated by multiplying SLE by the ARO. In our case, it is $25,000 (SLE) multiplied by 11 (ARO), or $275,000.

Table 1.4 summarizes the equations used to determine the ALE.

TOTAL COST OF OWNERSHIP

The TCO is the total cost of a mitigating safeguard. TCO combines upfront costs (often a one-time capital expense) plus the annual cost of maintenance, including staff hours, vendor maintenance fees, software subscriptions, etc. These ongoing costs are usually considered operational expenses.

Using our laptop encryption example, the upfront cost of laptop encryption software is $100/laptop, or $100,000 for 1000 laptops. The vendor charges a 10% annual support fee, or $10,000 per year. You estimate that it will take four staff hours per laptop to install the software, or 4000 staff hours. The staff members who will perform this work make $50 per hour plus benefits. Including benefits, the staff cost per hour is $70 multiplied by 4000 hours, which is $280,000.

Your company uses a 3-year technology refresh cycle, so you calculate the TCO over 3 years:

- Software cost: $100,000
- Three years of vendor support: $10,000×3=$30,000
- Hourly staff cost: $280,000
- TCO over 3 years: $410,000
- TCO per year: $410,000/3 = $136,667 per year

Your TCO for the laptop encryption project is $136,667 per year.

RETURN ON INVESTMENT

The ROI is the amount of money saved by implementing a safeguard. If your annual TCO is less than your ALE, you have a positive ROI and have made a good choice with your safeguard implementation. If the TCO is higher than your ALE, you have made a poor choice.

Table 1.5 Annualized Loss Expectancy of Unencrypted Laptops

	Formula	Value
Asset value (AV)	AV	$25,000
Exposure factor (EF)	EF	100%
Single-loss expectancy (SLE)	AV×EF	$25,000
Annual rate of occurrence (ARO)	ARO	11
Annualized loss expectancy (ALE)	SLE×ARO	$275,000

The annual TCO of laptop encryption is $136,667; the ALE for lost or stolen unencrypted laptops is $275,000. The math is summarized in Table 1.5.

Implementing laptop encryption will change the EF. The laptop hardware is worth $2500, and the exposed PII costs an additional $22,500, for a $25,000 AV. If an unencrypted laptop is lost or stolen, the EF is 100%, because all the hardware and data are exposed. Laptop encryption mitigates the PII exposure risk, lowering the EF from 100% (the laptop and all data) to 10% (just the laptop hardware).

The lower EF lowers the ALE from $275,000 to $27,500, as shown in Table 1.6.

You will save $247,500 per year (the old ALE, $275,000, minus the new ALE, $27,500) by making an investment of $136,667. Your ROI is $110,833 per year ($247,500 minus $136,667). The laptop encryption project has a positive ROI and is a wise investment.

BUDGET AND METRICS

When combined with risk analysis, the TCO and ROI calculations factor into proper budgeting. Metrics can greatly assist the information security budgeting process. They help illustrate potentially costly risks and demonstrate the effectiveness and potential cost savings of existing controls. They can also help champion the cause of information security.

RISK CHOICES

Once we have assessed risk, we must decide what to do. Options include accepting the risk, mitigating or eliminating the risk, transferring the risk, and avoiding the risk.

Table 1.6 Annualized Loss Expectancy of Encrypted Laptops

	Formula	Value
Asset value (AV)	AV	$25,000
Exposure factor (EF)	EF	10%
Single-loss expectancy (SLE)	AV×EF	$2,500
Annual rate of occurrence (ARO)	ARO	11
Annualized loss expectancy (ALE)	SLE×ARO	$27,500

Accept the risk
Some risks may be accepted. In some cases, it is cheaper to leave an asset unprotected due to a specific risk, rather than make the effort and spend the money required to protect it. This cannot be an ignorant decision; all options must be considered before accepting the risk.

Risk acceptance criteria
Low likelihood/low consequence risks are candidates for risk acceptance. High and extreme risks cannot be accepted. There are cases where accepting the risk is not an option, such as data protected by laws or regulations and risk to human life or safety.

Mitigating risk
Mitigating risk means lowering the risk to an acceptable level. Lowering risk is also called risk reduction, and the process of lowering risk is also called reduction analysis. The laptop encryption example given in the previous ALE section is an example of mitigating the risk. The risk of lost PII due to stolen laptops was mitigated by encrypting the data on the laptops. The risk has not been eliminated entirely; a weak or exposed encryption password could expose the PII, but the risk has been reduced to an acceptable level.

In some cases, it is possible to remove specific risks entirely; this is called eliminating the risk.

Transferring risk
The insurance model depicts transferring risk. Most homeowners do not assume the risk of fire for their houses; they pay an insurance company to assume that risk for them. The insurance companies are experts in risk analysis; buying risk is their business.

Risk avoidance
A thorough risk analysis should be completed before taking on a new project. If the risk analysis discovers high or extreme risks that cannot be easily mitigated, avoiding the risk (and the project) may be the best option.

QUANTITATIVE AND QUALITATIVE RISK ANALYSIS
Quantitative and qualitative risk analysis are two methods for analyzing risk. Quantitative risk analysis uses hard metrics, such as dollar amounts, while qualitative risk analysis uses simple approximate values. Quantitative is more objective; qualitative is more subjective. *Hybrid risk analysis* combines the two by using quantitative analysis for risks that may be easily expressed in hard numbers, such as money, and qualitative analysis for the remainder.

Calculating the ALE is an example of quantitative risk analysis. The risk analysis matrix (shown previously in Table 1.3) is an example of qualitative risk analysis.

THE RISK MANAGEMENT PROCESS

The US National Institute of Standards and Technology (NIST) published *Special Publication 800-30, Risk Management Guide for Information Technology Systems* (see http://csrc.nist.gov/publications/nistpubs/800-30/sp800-30.pdf). The guide describes a nine-step risk analysis process:

1. System Characterization
2. Threat Identification
3. Vulnerability Identification
4. Control Analysis
5. Likelihood Determination
6. Impact Analysis
7. Risk Determination
8. Control Recommendations
9. Results Documentation[6]

TYPES OF ATTACKERS

Controlling access is not limited to the control of authorized users; it also includes preventing unauthorized access. Information systems may be attacked by a variety of attackers, ranging from script kiddies to worms to militarized attacks. Attackers may use a variety of methods in their attempts to compromise the confidentiality, integrity, and availability of systems.

HACKERS

The term "hacker" is often used in the media to describe a malicious individual who attacks computer systems. The term originally described a nonmalicious explorer who used technologies in ways its creators did not intend.

While some simply use the term "hacker" to describe a malicious computer attacker, better terms include "malicious hacker," or "*black hat.*" *White hat* hackers are the good guys, including professional penetration testers who break into systems with permission, or malware researchers who research malicious code to provide better understanding and ethically disclose vulnerabilities to vendors.

A *hacktivist* is a hacker activist who attacks computer systems for political reasons. "Hacktivism" is hacking activism.

Script kiddies attack computer systems with tools of which they have little or no understanding.

OUTSIDERS

Outsiders are attackers with no authorized privileged access to a system or organization. The outsider seeks to gain unauthorized access. Outsiders launch the majority of attacks, but most are usually mitigated by defense-in-depth perimeter controls.

INSIDERS

An insider attack is launched by an internal user who may be authorized to use the system that is attacked. An insider attack may be intentional or accidental. Insider attackers range from poorly trained administrators who make mistakes to malicious individuals who intentionally compromise the security of systems. An authorized insider who attacks a system may be in a position to cause significant impact.

BOTS AND BOTNETS

A *bot* (short for robot) is a computer system running malware that is controlled via a *botnet*. A botnet contains a central command and control (C&C) network, managed by humans called bot herders. The term *zombie* is sometimes used to describe a bot.

PHISHERS AND SPEAR PHISHERS

A phisher ("fisher" spelled with the hacker spelling of "ph" instead of "f") is malicious attacker who attempts to trick users into divulging account credentials or PII. Phishing is a social engineering attack that sometimes includes other attacks, including client-side attacks. Users who click links in phishing emails may be subject to client-side attacks and theft of credentials. Simply visiting a phishing site is dangerous, and the client may be automatically compromised.

SUMMARY OF EXAM OBJECTIVES

Information security governance ensures that an organization has the correct information structure, leadership, and guidance. Governance helps ensure that a company has the proper administrative controls to mitigate risk. Risk analysis helps ensure that an organization properly identifies, analyzes, and mitigates risk. Accurately assessing risk and understanding terms such as ALE, TCO, and ROI will not only help you on the exam, but also to advance your information security career.

An understanding and appreciation of legal systems, concepts, and terms are required of an information security practitioner working in the information-centric world today. The impact of the ubiquity of information systems on legal systems cannot be overstated. Whether the major legal system is civil, common, religious, or a hybrid, information systems have made a lasting impact on legal systems throughout the world, causing the creation of new laws and reinterpretation of existing laws, as well as a new appreciation for the unique aspects that computers bring to the courts.

Finally, the nature of information security and the inherent sensitivity therein makes ethical frameworks an additional point requiring attention. This chapter presented the IAB's RFC, *Ethics and the Internet*, the Computer Ethics Institute's *Ten Commandments of Computer Ethics*, and The (ISC)²® *Code of Ethics*. The CISSP® exam will, no doubt, emphasize the Code of Ethics proffered by (ISC)²®, which presents an ordered set of four canons that attend to matters of the public, the individual's behavior, the provision of competent service, and the profession as a whole.

TOP FIVE TOUGHEST QUESTIONS

Use the following scenario to answer questions 1 through 3:

   Your company sells Apple iPods online and has suffered many denial-of-service (DoS) attacks. Your company makes an average $20,000 profit per week, and a typical DoS attack lowers sales by 40%. You suffer seven DoS attacks on average per year. A DoS-mitigation service is available for a subscription fee of $10,000 per month. You have tested this service and believe it will mitigate the attacks.

1. What is the ARO in the above scenario?
   (a) $20,000
   (b) 40%
   (c) 7
   (d) $10,000
2. What is the ALE of lost iPod sales due to the DoS attacks?
   (a) $20,000
   (b) $8000
   (c) $84,000
   (d) $56,000
3. Is the DoS mitigation service a good investment?
   (a) Yes, it will pay for itself.
   (b) Yes, $10,000 is less than the $56,000 ALE.
   (c) No, the annual TCO is higher than the ALE.
   (d) No, the annual TCO is lower than the ALE.

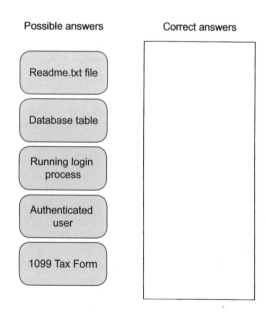

FIG. 1.5

Drag and drop.

4. Which canon of The (ISC)2® Code of Ethics should be considered the most important?

   (a) Protect society, the commonwealth, and the infrastructure
   (b) Advance and protect the profession
   (c) Act honorably, honestly, justly, responsibly, and legally
   (d) Provide diligent and competent service to principals

5. *Drag and drop*: Identify from the list below items that can be classified as objects. Drag and drop the objects from left to right (Fig. 1.5).

ANSWERS

1. Correct answer and explanation: C. The ARO is the number of attacks in a year.
   Incorrect answers and explanations: Answers A, B, and D are incorrect. The AV is $20,000. The EV is 40% and the monthly cost of the DoS service (used to calculate TCO) is $10,000.

2. Correct answer and explanation: D. The ALE is derived by first calculating the SLE, which is the AV, $20,000, multiplied by the EF, 40%. The SLE is $8000, which is multiplied by the ARO of 7 for an ALE of $56,000.
   Incorrect answers and explanations: Answers A, B, and C are incorrect. $20,000 is the AV, while $8000 is the SLE.

3. Correct answer and explanation: C. The TCO of the DoS mitigation service is higher than ALE of lost sales due to DoS attacks. This means it is less expensive to accept the risk of DoS attacks or to find a less expensive mitigation strategy.
   Incorrect answers and explanations: Answers A, B, and D are incorrect. The annual TCO is higher, not lower. $10,000 is the monthly TCO; you must calculate yearly TCO to compare with the ALE.

4. Correct answer and explanation: A. The canons are applied in order and "To protect society, the commonwealth, and the infrastructure" is the first canon, and is thus the most important of the four canons of The (ISC)²® Code of Ethics.
   Incorrect answers and explanations: Answers B, C, and D are incorrect. The canons of The (ISC)²® Code of Ethics are presented in order of importance. The second canon requires the security professional to act honorably, honestly, justly, responsibly, and legally. The third mandates that professionals provide diligent and competent service to principals. The final and therefore least important canon wants professionals to advance and protect the profession.

5. Correct answer and explanation: Files, database tables, and tax forms are example of objects, so they should be dragged to the right (Fig. 1.6).
   Incorrect answers and explanations: A running process and a user are examples of subjects.

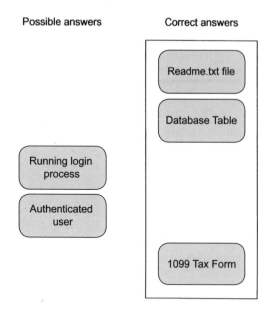

Possible answers   Correct answers

FIG. 1.6

Drag and drop answer.

ENDNOTES

1. *(ISC)²® Code of Ethics.* Available from http://www.isc2.org/ethics/default.aspx [accessed 25.04.16].
2. *Computer Ethics Institute. Ten Commandments of Computer Ethics.* Available from http://computerethicsinstitute.org/publications/tencommandments.html; 1992 [accessed 25.04.16].
3. *Internet Activities Board. RFC 1087—Ethics and the Internet.* Available from http://tools. ietf.org/html/rfc1087; 1989 [accessed 25.04.16].
4. *National Museum of Australia Collection Care and Preservation Policy.* Available from http://www.nma.gov.au/about_us/ips/policies/collection_care_and_preservation_policy [accessed 25.04.16].
5. *Intangible Assets—Recognising their Value.* http://www2.deloitte.com/content/dam/ Deloitte/ie/Documents/Finance/Corporate%20Finance/2009_valuing_intangible_assets_ deloitte_ireland.pdf [accessed 25.04.16].
6. *Risk Management Guide for Information Technology Systems.* http://csrc.nist.gov/publica-tions/nistpubs/800-30/sp800-30.pdf [accessed 25.04.16].

Domain 2: Asset security

CHAPTER OUTLINE

Eleventh Hour CISSP®. http://dx.doi.org/10.1016/B978-0-12-811248-9.00002-4

INTRODUCTION

The Asset Security (Protecting Security of Assets) domain focuses on controls such as data classification, clearances, labels, retention, and ownership of data. We will discuss data remanence, including newly testable material such as the remanence properties of solid-state drives (SSDs), which are a combination of electrically erasable programmable read-only memory (EEPROM) and random-access memory (RAM) and have remanence properties that are quite different in comparison to magnetic drives. The domain wraps up with a discussion of controls determination, including standards, scoping, and tailoring.

CLASSIFYING DATA

The day-to-day management of access control requires management of labels, clearances, formal access approval, and need to know. These formal mechanisms are typically used to protect highly sensitive data, such as government or military data.

LABELS

Objects have labels and subjects have clearances. The object labels used by many world governments are confidential, secret, and top-secret. According to Executive Order 12356—National Security Information:

- "Top Secret" shall be applied to information, of which the unauthorized disclosure could reasonably be expected to cause exceptionally grave damage to national security.
- "Secret" shall be applied to information, of which the unauthorized disclosure could reasonably be expected to cause serious damage to national security.
- "Confidential" shall be applied to information, of which the unauthorized disclosure could reasonably be expected to cause damage to national security.[1]

Private sector companies use labels such as "Internal Use Only" and "Company Proprietary" to categorize information.

CLEARANCE

A *clearance* is a formal determination of whether a user can be trusted with a specific level of information. Clearances must determine the subject's current and potential future trustworthiness; the latter is harder (and more expensive) to assess. Some higher-level clearances include access to compartmented information. *Compartmentalization* is a technical method for enforcing *need to know*.

FORMAL ACCESS APPROVAL

Formal access approval is documented approval from the data owner for a subject to access certain objects, requiring the subject to understand all of the rules and requirements for accessing data, as well as the consequences should the data become lost, destroyed, or compromised.

NEED TO KNOW

Need to know refers to answering the question: does the user "need to know" the specific data they may attempt to access? Most computer systems rely on least privilege and require the users to police themselves by following the set policy and therefore only attempting to obtain access to information of which they have a need to know. Need to know is more granular than least privilege: unlike least privilege, which typically groups objects together, need to know access decisions are based on each individual object.

SENSITIVE INFORMATION/MEDIA SECURITY

Though security and controls related to the people within an enterprise are vitally important, so is having a regimented process for handling sensitive information, including media security. This section discusses concepts that are an important component of a strong overall information security posture.

Sensitive information

All organizations have sensitive information that requires protection, and that sensitive information physically resides on some form of media. In addition to primary storage, backup storage must also be considered. Wherever data exists, there must be processes in place to ensure that the data is not destroyed or inaccessible (breach of availability), disclosed (breach of confidentiality), or altered (breach of integrity).

Handling

People handling sensitive media should be trusted individuals who have been vetted by the organization. They must understand their role in the organization's information security posture. Sensitive media should have strict policies regarding its handling. Policies should require the inclusion of written logs detailing the person responsible for the media. Historically, backup media has posed a significant problem for organizations.

Retention

Media and information have a limited period of usefulness. Retention of sensitive information should not persist beyond this period or legal requirement (whichever is greater), as it needlessly exposes the data to threats of disclosure when the data is no longer needed by the organization. Keep in mind there may be regulatory or other legal reasons that may compel the organization to maintain such data far beyond its time of utility.

OWNERSHIP

Primary information security roles include business or mission owners, data owners, system owners, custodians, and users. Each role has a different set of responsibilities in securing an organization's assets.

BUSINESS OR MISSION OWNERS

Business owners and mission owners (senior management) create the information security program and ensure that it is properly staffed and funded, as well as given appropriate organizational priority. These owners are responsible for ensuring that all organizational assets are protected.

DATA OWNERS

The data owner (also called information owner) is a manager responsible for ensuring that specific data is protected. Data owners determine data sensitivity labels and the frequency of data backup. They focus on the data itself, whether in electronic or paper format. A company with multiple lines of business may have multiple data owners. The data owner performs management duties, while custodians, which will be discussed shortly perform the hands-on protection of data.

SYSTEM OWNER

The system owner is a manager who is responsible for the actual computers that house data. This includes the hardware and software configuration, including updates, patching, etc. The system owners ensure that the hardware is physically secure, operating systems are patched and up to date, the system is hardened, etc. Technical hands-on responsibilities are delegated to custodians, discussed in the next section.

CUSTODIAN

A custodian provides hands-on protection of assets, such as data. They perform data backups and restoration, patch systems, configure antivirus software, etc. The custodians follow detailed orders and do not make critical decisions on how data is protected. The data owner may dictate, "The data owner may dictate that all data must be backed up every 24 h." The custodians would then deploy and operate a backup solution that meets the data owner's requirements.

USERS

Users must follow the rules; they must comply with mandatory policies, procedures, standards, etc. For example, users must not write their passwords down or share accounts. Users must be made aware of these risks and requirements. They must also be made aware of the penalty for failing to comply with mandatory directives and policies.

DATA CONTROLLERS AND DATA PROCESSORS

Data controllers create and manage sensitive data within an organization. Human resources employees are often data controllers, as they create and manage sensitive data, such as salary and benefit data, reports from employee sanctions, etc.

Data processors manage data on behalf of data controllers. An outsourced payroll company is an example of a data processor. Data processors manage payroll data, which is used to determine the amount to pay individual employees, on behalf of a data controller, such as an HR department.

DATA COLLECTION LIMITATION

Organizations should collect the minimum amount of sensitive information that is required.

The Organisation for Economic Co-operation and Development (OECD) Collection Limitation Principle discusses data limitation: "There should be limits to the collection of personal data and any such data should be obtained by lawful and fair means and, where appropriate, with the knowledge or consent of the data subject."[2]

MEMORY AND REMANENCE

The 2015 exam update added timely topics such as remanence properties of SSDs, discussed next, followed by a discussion of computer memory itself.

DATA REMANENCE

It is important to understand data remanence when discussing media sanitization and data destruction. Data remanence is data that persists beyond noninvasive means to delete it. Though data remanence is sometimes used specifically to refer to residual data that persists on magnetic storage, remanence concerns go beyond just that of magnetic storage media.

MEMORY

Memory is a series of on/off switches representing bits: 0s (off) and 1s (on). Memory may be chip based, disk based, or tape based. RAM is random-access memory: "random" means the CPU may randomly access or jump to any location in memory. Sequential memory, such as tape, must sequentially read memory, beginning at offset zero, to the desired portion of memory. Volatile memory, such as RAM, loses integrity after a power loss; nonvolatile memory (such as read-only memory (ROM), disk, or tape) maintains integrity without power.

Real or primary memory, such as RAM, is directly accessible by the CPU and is used to hold instructions and data for currently executing processes. Secondary memory, such as disk-based memory, is not directly accessible.

Cache memory

Cache memory is the fastest system memory, required to keep up with the CPU as it fetches and executes instructions. The data most frequently used by the CPU is stored in cache memory. The fastest portion of the CPU cache is the *register* file, which contains multiple registers. Registers are small storage locations used by the CPU to store instructions and data.

The next fastest form of cache memory is Level 1 cache, located on the CPU itself. Finally, Level 2 cache is connected to (but outside of) the CPU. Static random-access memory (SRAM) is used for cache memory.

RAM and ROM

RAM is volatile memory used to hold instructions and data of currently running programs. It loses integrity after loss of power.

ROM is nonvolatile; data stored in ROM maintains integrity after loss of power. A computer *basic input/output system* (BIOS) *firmware* is stored in ROM. While ROM is "read only," some types of ROM may be written to via flashing.

DRAM and SRAM

SRAM is fast, expensive memory that uses small latches called "flip-flops" to store bits. Dynamic random-access Memory (DRAM) stores bits in small capacitors (like small batteries), and is slower and cheaper than SRAM. The capacitors used by DRAM leak charge, and so they must be continually refreshed to maintain integrity, typically every few to a few hundred milliseconds, depending on the type of DRAM. Refreshing reads and writes the bits back to memory. SRAM does not require refreshing and maintains integrity as long as power is supplied.

Firmware

Firmware stores programs that do not change frequently, such as a computer's BIOS (discussed below) or a router's operating system and saved configuration. Various types of ROM chips may store firmware, including programmable read-only memory (PROM), erasable programmable read-only memory (EPROM), and EEPROM, defined next.

PROM can be written to once, typically at the factory. EPROM and EEPROM may be "flashed," or erased and written to multiple times.

A programmable logic device (PLD) is a field-programmable device, which means it is programmed after it leaves the factory. EPROMs, EEPROMs, and flash memory are examples of PLDs.

Flash memory

Flash memory, such as a USB thumb drive, is a specific type of EEPROM that is used for storage. The difference is that any byte of an EEPROM may be written, while flash drives are written by larger sectors.

Solid-state drives

A SSD is a combination of flash memory (EEPROM) and DRAM. Degaussing (destroying data via a strong magnetic field, which we will discuss shortly) has no effect on SSDs. While physical disks have physical blocks (eg, Block 1 is on a specific physical location on a magnetic disk), blocks on SSDs are logical and are mapped to physical blocks. Also, SSDs do not overwrite blocks that contain data; the device will instead write data to an unused block and mark the previous block unallocated.

A process called garbage collection later takes care of these old blocks: "Working in the background, garbage collection systematically identifies which memory cells contain unneeded data and clears the blocks of unneeded data during off-peak times to maintain optimal write speeds during normal operations."[3]

The TRIM command improves garbage collection by more efficiently marking data "invalid" (requiring garbage collection), and skipping data that can be ignored. "TRIM is an attribute of the ATA Data Set Management Command. The TRIM function improves compatibility, endurance, and performance by allowing the drive to do garbage collection in the background. This collection eliminates blocks of data, such as deleted files."[4] While the TRIM command improves performance, it does not reliably destroy data.

A sector-by-sector overwrite behaves very differently on an SSD versus a magnetic drive, and it does not reliably destroy all data. Also, electronically shredding a file (ie, overwriting the file's data before deleting it, which we will discuss shortly) is not effective. Data on SSD drives that are not physically damaged may be securely removed via ATA Secure Erase.

The two valid options for destroying data on SSD drives are ATA Secure Erase and destruction. Destruction is the best method for SSD drives that are physically damaged.

DATA DESTRUCTION

All forms of media should be securely cleaned or destroyed before disposal to prevent *object reuse*, which is the act of recovering information from previously used objects, such as computer files. Objects may be physical, such as paper files in manila folders, or electronic, such as data on a hard drive.

Object reuse attacks range from nontechnical attacks, such as *dumpster diving* (searching for information by rummaging through unsecured trash), to technical attacks, such as recovering information from unallocated blocks on a disk drive.

OVERWRITING

Simply "deleting" a file removes the entry from a file allocation table (FAT) and marks the data blocks as "unallocated." Reformatting a disk destroys the old FAT and replaces it with a new one. In both cases, data itself usually remains and can be recovered through the use of forensic tools. This issue is called *data remanence*, referring to "remnants" of data left behind.

The act of overwriting actually writes over every character of a file or entire disk drive and is far more secure than deleting or formatting a disk drive. Common methods include writing all zeroes or writing random characters. Electronic "*shredding*" or "*wiping*" overwrites the file's data before removing the FAT entry.

DEGAUSSING

Degaussing destroys the integrity of magnetic medium, such as a tape or disk drive, by exposing it to a strong magnetic field, which destroys the integrity of the medium and the data it contains.

DESTRUCTION

Destruction physically destroys the integrity of media by damaging or destroying the media itself, such as the platters of a disk drive. Destructive measures include incineration, pulverizing, and shredding, as well as bathing metal components in acid.

Destroying objects is more secure than overwriting them. It may not be possible to overwrite damaged media, though data may still be recoverable. Highly sensitive data should be degaussed or destroyed, perhaps in addition to overwriting.

SHREDDING

A simple form of media sanitization is shredding, a type of physical destruction. Though this term is sometimes used in relation to overwriting of data, here shredding refers to the process of making unrecoverable any data printed on hard copy or on smaller objects, such as floppy or optical disks.

DETERMINING DATA SECURITY CONTROLS

Determining which data security controls to employ is a critical skill. Standards, scoping, and tailoring are used to choose and customize which controls are employed. Also, the determination of controls will be dictated by whether the data is at rest or in motion.

CERTIFICATION AND ACCREDITATION

Certification means a system has been certified to meet the security requirements of the data owner. Certification considers the system, the security measures taken to protect the system, and the residual risk represented by the system. *Accreditation* is the data owner's acceptance of the certification and of the residual risk, which is required before the system is put into production.

STANDARDS AND CONTROL FRAMEWORKS

A number of standards are available to determine security controls. Some, such as Payment Card Industry Data Security Standard (PCI-DSS), are industry specific; for example, vendors who use credit cards. Others, such as OCTAVE®, ISO 17799/27002, and Control objectives for information and related technology (COBIT), are more general and will be discussed shortly.

PCI-DSS

The PCI-DSS is a security standard created by the Payment Card Industry Security Standards Council. The council is comprised of American Express, Discover, Master Card, Visa, and others. PCI-DSS seeks to protect credit cards by requiring vendors who use them to take specific security precautions.

The core principles of PCI-DSS (available at https://www.pcisecuritystandards.org/security_standards/index.php) are

- Build and Maintain a Secure Network and Systems
- Protect Cardholder Data
- Maintain a Vulnerability Management Program
- Implement Strong Access Control Measures
- Regularly Monitor and Test Networks
- Maintain an Information Security Policy[5]

OCTAVE®

OCTAVE® stands for *Operationally Critical Threat, Asset, and Vulnerability Evaluation*[sm], a risk management framework from Carnegie Mellon University. OCTAVE® describes a three-phase process for managing risk. Phase 1 identifies staff knowledge, assets, and threats. Phase 2 identifies vulnerabilities and evaluates safeguards. Phase 3 conducts the risk analysis and develops the risk mitigation strategy.

The International Common Criteria

The *International Common Criteria* is an internationally agreed-upon standard for describing and testing the security of information technology (IT) products. It presents a hierarchy of requirements for a range of classifications and systems.

CRUNCH TIME

The Common Criteria uses specific terms when defining specific portions of the testing process.

- *Target of evaluation (ToE)*: The system or product that is being evaluated
- *Security target*: The documentation describing the ToE, including the security requirements and operational environment
- *Protection profile*: An independent set of security requirements and objectives for a specific category of products or systems, such as firewalls or intrusion detection systems
- *Evaluation assurance level* (EAL): The evaluation score of the tested product or system

Levels of evaluation

Within the Common Criteria, there are seven EALs, each building upon the previous level. For example, EAL3-rated products can be expected to meet or exceed the requirements of products rated EAL1 or EAL2.

FAST FACTS

The Common Criteria levels are

- EAL1: Functionally tested
- EAL2: Structurally tested
- EAL3: Methodically tested and checked
- EAL4: Methodically designed, tested, and reviewed
- EAL5: Semiformally designed, and tested
- EAL6: Semiformally verified, designed, and tested
- EAL7: Formally verified, designed, and tested[6]

ISO 17799 and the ISO 27000 Series

ISO 17799 was a broad-based approach for the information security code of practice by the International Organization for Standardization, based in Geneva, Switzerland. The full title is *ISO/IEC 17799:2005 Information technology—Security Techniques—Code of Practice for Information Security Management.* ISO 17799:2005 signifies the 2005 version of the standard, based on BS (British Standard) 7799 Part 1.

ISO 17799 had 11 areas, focusing on specific information security controls:

1. Policy
2. Organization of information security
3. Asset management
4. Human resources security
5. Physical and environmental security
6. Communications and operations management
7. Access control
8. Information systems acquisition, development, and maintenance
9. Information security incident management
10. Business continuity management
11. Compliance[7]

ISO 17799 was renumbered to ISO 27002 in 2005 in order to make it consistent with the 27000 series of ISO security standards. ISO 27001 is a related standard, formally called *ISO/IEC 27001:2005 Information technology—Security techniques—Information Security Management Systems—Requirements.* ISO 27001 was based on BS 7799 Part 2.

COBIT

COBIT is a control framework for employing information security governance best practices within an organization. COBIT was developed by the ISACA (Information Systems Audit and Control Association, see http://www.isaca.org).

COBIT has four domains: Plan and Organize, Acquire and Implement, Deliver and Support, and Monitor and Evaluate. There are 34 IT processes across the 4 domains. More information about COBIT is available at: http://www.isaca.org/Knowledge-Center/COBIT/Pages/Overview.aspx. Version 5 was released in Apr. 2012.

ITIL®

ITIL® (Information Technology Infrastructure Library) is a framework for providing best services in IT Service Management. More information about ITIL® is available at: http://www.itil-officialsite.com.

ITIL® contains five *Service Management Practices—Core Guidance* publications:

- Service Strategy
- Service Design
- Service Transition
- Service Operation
- Continual Service Improvement

Service Strategy helps IT provide services. Service Design details the infrastructure and architecture required to deliver IT services. Service Transition describes taking new projects and making them operational. Service Operation covers IT operations controls. Finally, Continual Service Improvement describes ways to improve existing IT services.

SCOPING AND TAILORING

Scoping is the process of determining which portions of a standard will be employed by an organization. For example, an organization that does not employ wireless equipment may declare the wireless provisions of a standard are out of scope and therefore do not apply.

Tailoring is the process of customizing a standard for an organization. It begins with controls selection, continues with scoping, and finishes with the application of compensating controls.

PROTECTING DATA IN MOTION AND DATA AT REST

Data at rest is stored data that resides on a disk and/or in a file. Data in motion is data that is being transferred across a network. Each form of data requires different controls for protection, which we will discuss next.

Drive and tape encryption

Drive and tape encryption protect data at rest and is one of the few controls that will protect data after physical security has been breached. These controls are recommended for all mobile devices and media containing sensitive information that may physically leave a site or security zone.

Whole-disk encryption of mobile device hard drives is recommended. Partially encrypted solutions, such as encrypted file folders or partitions, often risk exposing sensitive data stored in temporary files, unallocated space, swap space, etc.

Media storage and transportation

All sensitive backup data should be stored offsite, whether transmitted offsite via networks or physically moved as backup media. Sites using backup media should follow strict procedures for rotating media offsite.

Always use a bonded and insured company for offsite media storage. The company should employ secure vehicles and store media at a secure site. Ensure that the storage site is unlikely to be impacted by the same disaster that may strike the primary site, such as a flood, earthquake, or fire. Never use informal practices, such as storing backup media at employees' houses.

Protecting data in motion

Data in motion is best protected via standards-based end-to-end encryption, such as IPsec VPN. This includes data sent over untrusted networks such as the Internet, but VPNs may also be used as an additional defense-in-depth measure on internal networks like a private corporate WAN or private circuits like T1s leased from a service provider.

SUMMARY OF EXAM OBJECTIVES

We described the concept of data classification, in use for millennia. We discussed the roles required to protect data, including business or mission owners, data owners, system owners, custodians, and users.

An understanding of the remanence properties of volatile and nonvolatile memory and storage media are critical security concepts to master. We discussed RAM, ROM, types of PROMs, flash memory, and SSDs, including remanence properties and secure destruction methods. Finally, we discussed well-known standards, including PCI-DSS and the ISO 27000 series, as well as standards processes including scoping and tailoring.

TOP FIVE TOUGHEST QUESTIONS

1. A company outsources payroll services to a third-party company. Which of the following roles most likely applies to the third-party payroll company?
   A. Data controller
   B. Data hander

    C. Data owner

    D. Data processor

2. Which managerial role is responsible for the actual computers that house data, including the security of hardware and software configurations?

    A. Custodian

    B. Data owner

    C. Mission owner

    D. System owner

3. What method destroys the integrity of magnetic media, such as tapes or disk drives, and the data they contain by exposing them to a strong magnetic field?

    A. Bit-level overwrite

    B. Degaussing

    C. Destruction

    D. Shredding

4. What type of relatively expensive and fast memory uses small latches called "flip-flops" to store bits?

    A. DRAM

    B. EPROM

    C. SRAM

    D. SSD

5. What type of memory stores bits in small capacitors (like small batteries)?

    A. DRAM

    B. EPROM

    C. SRAM

    D. SSD

ANSWERS

1. Correct answer and explanation: D. A third-party payroll company is an example of a data processor.

Incorrect answers and explanations: Answers A, B, and C are incorrect. A data controller is someone who creates PII, such as an HR department. "Data handler" is not a formal term and is a distractor answer. A data owner is a management employee responsible for assuring that specific data is protected.

2. Correct answer and explanation: D. A system owner is responsible for the actual computers that house data, including the security of hardware and software configurations.

Incorrect answers and explanations: Answers A, B, and C are incorrect. A custodian is a nonmanager who provides hands-on protection of assets. A data owner is a manager responsible for assuring that specific data is protected. A mission owner is a member of senior management who creates the information security program and ensures that it is properly staffed and funded and has the appropriate organizational priority.

3. Correct answer and explanation: B. Degaussing destroys the integrity of magnetic media, such as tapes or disk drives, and the data they contain by exposing them to a strong magnetic field.

   Incorrect answers and explanations: Answers A, C, and D are incorrect. A bit-level overwrite removes data by overwriting every sector of a disk. Destruction physically destroys data; for example, via incineration. Shredding electronic data involves overwriting a file's contents before deleting the file.

4. Correct answer and explanation: C. SRAM is relatively expensive and fast memory that uses small latches called "flip-flops" to store bits.

   Incorrect answers and explanations: Answers A, B, and D are incorrect. DRAM is relatively inexpensive memory that uses capacitors. EPROM may be erased with ultraviolet light. A SSD is a combination of DRAM and EEPROM.

5. Correct answer and explanation: A. DRAM stores bits in small capacitors (like small batteries).

   Incorrect answers and explanations: Answers B, C, and D are incorrect. EPROM may be erased with ultraviolet light. SRAM is relatively expensive and fast memory that uses small latches called "flip-flops" to store bits. A SSD is a combination of DRAM and EEPROM.

ENDNOTES

1. *Executive Order 12356—National security information.* http://www.archives.gov/federal-register/codification/executive-order/12356.html [accessed 25.04.16].
2. *OECD privacy principles.* http://oecdprivacy.org/ [accessed 25.04.16].
3. *SSD garbage collection briefly explained.* http://www.ryli.net/ssd-garbage-collection-briefly-explained/ [accessed 25.04.16].
4. *What is TRIM?* http://www.intel.com/support/ssdc/hpssd/sb/CS-031242.htm?wapkw=(TRIM) [accessed 25.04.16].
5. *Payment Card Industry (PCI) Data Security Standard requirements and security assessment procedures (Version 3.1).* https://www.pcisecuritystandards.org/documents/PCI_DSS_v3-1.pdf [accessed 25.04.16].
6. *Common Criteria (ISO/IEC 15408) certification.* http://www.kyoceradocumentsolutions.com/security/cc.html [accessed 25.04.16].
7. ISO/IEC 17799:2005 http://www.iso.org/iso/catalogue_detail?csnumber=39612 [accessed 25.04.16].

Domain 3: Security engineering

CHAPTER OUTLINE

Eleventh Hour CISSP®. http://dx.doi.org/10.1016/B978-0-12-811248-9.00003-6

INTRODUCTION

We begin this domain with security architecture concepts, including security models, as well as secure system components in hardware and software. Next comes cryptography, including core concepts of symmetric encryption, asymmetric encryption, and hash functions. Finally, we will discuss physical security, where we will learn that safety of personnel is paramount.

SECURITY MODELS

Security models provide rules of the road for security in operating systems. The canonical example is Bell-LaPadula, which includes "no read up" (NRU), also known as the Simple Security Property. This is the rule that forbids a secret-cleared subject from reading a top-secret object. While Bell-LaPadula, which is discussed shortly, is focused on protecting confidentiality, other models like Biba are focused on integrity.

READING DOWN AND WRITING UP

The concepts of reading down and writing up apply to mandatory access control models such as Bell-LaPadula. Reading down occurs when a subject reads an object at a lower sensitivity level, such as a top-secret subject reading a secret object.

There are instances when a subject has information and passes that information up to an object, which has higher sensitivity than the subject has permission to access. This is called writing up.

BELL-LAPADULA MODEL

The *Bell-LaPadula* model was originally developed for the US Department of defense (DoD). It is focused on maintaining the confidentiality of objects. Protecting confidentiality means users at a lower security level are denied access to objects at a higher security level.

FAST FACTS

Bell-LaPadula includes the following rules and properties:

- *Simple Security Property*: "No read up"; a subject at a specific clearance level cannot read an object at a higher classification level. Subjects with a Secret clearance cannot access Top Secret objects, for example.
- *Security Property*: "No write down"; a subject at a higher clearance level cannot write to a lower classification level. For example: subjects who are logged into a Top Secret system cannot send emails to a Secret system.
- *Strong Tranquility Property*: Security labels will not change while the system is operating.
- *Weak Tranquility Property*: Security labels will not change in a way that conflicts with defined security properties.

LATTICE-BASED ACCESS CONTROLS

Lattice-based access control allows security controls for complex environments. For every relationship between a subject and an object, there are defined upper and lower access limits implemented by the system. This lattice, which allows reaching higher and lower data classification, depends on the need of the subject, the label of the object, and the role the subject has been assigned. Subjects have a least upper bound (LUB) and greatest lower bound (GLB) of access to the objects based on their lattice position.

INTEGRITY MODELS

Models such as Bell-LaPadula focus on confidentiality, sometimes at the expense of integrity. The Bell-LaPadula "no write down" rule means subjects can write up; that is, a Secret subject can write to a Top Secret object. What if the Secret subject writes erroneous information to a Top Secret object? Integrity models such as Biba address this issue.

Biba model

While many governments are primarily concerned with confidentiality, most businesses desire to ensure that the integrity of the information is protected at the highest level. *Biba* is the model of choice when integrity protection is vital.

FAST FACTS

The Biba model has two primary rules: the Simple Integrity Axiom and the * Integrity Axiom.

- *Simple Integrity Axiom*: "No read down"; a subject at a specific clearance level cannot *read* data at a lower classification. This prevents subjects from accessing information at a lower integrity level. This protects integrity by preventing bad information from moving up from lower integrity levels.
- ** Integrity Axiom*: "No write up"; a subject at a specific clearance level cannot *write* data to a higher classification. This prevents subjects from passing information up to a higher integrity level than they have clearance to change. This protects integrity by preventing bad information from moving up to higher integrity levels.

Biba is often used where integrity is more important than confidentiality. Examples include time and location-based information.

DID YOU KNOW?

Biba takes the Bell-LaPadula rules and reverses them, showing how confidentiality and integrity are often at odds. If you understand Bell-LaPadula (no read up; no write down), you can extrapolate Biba by reversing the rules: "no read down"; "no write up."

Clark-Wilson

Clark-Wilson is a real-world integrity model that protects integrity by requiring subjects to access objects via programs. Because the programs have specific limitations to what they can and cannot do to objects, Clark-Wilson effectively limits the capabilities of the subject. Clark-Wilson uses two primary concepts to ensure that security policy is enforced: well-formed transactions and separation of duties. The concept of well-formed transactions provides integrity. The process is comprised of what is known as the access control triple: user, transformation procedure, and constrained data item.

CHINESE WALL MODEL

The Chinese Wall model (also known as Brewer-Nash) is designed to avoid conflicts of interest by prohibiting one person, such as a consultant, from accessing multiple conflict of interest categories (CoIs).

ACCESS CONTROL MATRIX

An access control matrix is a table that defines the access permissions that exist between specific subjects and objects. A matrix is a data structure that acts as a lookup table for the operating system. The table's rows, or capability lists, show the capabilities of each subject. The columns of the table show the access control list (ACL) for each object or application.

SECURE SYSTEM DESIGN CONCEPTS

Secure system design transcends specific hardware and software implementations and represents universal best practices.

LAYERING

Layering separates hardware and software functionality into modular tiers. The complexity of an issue, such as reading a sector from a disk drive, is contained to one layer; in this case, the hardware layer. One layer, such as the application layer, is not directly affected by a change to another.

FAST FACTS

A generic list of security architecture layers is as follows:

1. Hardware
2. *Kernel* and device drivers
3. *Operating system (OS)*
4. Applications

ABSTRACTION

Abstraction hides unnecessary details from the user. As Bruce Schneier said, "Complexity is the enemy of security"[1]; that is, the more complex a process, the less secure it is. That said, computers are tremendously complex machines, and abstraction provides a way to manage that complexity.

SECURITY DOMAINS

A *security domain* is the list of objects a subject is allowed to access. More broadly defined, domains are groups of subjects and objects with similar security requirements. Confidential, Secret, and Top Secret are three security domains used by the US DoD, for example.

THE RING MODEL

The *ring model* is a form of central processing unit (CPU) hardware layering that separates and protects domains, such as kernel mode and user mode, from each other. Many CPUs, such as the Intel x86 family, have four rings, ranging from Ring 0 (kernel) to Ring 3 (user), shown in Fig. 3.1. The innermost ring is the most trusted, and each successive outer ring is less trusted.

Processes communicate between the rings via *system calls*, which allow processes to communicate with the kernel and provide a window between the rings.

FAST FACTS

The rings are (theoretically) used as follows:

- *Ring 0*: Kernel
- *Ring 1*: Other OS components that do not fit into Ring 0
- *Ring 2*: Device drivers
- *Ring 3*: User applications

While x86 CPUs have four rings and can be used as described above, this usage is considered theoretical because most x86 operating systems, including Linux and Windows, use Rings 0 and 3 only. A new mode called hypervisor mode (and informally called "Ring −1") allows virtual guests to operate in Ring 0, controlled by the hypervisor one ring "below." The Intel Virtualization Technology (Intel VT, aka "Vanderpool"), and AMD-Virtualization (AMD-V, aka "Pacifica") CPUs support a hypervisor.

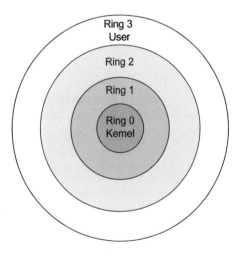

FIG. 3.1

The ring model.

OPEN AND CLOSED SYSTEMS

An *open system* uses open hardware and standards, using standard components from a variety of vendors. An IBM-compatible PC is an open system, using a standard motherboard, memory, BIOS, CPU, etc. You may build an IBM-compatible PC by purchasing components from a multitude of vendors. A *closed system* uses proprietary hardware or software.

DID YOU KNOW?

An open system is not the same as open source. An open system uses standard hardware and software, while open-source software makes source code publicly available.

SECURE HARDWARE ARCHITECTURE

Secure hardware architecture focuses on the physical computer hardware required to have a secure system. The hardware must provide confidentiality, integrity, and availability for processes, data, and users.

THE SYSTEM UNIT AND MOTHERBOARD

The *system unit* is the computer's case; it contains all of the internal electronic computer components, including the motherboard, internal disk drives, power supply, etc. The *motherboard* contains hardware including the CPU, memory slots, firmware, and peripheral slots, such as peripheral component interconnect slots. The keyboard unit is the external keyboard.

THE COMPUTER BUS

A *computer bus*, shown in Fig. 3.2, is the primary communication channel on a computer system. Communication between the CPU, memory, and input/output devices such as keyboard, mouse, and display occurs via the bus.

THE CPU

The central processing unit (CPU) is the brains of the computer, capable of controlling and performing mathematical calculations. Ultimately, everything a computer does is mathematical: adding numbers, which can be extended to subtraction, multiplication, division, etc.; performing logical operations; accessing memory locations by address; etc. CPUs are rated by the number of clock cycles per second. A 4-GHz CPU has four billion clock cycles per second.

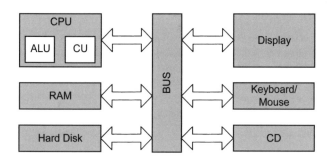

FIG. 3.2

Simplified computer bus.

Arithmetic logic unit and control unit

The *arithmetic logic unit* (ALU) performs mathematical calculations; it is the part that computes. The ALU is fed instructions by the *control unit*, which acts as a traffic cop, sending instructions to the ALU.

Fetch and execute

CPUs fetch machine language instructions (such as "add 1 + 1") and execute them (add the numbers, for answer of "2"). The *"fetch and execute"* (also called the fetch-decode-execute cycle or FDX) process actually takes four steps:

1. Fetch Instruction 1
2. Decode Instruction 1
3. Execute Instruction 1
4. Write (save) Result 1

These four steps take one clock cycle to complete.

Pipelining

Pipelining combines multiple CPU steps into one process, allowing simultaneous FDX and write steps for different instructions. Each part is called a pipeline stage; the pipeline depth is the number of simultaneous stages that may be completed at once.

Given our previous fetch-and-execute example of adding 1 + 1, a CPU without pipelining would have to wait an entire cycle before performing another computation. A four-stage pipeline can combine the stages of four other instructions:

1. Fetch Instruction 1
2. Fetch Instruction 2, Decode Instruction 1
3. Fetch Instruction 3, Decode Instruction 2, Execute Instruction 1
4. Fetch Instruction 4, Decode Instruction 3, Execute Instruction 2, Write (save) result 1
5. Fetch Instruction 5, Decode Instruction 4, Execute Instruction 3, Write (save) result 2, etc.

Pipelining is like an automobile assembly line; instead of building one car at a time, from start to finish, lots of cars enter the assembly pipeline, and discrete phases (like installing tires) occur on one car after another. This increases the throughput.

Interrupts

An *interrupt* indicates that an asynchronous event has occurred. A CPU interrupt is a form of hardware interrupt that causes the CPU to stop processing its current task, save the state, and begin processing a new request. When the new task is complete, the CPU will complete the prior task.

Processes and threads

A *process* is an executable program and its associated data loaded and running in memory. A heavyweight process (HWP) is also called a task. A parent process may spawn additional child processes called *threads*. A thread is a lightweight process (LWP). Threads are able to share memory, resulting in lower overhead compared to heavy weight processes.

Multitasking and multiprocessing

Applications run as processes in memory, comprised of executable code and data. *Multitasking* allows multiple tasks (heavyweight processes) to run simultaneously on one CPU. Older and simpler operating systems, such as MS-DOS, are non-multitasking, in that they run one process at a time. Most modern operating systems, such as Linux, Windows 10, and OS X support multitasking.

Multiprocessing has a fundamental difference from multitasking: it runs multiple processes on multiple CPUs. Two types of multiprocessing are symmetric multiprocessing (SMP) and asymmetric multiprocessing (AMP; some sources use ASMP). SMP systems have one operating system to manage all CPUs. AMP systems have one operating system image per CPU, essentially acting as independent systems.

CISC and RISC

CISC (complex instruction set computer) and RISC (reduced instruction set computer) are two forms of CPU design. CISC uses a large set of complex machine language instructions, while RISC uses a reduced set of simpler instructions. x86 CPUs, among many others, are CISC; ARM (used in many cell phones and PDAs), PowerPC, Sparc, and others are RISC.

MEMORY PROTECTION

Memory protection prevents one process from affecting the confidentiality, integrity, or availability of another. This is a requirement for secure multiuser (ie, more than one user logged in simultaneously) and multitasking (ie, more than one process running simultaneously) systems.

Process isolation

Process isolation is a logical control that attempts to prevent one process from interfering with another. This is a common feature among multiuser operating systems such as Linux, UNIX, or recent Microsoft Windows operating systems. Older operating systems such as MS-DOS provide no process isolation, which means a crash in any MS-DOS application could crash the entire system.

Hardware segmentation

Hardware segmentation takes process isolation one step further by mapping processes to specific memory locations. This provides more security than logical process isolation alone.

Virtual memory

Virtual memory provides virtual address mapping between applications and hardware memory. Virtual memory provides many functions, including multitasking (multiple tasks executing at once on one CPU), swapping, and allowing multiple processes to access the same shared library in memory, among others.

Swapping and paging

Swapping uses virtual memory to copy contents of primary memory (RAM) to or from secondary memory (not directly addressable by the CPU, on disk). Swap space is often a dedicated disk partition that is used to extend the amount of available memory. If the kernel attempts to access a page (a fixed-length block of memory) stored in swap space, a page fault occurs, which means that the page is not located in RAM and the page is "swapped" from disk to RAM.

Basic input/output system

The IBM PC-compatible basic input/output system (BIOS) contains code in firmware that is executed when a PC is powered on. It first runs the *power-on self-test* (POST), which performs basic tests, including verifying the integrity of the BIOS itself, testing the memory, and identifying system devices, among other tasks. Once the POST process is complete and successful, it locates the boot sector (for systems that boot off disks), which contains the machine code for the operating system kernel. The kernel then loads and executes, and the operating system boots up.

WORM storage

WORM (write once, read many) storage, like its name suggests, can be written to once and read many times. It is often used to support records retention for legal or regulatory compliance. WORM storage helps assure the integrity of the data it contains; there is some assurance that it has not been and cannot be altered, short of destroying the media itself.

TRUSTED PLATFORM MODULE

A trusted platform module (TPM) chip is a processor that can provide additional security capabilities at the hardware level. Not all computer manufacturers employ TPM chips, but the adoption has steadily increased. If included, a TPM chip is typically found on a system's motherboard.

The TPM chip allows for hardware-based cryptographic operations. Security functions can leverage the TPM for random number generation; the use of symmetric, asymmetric, and hashing algorithms; and secure storage of cryptographic keys and message digests. The most commonly referenced use case for the TPM chip is ensuring boot integrity. By operating at the hardware level, the TPM chip can help ensure that kernel-mode rootkits are less likely to be able to undermine operating system security. In addition to boot integrity, TPM is also commonly associated with some implementations of full disk encryption.

DATA EXECUTION PREVENTION AND ADDRESS SPACE LAYOUT RANDOMIZATION

One of the main goals in attempting to exploit software vulnerabilities is to achieve some form of code execution capability. The two most prominent protections against this attack are data execution prevention (DEP) and address space location randomization (ASLR). DEP, which can be enabled within hardware and/or software, attempts to prevent code execution in memory locations that are not predefined to contain executable content.

Another protection mechanism, ASLR, seeks to make exploitation more difficult by randomizing memory addresses. For example, imagine an adversary develops a successful working exploit on his or her own test machine. When the code is run on a different system using ASLR, the addresses will change, which will probably cause the exploit to fail.

SECURE OPERATING SYSTEM AND SOFTWARE ARCHITECTURE

Secure operating system and software architecture builds upon the secure hardware described in the previous section, providing a secure interface between hardware and the applications, as well as the users, that access the hardware. Operating systems provide memory, resource, and process management.

THE KERNEL

The kernel is the heart of the operating system, which usually runs in ring 0. It provides the interface between hardware and the rest of the operating system, including applications. As discussed previously, when an IBM-compatible PC is started or rebooted, the BIOS locates the boot sector of a storage device, such as a hard drive. That boot sector contains the beginning of the software kernel machine code, which is then executed.

Reference monitor

A core function of the kernel is running the *reference monitor*, which mediates all access between subjects and objects. It enforces the system's security policy, such as preventing a normal user from writing to a restricted file, like the system password file.

VIRTUALIZATION AND DISTRIBUTED COMPUTING

Virtualization and distributed computing have revolutionized the computing world, bringing wholesale changes to applications, services, systems data, and data centers.

VIRTUALIZATION

Virtualization adds a software layer between an operating system and the underlying computer hardware. This allows multiple "guest" operating systems to run simultaneously on one physical "host" computer.

Hypervisor

The key to virtualization security is the *hypervisor*, which controls access between virtual guests and host hardware. A Type 1 hypervisor, also called bare metal, is part of an operating system that runs directly on host hardware. A Type 2 hypervisor runs as an application on a normal operating system, such as Windows 10.

Many virtualization exploits target the hypervisor, including hypervisor-controlled resources shared between host and guests, or guest and guest. These include cut-and-paste, shared drives, and shared network connections.

Virtualization security issues

Virtualization software is complex and relatively new. As discussed previously, complexity is the enemy of security[1]; the sheer complexity of virtualization software may cause security problems.

Combining multiple guests onto one host may also raise security issues. Virtualization is no replacement for a firewall; never combine guests with different security requirements (such as DMZ and internal) onto one host. The risk of virtualization escape is called VMEscape, where an attacker exploits the host OS or a guest from another guest.

Many network-based security tools, such as network intrusion detection systems, can be blinded by virtualization.

CLOUD COMPUTING

Public cloud computing outsources IT infrastructure, storage, or applications to a third-party provider. A cloud also implies geographic diversity of computer resources. The goal of cloud computing is to allow large providers to leverage their economies of scale to provide computing resources to other companies that typically pay for these services based on their usage.

Table 3.1 Example Cloud Service Levels

Type	Example
Infrastructure as a Service (IaaS)	Linux server hosting
Platform as a Service (PaaS)	Web service hosting
Software as a Service (SaaS)	Web mail

Three commonly available levels of service provided by cloud providers are infrastructure as a service (IaaS), platform as a service (PaaS), and software as a service (SaaS). IaaS provides an entire virtualized operating system, which the customer configures from the OS on up. PaaS provides a preconfigured operating system and the customer configures the applications. Finally, SaaS is completely configured, from the operating system to applications, and the customer simply uses the application. In all three cases, the cloud provider manages hardware, virtualization software, network, backups, etc. See Table 3.1 for typical examples of each.

Private clouds house data for a single organization and may be operated by a third party or by the organization itself. Government clouds keep data and resources geographically contained within the borders of one country, designed for the government of the respective country.

Benefits of cloud computing include reduced upfront capital expenditure, reduced maintenance costs, robust levels of service, and overall operational cost savings.

From a security perspective, taking advantage of public cloud computing services requires strict service level agreements and an understanding of new sources of risk. One concern is that if multiple organizations' guests are running on the same host, the compromise of one cloud customer could lead to the compromise of other customers.

Organizations should also negotiate specific rights before signing a contract with a cloud computing provider. These rights include the right to audit, the right to conduct a vulnerability assessment, and the right to conduct a penetration test, both electronic and physical, of data and systems placed in the cloud.

GRID COMPUTING

Grid computing represents a distributed computing approach that attempts to achieve high computational performance by nontraditional means. Rather than achieving high-performance computational needs by having large clusters of similar computing resources or a single high-performance system, such as a supercomputer, grid computing attempts to harness the computational resources of a large number of dissimilar devices.

LARGE-SCALE PARALLEL DATA SYSTEMS

The primary purpose of large-scale parallel systems is to allow for increased performance through economies of scale. One of the key security concerns with parallel systems is ensuring the maintenance of data integrity throughout the processing.

Often parallel systems will leverage some degree of shared memory on which they operate. This shared memory, if not appropriately managed, can expose potential race conditions that introduce integrity challenges.

PEER-TO-PEER NETWORKS

Peer-to-peer (P2P) networks alter the classic client/server computer model. Any system may act as a client, a server, or both, depending on the data needs. Decentralized peer-to-peer networks are resilient; there are no central servers that can be taken offline.

Integrity is a key P2P concern. With no central repository of data, what assurance do users have of receiving legitimate data? Cryptographic hashes are a critical control and should be used to verify the integrity of data downloaded from a P2P network.

THIN CLIENTS

Thin clients are simpler than normal computer systems, which have hard drives, full operating systems, locally installed applications, etc. Thin clients rely on central servers, which serve applications and store the associated data. Thin clients allow centralization of applications and their data, as well as the associated security costs of upgrades, patching, data storage, etc. Thin clients may be hardware based (such as diskless workstations) or software based (such as thin client applications).

SYSTEM VULNERABILITIES, THREATS, AND COUNTERMEASURES

System threats, vulnerabilities, and countermeasures describe security architecture and design vulnerabilities, as well as the corresponding exploits that may compromise system security. We will also discuss countermeasures, or mitigating actions that reduce the associated risk.

COVERT CHANNELS

A *covert channel* is any communication that violates security policy. The communication channel used by malware installed on a system that locates personally identifiable information (PII) such as credit card information and sends it to a malicious server is an example of a covert channel. Two specific types of covert channels are *storage channels* and *timing channels*.

BACKDOORS

A *backdoor* is a shortcut in a system that allows a user to bypass security checks, such as username/password authentication, to log in. Attackers will often install a backdoor after compromising a system.

Maintenance hooks are a type of backdoor; they are shortcuts installed by system designers and programmers to allow developers to bypass normal system checks during development, such as requiring users to authenticate.

MALICIOUS CODE (MALWARE)

Malicious code or *malware* is the generic term for any type of software that attacks an application or system. There are many types of malicious code; viruses, worms, Trojans, and logic bombs can all cause damage to targeted systems. Zero-day exploits are malicious code (ie, a threat) for which there is no vendor-supplied patch, meaning there is an unpatched vulnerability.

Computer viruses

Computer viruses are malware that does not spread automatically; they require a host (such as a file) and a carrier to spread the virus from system to system (usually a human).

FAST FACTS

Types of viruses include:

- *Macro virus*: virus written in macro language (such as Microsoft Office or Microsoft Excel macros).
- *Boot sector virus*: virus that infects the boot sector of a PC, which ensures that the virus loads upon system startup.
- *Stealth virus*: a virus that hides itself from the OS and other protective software, such as antivirus software.
- *Polymorphic virus*: a virus that changes its signature upon infection of a new system, attempting to evade signature-based antivirus software.
- *Multipartite virus*: a virus that spreads via multiple vectors. Also called multipart virus.

Worms

Worms are malware that self-propagates (spreads independently). Worms typically cause damage two ways: first by the malicious code they carry and then the loss of network availability due to aggressive self-propagation.

Trojans

A Trojan (also called a Trojan horse) is malware that performs two functions: one benign, such as a game, and one malicious. The term derives from the Trojan horse described in Virgil's poem *The Aeneid*.

Rootkits

A rootkit is malware that replaces portions of the kernel and/or operating system. A user-mode rootkit operates in ring 3 on most systems, replacing operating system components in "userland." A kernel-mode rootkit replaces the kernel, or loads malicious loadable kernel modules. Kernel-mode rootkits operate in ring 0 on most operating systems.

Packers

Packers provide runtime compression of executables. The original executable is compressed, and a small decompresser is prepended to the executable. Upon execution, the decompresser unpacks the compressed executable machine code and runs it. Packers are a neutral technology that is used to shrink the size of executables. Many types of malware use packers, which can be used to evade signature-based malware detection.

Logic bombs

A *logic bomb* is a malicious program that is triggered when a logical condition is met, such as after a number of transactions have been processed, or on a specific date (also called a time bomb). Malware such as worms often contain logic bombs, behaving in one manner, then changing tactics on a specific date and time.

Antivirus software

Antivirus software is designed to prevent and detect malware infections. Signature-based antivirus software uses static signatures of known malware. Heuristic-based antivirus uses anomaly-based detection to attempt to identify behavioral characteristics of malware, such as altering the boot sector.

SERVER-SIDE ATTACKS

Server-side attacks (also called service-side attacks) are launched directly from an attacker (the client) to a listening service. Patching, system hardening, firewalls, and other forms of defense-in-depth mitigate server-side attacks. Organizations should not allow direct access to server ports from untrusted networks such as the Internet, unless the systems are hardened and placed on DMZ networks.

CLIENT-SIDE ATTACKS

Client-side attacks occur when a user downloads malicious content. The flow of data is reversed compared to server-side attacks: client-side attacks initiate from the victim who downloads content from the attacker.

Client-side attacks are difficult to mitigate for organizations that allow Internet access. Clients include word processing software, spreadsheets, media players, Web browsers, etc. Most firewalls are far more restrictive inbound compared to outbound; they were designed to "keep the bad guys out," and mitigate server-side attacks originating from untrusted networks. They often fail to prevent client-side attacks.

WEB ARCHITECTURE AND ATTACKS

The World Wide Web of 10 or more years ago was simpler. Most web pages were static, rendered in Hypertext Markup Language, or HTML. The advent of "Web 2.0," with dynamic content, multimedia, and user-created data has increased the attack surface of the Web, creating more attack vectors.

Applets

Applets are small pieces of mobile code that are embedded in other software such as web browsers. Unlike HTML, which provides a way to display content, applets are executables. The primary security concern is that applets are downloaded from servers, then run locally. Malicious applets may be able to compromise the security of the client.

Applets can be written in a variety of programming languages; two prominent applet languages are *Java* (by Oracle/Sun Microsystems) and *ActiveX* (by Microsoft). The term "applet" is used for Java and "control" for ActiveX, although they are functionally similar.

Java

Java is an object-oriented language used not only as a way to write applets, but also as a general-purpose programming language. Java platform-independent bytecode is interpreted by the Java Virtual Machine (JVM). The JVM is available for a variety of operating systems, including Linux, FreeBSD, and Microsoft Windows.

Java applets run in a sandbox, which segregates the code from the operating system. The sandbox is designed to prevent an attacker who is able to compromise a java applet from accessing system files, such as the password file.

ActiveX

ActiveX controls are the functional equivalent of Java applets. They use digital certificates instead of a sandbox to provide security. Unlike Java, ActiveX is a Microsoft technology that works on Microsoft Windows operating systems only.

Open web application security project

The Open Web Application Security Project (OWASP, see: http://www.owasp.org) represents one of the best application security resources. OWASP provides a tremendous number of free resources dedicated to improving organizations' application security posture. One of their best-known projects is the OWASP Top 10 project, which provides consensus guidance on what are considered to be the 10 most significant application security risks. The OWASP Top 10 is available at https://www.owasp.org/index.php/Category:OWASP_Top_Ten_Project.

In addition to the wealth of information about application security threats, vulnerabilities, and defenses, OWASP also maintains a number of security tools available for free download including a leading interception proxy called the Zed Attack Proxy (ZAP).

Extensible markup language

Extensible markup language, or XML, is a markup language designed as a standard way to encode documents and data. XML is similar to HTML, but it is more universal. XML is used on the web, but is not tied to it; XML can be used to store application configuration and output from auditing tools, among other things. Extensible means users may use XML to define their own data formats.

Service-oriented architecture

Service-oriented architecture (SOA) attempts to reduce application architecture down to a functional unit of a service. SOA is intended to allow multiple heterogeneous applications to be consumers of services. The service can be used and reused throughout an organization rather than built within each individual application that needs the functionality offered by the service.

Services are expected to be platform independent and able to be called in a generic way that is also independent of a particular programming language. The intent is that that any application may leverage the service simply by using standard means available within their programming language of choice. Services are typically published in some form of a directory that provides details about how the service can be used and what the service provides.

Though web services are not the only example, they are the most common example provided for the SOA model. XML or JavaScript Object Notation (JSON) is commonly used for the underlying data structures of web services. SOAP, originally an acronym for Simple Object Access Protocol, but now simply SOAP, or REST (Representational State Transfer) provides the connectivity, and the WSDL (Web Services Description Language) provides details about how the web services are to be invoked.

DATABASE SECURITY

Databases present unique security challenges. The sheer amount of data that may be housed in a database requires special security consideration. As we will see shortly in the "Inference and Aggregation" section, the logical connections database users may make by creating, viewing, and comparing records may lead to inference and aggregation attacks, requiring database security precautions such as *inference* controls and *polyinstantiation*.

Polyinstantiation

Polyinstantiation allows two different objects to have the same name. The word polyinstantiation is based on the Latin roots for multiple (poly) and instances (instantiation). Database polyinstantiation means two rows may have the same primary key, but different data.

Inference and aggregation

Inference and *aggregation* occur when a user is able to use lower-level access to learn restricted information. These issues occur in multiple realms, including database security.

Inference requires deduction. There is a mystery to be solved, and lower level details provide the clues. Aggregation is a mathematical process; a user asks every question, receives every answer, and derives restricted information.

Data mining

Data mining searches large amounts of data to determine patterns that would otherwise get "lost in the noise." Credit card issuers have become experts in data mining, searching millions of credit card transactions stored in their databases to discover signs of fraud. Simple data mining rules, such as "X or more purchases, in Y time, in Z places" are useful in discovering stolen credit cards.

MOBILE DEVICE ATTACKS

A recent information security challenge is the number of mobile devices ranging from USB flash drives to laptops that are infected with malware outside of a security perimeter, then carried into an organization. Traditional network-based protection, such as firewalls and intrusion detection systems, are powerless to prevent the initial attack.

Mobile device defenses

Defenses include administrative controls such as restricting the use of mobile devices via policy. Technical controls to mitigate infected mobile computers include requiring authentication at OSI model Layer 2 via 802.1X. 802.1X authentication may be bundled with additional security functionality, such as verification of current patches and antivirus signatures.

Another mobile device security concern is the loss or theft of a mobile device, which threatens the confidentiality, integrity, and availability of the device and the data that resides on it. Backups can assure the availability and integrity of mobile data.

Full disk encryption (also known as whole disk encryption) ensures the confidentiality of mobile device data.

Remote wipe capability is another critical control, which describes the ability to erase and sometimes disable a mobile device that is lost or stolen.

CORNERSTONE CRYPTOGRAPHIC CONCEPTS

Cryptography is secret writing, a type of secure communication understood by the sender and intended recipient only. While it may be known that the data is being transmitted, the content of that data should remain unknown to third parties. Data in motion (moving on a network) and data at rest (stored on a device, such as a disk) may be encrypted for security.

KEY TERMS

Cryptology is the science of secure communications. *Cryptography* creates messages with hidden meaning; *cryptanalysis* is the science of breaking those encrypted messages to recover their meaning. Many use the term cryptography in place of cryptology; however, it is important to remember that cryptology encompasses both cryptography and cryptanalysis.

A *cipher* is a cryptographic algorithm. A *plaintext* is an unencrypted message. *Encryption* converts a plaintext to a *ciphertext*. *Decryption* turns a ciphertext back into a plaintext.

CONFIDENTIALITY, INTEGRITY, AUTHENTICATION, AND NONREPUDIATION

Cryptography can provide confidentiality (secrets remain secret) and integrity (data is not altered without authorization). It is important to note that it does not directly provide availability. Cryptography can also provide authentication, which proves an identity claim.

Additionally, cryptography can provide *nonrepudiation*, which is an assurance that a specific user performed a specific transaction that did not change.

CONFUSION, DIFFUSION, SUBSTITUTION, AND PERMUTATION

Diffusion means the order of the plaintext should be "diffused" or dispersed in the ciphertext. *Confusion* means that the relationship between the plaintext and ciphertext should be as confused or random as possible.

Cryptographic *substitution* replaces one character for another; this provides the confusion. *Permutation*, also called transposition, provides diffusion by rearranging the characters of the plaintext, anagram-style. For example, "ATTACKATDAWN" can be rearranged to "CAAKDTANTATW."

DID YOU KNOW?

Strong encryption destroys patterns. If a single bit of plaintext changes, the odds of every bit of resulting ciphertext changing should be 50/50. Any signs of nonrandomness can be clues for a cryptanalyst, hinting at the underlying order of the original plaintext or key.

CRYPTOGRAPHIC STRENGTH

Good encryption is strong. For key-based encryption, it should be very difficult (ideally, impossible) to convert a ciphertext back to a plaintext without the key. The *work factor* describes how long it will take to break a cryptosystem (decrypt a ciphertext without the key).

Secrecy of the cryptographic algorithm does not provide strength; in fact, secret algorithms are often proven quite weak. Strong crypto relies on math, not secrecy, to provide strength. Ciphers that have stood the test of time are public algorithms, such as the *Triple Data Encryption Standard* (TDES) and the Advanced Encryption Standard (AES).

MONOALPHABETIC AND POLYALPHABETIC CIPHERS

A *monoalphabetic cipher* uses one alphabet, in which a specific letter substitutes for another. A *polyalphabetic cipher* uses multiple alphabets; for example, E substitutes for X one round, then S the next round.

Monoalphabetic ciphers are susceptible to frequency analysis. Polyalphabetic ciphers attempt to address this issue via the use of multiple alphabets.

EXCLUSIVE OR

Exclusive OR (XOR) is the "secret sauce" behind modern encryption. Combining a key with a plaintext via XOR creates a ciphertext. XORing the same key to the ciphertext restores the original plaintext. XOR math is fast and simple, so simple that it can be implemented with phone relay switches.

Two bits are true (or 1) if one or the other (exclusively, not both) is 1. In other words: if two bits are different, the answer is 1 (true). If two bits are the same, the answer is 0 (false). XOR uses a *truth table*, shown in Table 3.2. This dictates how to combine the bits of a key and plaintext.

DATA AT REST AND DATA IN MOTION

Cryptography protects data at rest and data in motion, or data in transit. Full disk encryption (also called whole disk encryption) of a magnetic disk drive using software such as BitLocker or PGP Whole Disk Encryption is an example of encrypting data at rest. An SSL or IPsec VPN is an example of encrypting data in motion.

PROTOCOL GOVERNANCE

Cryptographic *protocol governance* describes the process of selecting the right method (ie, cipher) and implementation for the right job, typically on an organization-wide scale. For example, as we will learn later this chapter, a digital signature provides authentication and integrity, but not confidentiality. Symmetric ciphers are primarily used for confidentiality, and AES is preferable over DES due to its strength and performance.

TYPES OF CRYPTOGRAPHY

There are three primary types of modern encryption: *symmetric*, *asymmetric*, and *hashing*. Symmetric cryptography uses a single key to encrypt and decrypt. Asymmetric cryptography uses two keys, one to encrypt and the other to decrypt. Hashing is a one-way cryptographic transformation using an algorithm, but no key.

Table 3.2 XOR Truth Table

X	Y	X XOR Y
0	0	0
0	1	1
1	0	1
1	1	0

SYMMETRIC ENCRYPTION

Symmetric encryption uses a single key to encrypt and decrypt. If you encrypt a zip file, then decrypt with the same key, you are using symmetric encryption. Symmetric encryption is also called "secret key" encryption because the key must be kept secret from third parties. Strengths of this method include speed and cryptographic strength per bit of key; however, the major weakness is that the key must be securely shared before two parties may communicate securely.

Stream and block ciphers

Symmetric encryption may have stream and block modes. Stream mode means each bit is independently encrypted in a "stream." Block mode ciphers encrypt blocks of data each round; for example, 64 bits for the Data Encryption Standard (DES), and 128 bits for AES. Some block ciphers can emulate stream ciphers by setting the block size to 1 bit; they are still considered block ciphers.

Initialization vectors and chaining

Some symmetric ciphers use an initialization vector to ensure that the first encrypted block of data is random. This ensures that identical plaintexts encrypt to different ciphertexts. Also, as Bruce Schneier notes in *Applied Cryptography*, "Even worse, two messages that begin the same will encrypt the same way up to the first difference. Some messages have a common header: a letterhead, or a 'From' line, or whatever."[2] Initialization vectors solve this problem.

Chaining (called *feedback* in stream modes) seeds the previous encrypted block into the next block ready for encryption. This destroys patterns in the resulting ciphertext. DES *Electronic Code Book* mode (see below) does not use an initialization vector or chaining, and patterns can be clearly visible in the resulting ciphertext.

DES

DES is the data encryption standard, which describes the *data encryption algorithm* (DEA). IBM designed DES, based on their older Lucifer symmetric cipher, which uses a 64-bit block size (ie, it encrypts 64 bits each round) and a 56-bit key.

EXAM WARNING

Even though DES is commonly referred to as an algorithm, it is technically the name of the published standard that describes DEA. It may sound like splitting hairs, but that is an important distinction to keep in mind on the exam. DEA may be the best answer for a question regarding the algorithm itself.

Modes of DES

DES can use five different modes to encrypt data. The modes' primary difference is block versus emulated stream, the use of initialization vectors, and whether errors in encryption will propagate to subsequent blocks.

FAST FACTS

The five modes of DES are:

- Electronic Code Book (ECB)
- Cipher Block Chaining (CBC)
- Cipher Feedback (CFB)
- Output Feedback (OFB)
- Counter (CTR) Mode

ECB is the original mode of DES. CBC, CFB, and OFB were added later. CTR mode is the newest mode, described in *NIST Special Publication 800-38a* (see http://csrc.nist.gov/publications/nistpubs/800-38a/sp800-38a.pdf).

Electronic code book

ECB is the simplest and weakest form of DES. It uses no initialization vector or chaining. Identical plaintexts with identical keys encrypt to identical ciphertexts. Two plaintexts with partial identical portions, such as the header of a letter, encrypted with the same key will have partial identical ciphertext portions.

Cipher block chaining

CBC mode is a block mode of DES that XORs the previous encrypted block of ciphertext to the next block of plaintext to be encrypted. The first encrypted block is an initialization vector that contains random data. This "chaining" destroys patterns. One limitation of the CBC mode is that encryption errors will propagate; an encryption error in one block will cascade through subsequent blocks due to the chaining, therefore destroying their integrity.

Cipher feedback

CFB mode is very similar to CBC, but the primary difference is that CFB is a stream mode. It uses feedback, which is the name for chaining when used in stream modes, to destroy patterns. Like CBC, CFB uses an initialization vector and destroys patterns, and so errors propagate.

Output feedback

OFB mode differs from CFB in the way feedback is accomplished. CFB uses the previous ciphertext for feedback. The previous ciphertext is the subkey XORed to the plaintext. OFB uses the subkey *before* it is XORed to the plaintext. Since the subkey is not affected by encryption errors, errors will not propagate.

Counter

CTR mode is like OFB; the difference again is the feedback. CTR mode uses a counter, so this mode shares the same advantages as OFB in that patterns are destroyed and errors do not propagate. However, there is an additional advantage: since the feedback can be as simple as an ascending number, CTR mode encryption can be executed in parallel.

Table 3.3 summarizes the five modes of DES.

Table 3.3 Modes of DES Summary

	Type	Initialization Vector	Error Propagation?
Electronic code book (ECB)	Block	No	No
Cipher block chaining (CBC)	Block	Yes	Yes
Cipher feedback (CFB)	Stream	Yes	Yes
Output feedback (OFB)	Stream	Yes	No
Counter mode (CTR)	Stream	Yes	No

Single DES

Single DES is the original implementation of DES, encrypting 64-bit blocks of data with a 56-bit key, using 16 rounds of encryption. The work factor required to break DES was reasonable in 1976, but advances in CPU speed and parallel architecture have made DES weak to a *brute-force* key attack today, where every possible key is generated and attempted.

Triple DES

Triple DES applies single DES encryption three times per block. Formally called the "triple data encryption algorithm (TDEA) and commonly called TDES," it became a recommended standard in 1999.

International data encryption algorithm

The international data encryption algorithm (IDEA) is a symmetric block cipher designed as an international replacement to DES. It uses a 128-bit key and 64-bit block size. The IDEA has patents in many countries.

Advanced encryption standard

The advanced encryption standard (AES) is the current US standard in symmetric block ciphers. AES uses 128-bit (with 10 rounds of encryption), 192-bit (with 12 rounds of encryption), or 256-bit (with 14 rounds of encryption) keys to encrypt 128-bit blocks of data.

Choosing AES

The US National Institute of Standards and Technology (NIST) solicited input on a replacement for DES in the *Federal Register* in January 1997. Fifteen AES candidates were announced in August 1998, and the list was reduced to five in August 1999. Table 3.4 lists the five AES finalists.

Rijndael was chosen and became AES. AES has four functions: SubBytes, ShiftRows, MixColumns, and AddRoundKey.

Blowfish and Twofish

Blowfish and Twofish are symmetric block ciphers created by teams lead by Bruce Schneier, author of *Applied Cryptography*. Blowfish uses from 32- through 448-bit keys (the default is 128-bit) to encrypt 64 bits of data. Twofish was an AES finalist,

Table 3.4 Five AES Finalists

Name	Author
MARS	IBM (11 authors)
RC6	RSA (Rivest, Robshaw, Sidney, Yin)
Rijndael	Daemen, Rijmen
Serpent	Anderson, Biham, Knudsen
Twofish	Schneier, Kelsey, Hall, Ferguson, Whiting, Wagner

encrypting 128-bit blocks using 128-bit through 256-bit keys. Both are open algorithms, meaning they are unpatented and freely available.

RC5 and RC6

RC5 and RC6 are symmetric block ciphers by RSA Laboratories. RC5 uses 32-bit (testing purposes), 64-bit (replacement for DES), or 128-bit blocks. The key size ranges from zero to 2040 bits.

RC6 was an AES finalist. RC6 is based on RC5 and is altered to meet the AES requirements. It is also stronger than RC5, encrypting 128-bit blocks using 128-, 192-, or 256-bit keys.

ASYMMETRIC ENCRYPTION

Asymmetric encryption uses two keys, one for encryption and the other for decryption. The public key, as its name indicates, is made public, and asymmetric encryption is also called public key encryption for this reason. Anyone who wants to communicate with you may simply download your posted public key and use it to encrypt their plaintext. Once encrypted, your public key cannot decrypt the plaintext, but your *private key* can do so. As the name implies, your private key must be kept private and secure.

Additionally, any message encrypted with the private key may be decrypted with the public key, as it is for digital signatures, as we will see shortly.

Asymmetric methods

Math lies behind the asymmetric breakthrough. These methods use one-way functions, which are easy to compute one way but are difficult to compute in the reverse direction.

Factoring prime numbers

An example of a one-way function is factoring a composite number into its primes. Multiplying the prime number 6269 by the prime number 7883 results in the composite number 49,418,527. That way is quite easy to compute, as it takes just milliseconds on a calculator. However, answering the question "Which prime number times which prime number equals 49,418,527" is *much* more difficult.

That computation is called factoring, and no shortcut has been found for hundreds of years. Factoring is the basis of the RSA algorithm.

Discrete logarithm

A logarithm is the opposite of exponentiation. Computing 7 to the 13th power (exponentiation) is easy on a modern calculator: 96,889,010,407. Asking the question "96,889,010,407 is 7 to what power," which means to find the logarithm, is more difficult. Discrete logarithms apply logarithms to groups, which is a much harder problem to solve. This one-way function is the basis of the *Diffie-Hellman* and *ElGamal* asymmetric algorithms.

Diffie-Hellman key agreement protocol

Key agreement allows two parties the security with which to agree on a symmetric key via a public channel, such as the Internet, with no prior key exchange. An attacker who is able to sniff the entire conversation is unable to derive the exchanged key. Whitfield Diffie and Martin Hellman created the Diffie-Hellman Key Agreement Protocol (also called the Diffie-Hellman Key Exchange) in 1976. Diffie-Hellman uses discrete logarithms to provide security.

Elliptic curve cryptography

ECC leverages a one-way function that uses discrete logarithms as applied to elliptic curves. Solving this problem is harder than solving discrete logarithms, so algorithms based on elliptic curve cryptography (ECC) are much stronger per bit than systems using discrete logarithms (and also stronger than factoring prime numbers). ECC requires less computational resources because it uses shorter keys comparison to other asymmetric methods. Lower-power devices often use ECC for this reason.

Asymmetric and symmetric tradeoffs

Asymmetric encryption is far slower than symmetric encryption, and it is weaker per bit of key length. The strength of asymmetric encryption is the ability to communicate securely without presharing a key.

HASH FUNCTIONS

A hash function provides encryption using an algorithm and no key. They are called one-way hash functions because there is no way to reverse the encryption. A variable-length plaintext is "hashed" into a fixed-length hash value, which is often called a "message digest" or simply a "hash." Hash functions are primarily used to provide integrity: if the hash of a plaintext changes, the plaintext itself has changed. Common older hash functions include *secure hash algorithm 1* (SHA-1), which creates a 160-bit hash and *Message Digest 5* (MD5), which creates a 128-bit hash. There are weaknesses in both MD5 and SHA-1, so newer alternatives such as SHA-2 are recommended.

Collisions

Hashes are not unique because the number of possible plaintexts is far larger than the number of possible hashes. Assume you are hashing documents that are a megabit long with MD5. Think of the documents as strings that are 1,000,000 bits long, and think of the MD5 hash as a string 128 bits long. The universe of potential 1,000,000-bit strings is clearly larger than the universe of 128-bit strings. Therefore, more than one document could have the same hash' this is called a *collision*.

MD5

MD5 is the Message Digest algorithm 5. It is the most widely used of the MD family of hash algorithms. MD5 creates a 128-bit hash value based on any input length. MD5 has been quite popular over the years, but there are weaknesses where collisions can be found in a more practical amount of time. MD6 is the newest version of the MD family of hash algorithms, first published in 2008.

Secure hash algorithm

Secure hash algorithm (SHA) is the name of a series of hash algorithms. SHA-1 creates a 160-bit hash value. SHA-2 includes SHA-224, SHA-256, SHA-384, and SHA-512, named after the length of the message digest each creates.

CRYPTOGRAPHIC ATTACKS

Cryptanalysts use cryptographic attacks to recover the plaintext without the key. Please remember that recovering the key (which is sometimes called "stealing" the key) is usually easier than breaking modern encryption. This is what law enforcement officials typically do when tracking a suspect who used cryptography; they obtain a search warrant and attempt to recover the key.

BRUTE FORCE

A brute-force attack generates the entire key space, which is every possible key. Given enough time, the plaintext will be recovered.

SOCIAL ENGINEERING

Social engineering uses the human mind to bypass security controls. This technique may recover a key by tricking the key holder into revealing the key. Techniques are varied; one way is to impersonate an authorized user when calling a help desk to request a password reset.

KNOWN PLAINTEXT

A known plaintext attack relies on recovering and analyzing a matching plaintext and ciphertext pair; the goal is to derive the key that was used. You may be wondering why you would need the key if you already have the plaintext, but recovering the key would allow you to also decrypt other ciphertexts encrypted with the same key.

CHOSEN PLAINTEXT AND ADAPTIVE CHOSEN PLAINTEXT

A cryptanalyst chooses the plaintext to be encrypted in a chosen plaintext attack; the goal is to derive the key. Encrypting without knowing the key is accomplished via an encryption oracle, or a device that encrypts without revealing the key.

Adaptive-chosen plaintext begins with a chosen plaintext attack in the first round. The cryptanalyst then "adapts" further rounds of encryption based on the previous round.

CHOSEN CIPHERTEXT AND ADAPTIVE CHOSEN CIPHERTEXT

Chosen ciphertext attacks mirror chosen plaintext attacks; the difference is that the cryptanalyst chooses the ciphertext to be decrypted. This attack is usually launched against asymmetric cryptosystems, where the cryptanalyst may choose public documents to decrypt that are signed (encrypted) with a user's private key.

Adaptive-chosen ciphertext also mirrors its plaintext cousin: it begins with a chosen ciphertext attack in the first round. The cryptanalyst then adapts further rounds of decryption based on the previous round.

KNOWN KEY

The term "known-key attack" is misleading, because if the cryptanalyst knows the key, the attack is over. Known key means the cryptanalyst knows something about the key and can use that knowledge to reduce the efforts used to attack it. If the cryptanalyst knows that the key is an uppercase letter and a number only, other characters can be omitted in the attack.

DIFFERENTIAL CRYPTANALYSIS

Differential cryptanalysis seeks to find the difference between related plaintexts that are encrypted. The plaintexts may differ by a few bits. It launches as an adaptive chosen plaintext attack; the attacker chooses the plaintext to be encrypted though he or she does not know the key and then encrypts related plaintexts.

LINEAR CRYPTANALYSIS

Linear cryptanalysis is a known plaintext attack where the cryptanalyst finds large amounts of plaintext/ciphertext pairs created with the same key. The pairs are studied to derive information about the key used to create them.

Both differential and linear analysis can be combined as *differential linear analysis*.

SIDE-CHANNEL ATTACKS

Side-channel attacks use physical data to break a cryptosystem, such as monitoring CPU cycles or power consumption used while encrypting or decrypting.

IMPLEMENTING CRYPTOGRAPHY

Symmetric, asymmetric, and hash-based cryptography do not exist in a vacuum; rather, they have real-world applications, often in combination with each other, in which they can provide confidentiality, integrity, authentication, and nonrepudiation.

DIGITAL SIGNATURES

Digital signatures are used to cryptographically sign documents. Digital signatures provide nonrepudiation, which includes authentication of the identity of the signer, and proof of the document's integrity (proving the document did not change). This means the sender cannot later deny or repudiate signing the document.

Roy wants to send a digitally signed email to Rick. Roy writes the email, which is the plaintext. He then uses the SHA-1 hash function to generate a hash value of the plaintext. He then creates the digital signature by encrypting the hash with his RSA private key. Fig. 3.3 shows this process. Roy then attaches the signature to his plaintext email and hits send.

Rick receives Roy's email and generates his own SHA-1 hash value of the plaintext email. Rick then decrypts the digital signature with Roy's RSA public key, recovering the SHA-1 hash Roy generated. Rick then compares his SHA-1 hash with Roy's. Fig. 3.4 shows this process.

FIG. 3.3

Creating a digital signature[3].

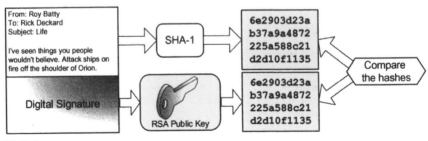

FIG. 3.4

Verifying a digital signature.

If the two hashes match, Rick knows a number of things:

1. Roy must have sent the email (only Roy knows his private key). This authenticates Roy as the sender.
2. The email did not change. This proves the integrity of the email.

If the hashes match, Roy cannot later deny having signed the email. This is nonrepudiation. If the hashes do not match, Rick knows either Roy did not send it, or that the email's integrity was violated.

PUBLIC KEY INFRASTRUCTURE

Public Key Infrastructure (PKI) leverages all three forms of encryption to provide and manage *digital certificates*. A digital certificate is a public key signed with a digital signature. Digital certificates may be server-based or client-based. If client and server certificates are used together, they provide mutual authentication and encryption. The standard digital certificate format is X.509.

Certificate authorities and organizational registration authorities

Digital certificates are issued by *certificate authorities* (CAs). Organizational registration authorities (ORAs) authenticate the identity of a certificate holder before issuing a certificate to them. An organization may operate as a CA or ORA (or both).

Certificate revocation lists

The CAs maintain *certificate revocation lists* (CRL), which, as the name implies, is a list of revoked certificates. A certificate may be revoked if the private key has been stolen, an employee is terminated, etc. A CRL is a flat file and does not scale well. The *Online Certificate Status Protocol* (OCSP) is a replacement for CRLs and uses client-server design that scales better.

Key management issues

CAs issue digital certificates and distribute them to certificate holders. The confidentiality and integrity of the holder's private key must be assured during the distribution process.

Public/private key pairs used in PKI should be stored centrally and securely. Users may lose their private key as easily as they may forget their password. A lost private key means that anything encrypted with the matching public key will be lost, short of cryptanalysis, as described previously.

Note that key storage is different than key escrow. Key storage means the organization that issued the public/private key pairs retains a copy. Key escrow means a copy is retained by a third-party organization (and sometimes multiple organizations), often for law enforcement purposes.

A retired key may not be used for new transactions, but one may be used to decrypt previously encrypted plaintexts. A destroyed key no longer exists and therefore cannot be used for any purpose.

SSL AND TLS

Secure Sockets Layer (SSL) brought the power of PKI to the web. SSL authenticates and provides confidentiality to web traffic. *Transport Layer Security* (TLS) is the successor to SSL. Both are commonly used as part of HTTPS (*Hypertext Transfer Protocol Secure*).

SSL was developed for the Netscape Web browser in the 1990s. SSL 2.0 was the first released version; SSL 3.0 fixed a number of security issues with version 2. TLS was based on SSL 3.0. TLS is very similar to that version, with some security improvements. Although typically used for HTTPS to secure web traffic, TLS may be used for other applications, such as Internet chat and email access.

IPsec

Internet Protocol Security (IPsec) is a suite of protocols that provide a cryptographic layer to both IPv4 and IPv6. It is one of the methods used to provide *virtual private networks* (VPN), which allow you to send private data over an insecure network, such as the Internet; the data crosses a public network, but is "virtually private." IPsec includes two primary protocols: *Authentication Header* (AH) and *Encapsulating Security Payload* (ESP). AH and ESP provide different and sometimes overlapping functionality.

Supporting IPsec protocols include *Internet Security Association and Key Management Protocol* (ISAKMP) and *Internet Key Exchange* (IKE).

AH and ESP

Authentication header (AH) provides authentication and integrity for each packet of network data. AH provides no confidentiality; it acts as a digital signature for the data. AH also protects against *replay attacks,* where data is sniffed off a network and resent, often in an attempt to fraudulently reuse encrypted authentication credentials.

ESP primarily provides confidentiality by encrypting packet data. It may also optionally provide authentication and integrity.

Security association and ISAKMP

AH and ESP may be used separately or in combination. An IPsec Security Association (SA) is a simplex (one-way) connection that may be used to negotiate ESP or AH parameters. If two systems communicate via ESP, they use two SAs, one for each direction. If the systems leverage AH in addition to ESP, they use two more SAs for a total of four. A unique 32-bit number called the security parameter index (SPI) identifies each simplex SA connection. The internet security association and key management protocol (ISAKMP) manages the SA creation process.

Tunnel and transport mode

IPsec is used in tunnel mode or transport mode. Security gateways use tunnel mode because they can provide point-to-point IPsec tunnels. ESP tunnel mode encrypts the entire packet, including the original packet headers. ESP transport mode only encrypts the data, not the original headers; this is commonly used when the sending and receiving system can "speak" IPsec natively.

> **CRUNCH TIME**
>
> AH authenticates the original IP headers, so it is often used (along with ESP) in transport mode because the original headers are not encrypted. Tunnel mode typically uses ESP alone, as the original headers are encrypted and thus protected by ESP).

IKE

IPsec can use a variety of encryption algorithms, such as MD5 or SHA-1 for integrity, and Triple DES or AES for confidentiality. The IKE negotiates the algorithm selection process. Two sides of an IPsec tunnel will typically use IKE to negotiate to the highest and fastest level of security, selecting AES over single DES for confidentiality if both sides support AES, for example.

PGP

Pretty Good Privacy (PGP), created by Phil Zimmerman in 1991, brought asymmetric encryption to the masses. PGP provides the modern suite of cryptography: confidentiality, integrity, authentication, and nonrepudiation. PGP can encrypt emails, documents, or an entire disk drive. PGP uses a *web of trust* model to authenticate digital certificates, instead of relying on a central CA.

S/MIME

MIME (multipurpose Internet mail extensions) provides a standard way to format email, including characters, sets, and attachments. Secure MIME (S/MIME) leverages PKI to encrypt and authenticate MIME-encoded email. The client or client's email server, called an S/MIME gateway, may perform the encryption.

ESCROWED ENCRYPTION

Escrowed encryption means a third-party organization holds a copy of a public/private key pair. The private key is often divided into two or more parts, each held in escrow by different trusted third-party organizations, which will only release their portion of the key with proper authorization, such as a court order. This provides separation of duties.

PERIMETER DEFENSES

Perimeter defenses help prevent, detect, and correct unauthorized physical access. Buildings, like networks, should employ defense in depth. Any one defense can fail, so critical assets should be protected by multiple physical security controls, such as fences, doors, walls, locks, etc. The ideal perimeter defense is safe, prevents unauthorized ingress, and offers both authentication and accountability, when applicable.

FENCES

Fences may range from simple deterrents (such as 3-foot/1-m tall fencing) to preventive devices, such as an 8-foot-tall (2.4 m) fence with barbed wire on top. Fences should be designed to steer ingress and egress to controlled points, such as exterior doors and gates.

GATES

Gates range in strength from Class 1, an ornamental gate designed to deter access, to a Class IV gate designed to prevent a car from crashing through entrances at airports and prisons.

FAST FACTS

Here are the four classes of gates:

- *Class I*: Residential (home use)
- *Class II*: Commercial/General Access (parking garage)
- *Class III*: Industrial/Limited Access (loading dock for 18-wheeler trucks)
- *Class IV*: Restricted Access (airport or prison)

LIGHTS

Lights can act as both a detective and deterrent control. A light that allows a guard to see an intruder is acting as a detective control. Types of lights include Fresnel lights, named after Augustine-Jean Fresnel. These are the same type of lights originally used in lighthouses, which used Fresnel lenses to aim light in a specific direction.

Light measurement terms include *lumen*, which is the amount of light one candle creates. Historically, light was measured in *foot-candles*, with one foot-candle measuring one lumen per square foot. *Lux*, based on the metric system, is more commonly used now; one lux is one lumen per square meter.

CCTV

Closed-circuit television (CCTV) is a detective device used to aid guards in detecting the presence of intruders in restricted areas. CCTVs using the normal light spectrum require sufficient visibility to illuminate the field of view that is visible to the camera. Infrared devices can "see in the dark" by displaying heat. Older "tube cameras" are analog devices. Modern cameras use charge-coupled discharge (CCD), which is digital.

Cameras have mechanical irises that act as human irises, controlling the amount of light that enters the lens by changing the size of the aperture. Key issues include *depth of field*, which is the area that is in focus, and *field of view*, which is the entire area viewed by the camera. More light allows a larger depth of field because a smaller aperture places more of the image in focus. Correspondingly, a wide aperture (used in lower light conditions) lowers the depth of field.

CCTV cameras may also have other typical camera features such as pan and tilt (moving horizontally and vertically).

LOCKS

Locks are a preventive physical security control, used on doors and windows to prevent unauthorized physical access. Locks may be mechanical, such as key locks or combination locks, while electronic locks are often used with smart cards or magnetic stripe cards.

Key locks

Key locks require a physical key to unlock. Keys are shared or sometimes copied, which lowers the accountability of key locks. A common type is the pin tumbler lock, which has driver pins and key pins. The correct key makes the pins line up with the shear line, allowing the lock tumbler (plug) to turn.

Ward or *warded locks* must turn a key through channels, or wards. A skeleton key can open varieties of warded locks.

Combination locks

Combination locks have dials that must be turned to specific numbers in a specific order (ie, alternating clockwise and counterclockwise turns) to unlock. Button or keypad locks also use numeric combinations. Limited accountability due to shared combinations is the primary security issue concerning these types of locks.

SMART CARDS AND MAGNETIC STRIPE CARDS

A *smart card* is a physical access control device that is often used for electronic locks, credit card purchases, or dual-factor authentication systems. "Smart" means the card contains a computer circuit; another term for a smart card is *integrated circuit card* (ICC).

Smart cards may be "contact" or "contactless." Contact cards use a smart card reader, while contactless cards are read wirelessly. One type of contactless card technology is *radio-frequency identification* (RFID). These cards contain RFID tags (also called transponders) that are read by RFID transceivers.

A *magnetic stripe* card contains a magnetic stripe that stores information. Unlike smart cards, magnetic stripe cards are passive devices that contain no circuits. These cards are sometimes called swipe cards because they are read when swiped through a card reader.

TAILGATING/PIGGYBACKING

Tailgating, also known as *piggybacking*, occurs when an unauthorized person follows an authorized person into a building after the authorized person unlocks and opens the door. Policy should forbid employees from allowing tailgating and security awareness efforts should describe this risk.

MANTRAPS AND TURNSTILES

A *mantrap* is a preventive physical control with two doors. The first door must close and lock before the second door may be opened. Each door typically requires a separate form of authentication to open, such as biometrics or a personal identification number (PIN). Without authentication, the intruder is trapped between the doors after entering the mantrap.

Turnstiles are designed to prevent tailgating by enforcing a "one person per authentication" rule, just as they do in subway systems. Secure data centers often use floor-to-ceiling turnstiles with interlocking blades to prevent an attacker from going over or under the turnstile. Secure revolving doors perform the same function.

CONTRABAND CHECKS

Contraband checks seek to identify objects that prohibited from entering a secure area. These checks often detect metals, weapons, or explosives. Contraband checks are casually thought to be detective controls, but their presence makes them a viable deterrent to actual threats.

MOTION DETECTORS AND OTHER PERIMETER ALARMS

Ultrasonic and *microwave motion detectors* work like Doppler radar used to predict the weather. A wave of energy is emitted, and the "echo" is returned when it bounces off an object. A motion detector that is 20 ft away from a wall will consistently receive an echo in the time it takes for the wave to hit the wall and bounce back to the receiver, for example. The echo will return more quickly when a new object, such as a person walking in range of the sensor, reflects the wave.

A *photoelectric motion sensor* sends a beam of light across a monitored space to a photoelectric sensor. The sensor alerts when the light beam is broken.

Ultrasonic, microwave, and infrared motion sensors are active sensors, which means they actively send energy. Consider a passive sensor as a read-only device; an example is a *passive infrared (PIR) sensor*, which detects infrared energy created by body heat.

DOORS AND WINDOWS

Always consider the relative strengths and weaknesses of doors, windows, walls, floors, ceilings, etc. All should be equally strong from a defensive standpoint, as attackers will target the weakest spot.

Egress must be unimpeded in case of emergency, so a simple push button or motion detectors are frequently used to allow egress. Outward-facing emergency doors should be marked for emergency use only and equipped with panic bars, which will trigger an alarm when used.

Glass windows are structurally weak and can be dangerous when shattered. Bullet-proof or explosive-resistant glass can be used for secured areas. Wire mesh or security film can lower the danger of shattered glass and provide additional strength. Alternatives to glass windows include polycarbonate such as Lexan™ and acrylic such as Plexiglas®.

WALLS, FLOORS, AND CEILINGS

The walls around any internal secure perimeter, such as a data center, should start at the floor slab and run to the ceiling slab. These are called slab-to-slab walls. Raised floors and drop ceilings can obscure where the walls truly start and stop. An attacker should not be able to crawl under a wall that stops at the top of the raised floor, or climb over a wall that stops at the drop ceiling.

GUARDS

Guards are a dynamic control in a variety of situations. Guards can inspect access credentials, monitor CCTVs and environmental controls, respond to incidents, and act as a general deterrent. All things being equal, criminals are more likely to target an unguarded building over a guarded building.

Professional guards have attended advanced training and/or schooling; amateur guards have not. The term *pseudo guard* means an unarmed security guard.

DOGS

Dogs provide perimeter defense duties, particularly in controlled areas, such as between the exterior building wall and a perimeter fence. The primary drawback to using dogs as a perimeter control is the legal liability.

SITE SELECTION, DESIGN, AND CONFIGURATION

Selection, design, and configuration describes the process of building a secure facility like a data center starting from the site selection process and going through the final design.

SITE SELECTION ISSUES

A greenfield is an undeveloped lot of land, which is the design equivalent of a blank canvas. In a similar way, site selection is the greenfield process of choosing a site to construct a building or data center.

Utility reliability

The reliability of local utilities is a critical concern for site selection purposes. Electrical outages are among the most common of all failures and disasters. Uninterruptible power supply (UPS) will provide protection against electrical failure for a short period (usually several hours or less). Generators provide longer protection but require refueling in order to operate for extended periods.

Crime

Local crime rates also factor into site selection. The primary issue is employee safety; all employees have the right to a safe working environment. Additional issues include theft of company assets.

SITE DESIGN AND CONFIGURATION ISSUES

Once the site has been selected, a number of design decisions must be made. Will the site be externally marked as a data center? Is there shared tenancy in the building? Where is the telecom demarcation point, or telecom *demark*?

Site marking

Many data centers are not externally marked in order to avoid drawing attention to the facility and its expensive contents. A modest building design might be an effective way to avoid attention.

Shared tenancy and adjacent buildings

Other tenants in a building can pose security issues, as they are already behind the physical security perimeter. A tenant's poor practices in visitor security can endanger your security.

Adjacent buildings pose a similar risk. Attackers can enter a less secure adjacent building and use that as a base to attack an adjacent building, often breaking in through a shared wall.

Shared demarc

A crucial issue to consider in a building with shared tenancy is a shared demarc, which is the demarcation point at which the Internet service provider (ISP) responsibility ends and the customer's begins. Most buildings have one demarc area where all external circuits enter the building. Access to the demarc allows attacks on the confidentiality, integrity, and availability of all circuits and the data flowing over them.

Media storage facilities

Offline storage of media for disaster recovery, potential legal proceedings, or other legal or regulatory purposes is commonplace. An off-site media storage facility will ensure that the data is accessible even after a physical disaster at the primary facility. The purpose of the media being stored offsite is to ensure continued access, which means the facility should be far enough removed from the primary facility to avoid the likelihood of a physical disaster affecting both the primary facility and the offsite storage location. Licensed and bonded couriers should transfer the media to and from the offsite storage facility.

SYSTEM DEFENSES

System defenses are one of the last lines of defense in a defense-in-depth strategy. These defenses assume that an attacker has physical access to the device or media containing sensitive information. In some cases, other controls may have failed and these controls are the final phase in data protection.

ASSET TRACKING

Detailed asset tracking databases enhance physical security. You cannot protect your data unless you know where and what it is. Detailed asset tracking databases support regulatory compliance by identifying where all regulated data is within a system. In case of employee termination, the asset database will show the exact equipment and data that the employee must return to the company. Data such as serial numbers and model numbers are useful in cases of loss due to theft or disaster.

PORT CONTROLS

Modern computers may contain multiple ports that may allow copying data to or from a system. Port controls are critical because large amounts of information can be placed on a device small enough to evade perimeter contraband checks. Ports can be physically disabled; examples include disabling ports on a system's motherboard, disconnecting internal wires that connect the port to the system, and physically obstructing the port itself.

ENVIRONMENTAL CONTROLS

Environmental controls provide a safe environment for personnel and equipment. Examples of environmental controls include power, HVAC, and fire safety.

ELECTRICITY

Reliable electricity is critical for any data center. It is one of the top priorities when selecting, building, and designing a site.

CRUNCH TIME

The following are common types of electrical faults:

- *Blackout*: prolonged loss of power
- *Brownout*: prolonged low voltage
- *Fault*: short loss of power
- *Surge*: prolonged high voltage
- *Spike*: temporary high voltage
- *Sag*: temporary low voltage

Surge protectors, UPS, and generators

Surge protectors protect equipment from damage due to electrical surges. They contain a circuit or fuse that is tripped during a power spike or surge, shorting the power or regulating it down to acceptable levels.

UPS provides temporary backup power in the event of a power outage. It may also "clean" the power, protecting against surges, spikes, and other forms of electrical faults.

Generators provide power longer than UPS and will run as long as fuel for the generator is available on site. Disaster recovery strategies should consider any negative impact on fuel supply and delivery.

EMI

Electricity generates magnetism, so any electrical conductor emits electromagnetic interference (EMI). This includes circuits, power cables, network cables, and many others. Network cables that are shielded poorly or are installed too closely together may suffer *crosstalk,* where magnetism from one cable crosses over to another nearby cable. This primarily affects the integrity of the network or voice data, but it might also affect the confidentiality.

Proper network cable management can mitigate crosstalk. Therefore, never route power cables close to network cables. The type of network cable used can also lower crosstalk. For example, *unshielded twisted pair* (UTP) cabling is far more susceptible than *shielded twisted pair* (STP) or *coaxial cable. Fiber optic cable* uses light instead of electricity to transmit data and is not susceptible to EMI.

HEATING, VENTILATION, AND AIR CONDITIONING

Heating, ventilation, and air conditioning (HVAC) controls keep the air at a reasonable temperature and humidity. They operate in a closed loop and recirculate treated air to help reduce dust and other airborne contaminants. HVAC units should employ positive pressure and drainage.

Data center HVAC units are designed to maintain optimum heat and humidity levels for computers. Humidity levels of 40–55% are recommended. A commonly recommended set point temperature range for a data center is 68–77 F (20–25°C).

Static and corrosion

The proper level of humidity can mitigate static by grounding all circuits in a proper manner and using antistatic sprays, wrist straps, and work surfaces. All personnel working with sensitive computer equipment such as boards, modules, or memory chips should ground themselves before performing any work.

High humidity levels can allow the water in the air to condense onto and into equipment, which may lead to corrosion. Maintaining proper humidity levels mitigates corrosion as well.

HEAT, FLAME, AND SMOKE DETECTORS

Heat detectors emit alerts when temperature exceeds an established safe baseline. They may trigger when a specific temperature is exceeded or when temperature changes at a specific rate (such as "10 F in less than 5 minutes").

Smoke detectors work through two primary methods: *ionization* and *photoelectric*. Ionization-based smoke detectors contain a small radioactive source that creates a small electric charge. Photoelectric sensors work in a similar fashion, except that they contain an LED (light-emitting diode) and a photoelectric sensor that generates a small charge while receiving light. Both types of alarms will sound when smoke interrupts the radioactivity or light by lowering or blocking the electric charge.

Flame detectors detect infrared or ultraviolet light emitted in fire. One drawback to this type of detection is that the detector usually requires line of sight to detect the flame; smoke detectors do not have this limitation.

PERSONNEL SAFETY, TRAINING, AND AWARENESS

Personnel safety is the primary goal of physical security. Safety training provides a skill set for personnel, such as learning to operate an emergency power system. Safety awareness can change user behavior in a positive manner. Both safety training and awareness are critical to ensure the success of a physical security program because you can never assume that personnel will know what to do and when to do it.

Evacuation routes

Post evacuation routes in a prominent location, as they are in hotel rooms, for example. Advise all personnel and visitors of the quickest evacuation route from their areas.

All sites should designate a meeting point, where all personnel will meet in the event of emergency. Meeting points are critical; tragedies have occurred when a person does not know another has already left the building and so he or she reenters the building for an attempted rescue.

Evacuation roles and procedures

The two primary evacuation roles are *safety warden* and *meeting point leader*. The safety warden ensures that all personnel safely evacuate the building in the event of an emergency or drill. The meeting point leader assures that all personnel are accounted for at the emergency meeting point. Personnel must follow emergency procedures, which includes following the posted evacuation route in case of emergency or drill.

Duress warning systems

Duress warning systems are designed to provide immediate alerts in the event of emergencies, such as severe weather, threat of violence, chemical contamination, etc. Duress systems may be local and include technologies such as use of overhead speakers or automated communications such as email or text messaging.

Travel safety

Personnel must be safe while working in all phases of business. This does not only refer to on-site work; it also includes authorized work from home and business travel. Telecommuters should have the proper equipment, including ergonomically safe workstations.

Business travel to certain areas can be dangerous. When organizations such as the US State Department Bureau of Consular Affairs issue travel warnings (http://travel.state.gov/), they should heeded by personnel before embarking on any travel to foreign countries.

ABCDK FIRES AND SUPPRESSION

The primary safety issue in case of fire is safe evacuation. Fire suppression systems extinguish fires, and different types of fires require different suppressive agents. These systems are typically designed with personnel safety as the primary concern.

Classes of fire and suppression agents

Class A fires are common combustibles such as wood and paper. This type of fire is the most common and should be extinguished with water or soda acid.

Class B fires are burning alcohol, oil, and other petroleum products such as gasoline. They are extinguished with gas or soda acid. You should never use water to extinguish a Class B fire.

Class C fires are electrical fires fed by electricity and may ignite in equipment or wiring. Electrical fires are conductive fires, and the extinguishing agent must be nonconductive, such as any type of gas. Many sources erroneously list soda acid as recommended for Class C fires, this is incorrect, as soda acid can conduct electricity.

Class D fires involve burning metals; use dry power to extinguish them.

Class K fires are kitchen fires, such as burning oil or grease. Extinguish class K fires with wet chemicals. Table 3.5 summarizes the classes of fire and suppression agents.

TYPES OF FIRE SUPPRESSION AGENTS

All fire suppression agents work via four possible methods, sometimes in combination: reducing the temperature of the fire, reducing the supply of oxygen, reducing the supply of fuel, and interfering with the chemical reaction within fire.

Water

Water suppresses fire by lowering the temperature below the *kindling point*, also called the *ignition point*. Water is the safest of all suppressive agents and therefore recommended for extinguishing common combustible fires such as burning paper or wood. It is important to cut electrical power when extinguishing a fire with water to reduce the risk of electrocution.

Table 3.5 Classes of Fire and Suppression Agents

US Class	Europe Class	Material	Suppression Agent
A	A	Ordinary combustibles such as wood and paper	Water or soda acid
B	B	Liquid	Halon/Halon substitute, CO_2, or soda acid
B	C	Flammable gases	Halon/Halon substitute, CO_2, or soda acid
C	E	Electrical equipment	Halon/Halon substitute, CO_2
D	D	Combustible metals	Dry powder
K	F	Kitchen (oil or fat) fires	Wet chemicals

Soda acid

Soda acid extinguishers are an older technology that use soda (sodium bicarbonate) mixed with water. There is a glass vial of acid suspended inside the extinguisher and an external lever breaks the vial. In addition to suppressing fire by lowering temperature, soda acid also has additional suppressive properties beyond plain water, as it creates foam that can float on the surface of some liquid fires, cutting off the oxygen supply.

Dry powder

Extinguishing a fire with dry powder, such as sodium chloride, works by lowering temperature and smothering the fire, starving it of oxygen. Dry powder is often used to extinguish metal fires. Flammable metals include sodium, magnesium, and many others.

Wet chemicals

Wet chemicals are primarily used to extinguish kitchen fires, which are Type K fires in the United States and Type F in Europe. However, wet chemicals may also be used on Type A (common combustible) fires. The chemical is usually potassium acetate mixed with water. This covers a grease or oil fire in a soapy film that lowers the temperature.

CO_2

Fires require oxygen as fuel, so removing oxygen smothers fires in CO_2 fire suppression. A major risk associated with CO_2 is that it is odorless and colorless, and our bodies will breathe it like air. By the time we begin suffocating due to lack of oxygen, it is often too late. This makes CO_2 a dangerous suppressive agent, so it is only recommended for use in unstaffed areas, such as electrical substations.

Halon and Halon substitutes

Halon extinguishes fire via a chemical reaction that consumes energy and lowers the temperature of the fire. However, Halon is currently being phased out in favor of replacements with similar properties.

Montreal accord

Halon has ozone-depleting properties. Because of this effect, the 1989 *Montreal Protocol* (formally called the *Montreal Protocol on Substances That Deplete the Ozone Layer*) banned production and consumption of new Halon in developed countries as of Jan. 1, 1994. However, existing Halon systems may be used, and while new Halon is not being produced, recycled Halon may be used.

FAST FACTS

Recommended replacements for Halon include the following systems:

- Argon
- FE-13
- FM-200
- Inergen

FE-13 is the newest of these agents, and comparatively safe. Breathing it in is safe in concentrations of up to 30%. Other Halon replacements are usually only safe for breathing up to a 10–15% concentration.

Sprinkler systems

Wet pipes have water right up to the sprinkler heads; therefore, the pipes are "wet." The sprinkler head contains a metal, which is common in older sprinklers, or small glass bulb designed to melt or break at a specific temperature. Once that occurs, the sprinkler head opens and water flows. Each head will open independently as the trigger temperature is exceeded.

Dry pipe systems also have closed sprinkler heads, but the difference is compressed air fills the pipes. A valve holds the water back and it will remain closed as long as sufficient air pressure remains in the pipes. As the dry pipe sprinkler heads open, the air pressure drops in each pipe, allowing the valve to open and send water to that head.

Deluge systems are similar to dry pipes, except the sprinkler heads are open and larger than dry pipe heads. The pipes are empty at normal air pressure; a deluge valve holds the water back. The valve opens when a fire alarm triggers.

Preaction systems are a combination of wet, dry, or deluge systems and require two separate triggers to release water. Single interlock systems release water into the pipes when a fire alarm triggers. The water releases once the head opens. Double interlock systems use compressed air, the same as dry pipes. However, the water will not fill the pipes until both the fire alarm triggers and the sprinkler head opens.

Portable fire extinguishers

All portable fire extinguishers should be marked with the type of fire they can extinguish. Portable extinguishers should be small enough so that any personnel who may need to use one can do so.

SUMMARY OF EXAM OBJECTIVES

In this large domain we began by describing fundamental logical hardware, operating systems, and software security components, as well as how to use those components to design, architect, and evaluate secure computer systems. Understanding these fundamental issues is critical for any information security professional.

We then moved on to cryptography, which dates to ancient times but is very much a part of our modern world, providing security for data in motion and at rest. Modern systems such as PKI put all the cryptographic pieces into play via the use of symmetric, asymmetric, and hash-based encryption to provide confidentiality, integrity, authentication, and nonrepudiation. You have learned how the pieces fit together; slower and weaker asymmetric ciphers such as RSA and Diffie-Hellman are used to exchange faster and stronger symmetric keys such as AES and DES. The symmetric keys are used as session keys to encrypt short-term sessions, such as web connections via HTTPS. Digital signatures employ public key encryption and hash algorithms such as MD5 and SHA-1 to provide nonrepudiation, authentication of the sender, and integrity of the message.

Finally, physical security is implicit in most other security controls, and it is often overlooked. We must always seek balance when implementing controls from all eight domains of knowledge. All assets should be protected by multiple defense-in-depth controls that span multiple domains. For example, a file server can be protected by policy, procedures, access control, patching, antivirus, OS hardening, locks, walls, HVAC, and fire suppression systems, among other controls). A thorough and accurate risk assessment should be conducted for all assets needing protection.

TOP FIVE TOUGHEST QUESTIONS

(1) Which of the following is true for digital signatures?
  (A) The sender encrypts the hash with a public key
  (B) The sender encrypts the hash with a private key
  (C) The sender encrypts the plaintext with a public key
  (D) The sender encrypts the plaintext with a private key
(2) Under which type of cloud service level would Linux hosting be offered?
  (A) IaaS
  (B) IDaaS
  (C) PaaS
  (D) SaaS
(3) A criminal deduces that an organization is holding an offsite meeting and there are few people in the building, based on the low traffic volume to and from the parking lot. The criminal uses the opportunity to break into the building to steal laptops. What type of attack has been launched?
  (A) Aggregation
  (B) Emanations
  (C) Inference
  (D) Maintenance Hook

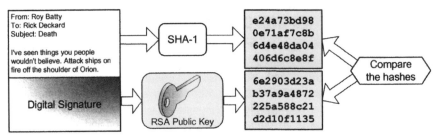

FIG. 3.5

Hotspot.

(4) EMI issues such as crosstalk primarily impact which aspect of security?

   (A) Confidentiality

   (B) Integrity

   (C) Availability

   (D) Authentication

(5) Hotspot: You receive the following signed email from Roy Batty. You determine that the email is not authentic, or it has changed since it was sent. Click on the locally generated message digest that proves the email lacks nonrepudiation (Fig. 3.5).

ANSWERS

1. *Correct Answer and Explanation*: B. The sender generates a hash of the plaintext and encrypts the hash with a private key. The recipient decrypts the hash with a public key.

   Incorrect Answers and Explanations: Answers A, C, and D are incorrect. The sender encrypts the hash with the private key, not public. The plaintext is hashed, and not encrypted.

2. *Correct Answer and Explanation*: A. Answer A is correct; IaaS (infrastructure as a service) provides an entire virtualized operating system, which the customer configures from the OS on up.

   Incorrect Answers and Explanations: Answers B, C, and D are incorrect. IDaaS (identity as a service) is also called cloud identity. IDaaS allows organizations to leverage cloud service for identity management. PaaS (platform as a service) provides a preconfigured operating system, and the customer configures the applications. SaaS (software as a service) is completely configured from the operating system to applications, and the customer simply uses the application.

3. *Correct Answer and Explanation*: C. Inference requires an attacker to "fill in the blanks" and deduce sensitive information from public information.

   Incorrect Answers and Explanations: Answers A, B, and D are incorrect. Aggregation is a mathematical operation where all questions are asked and

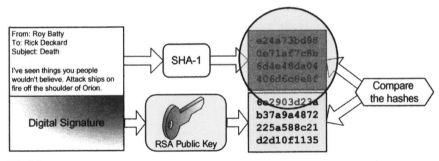

From: Roy Batty
To: Rick Deckard
Subject: Death

I've seen things you people wouldn't believe. Attack ships on fire off the shoulder of Orion.

Digital Signature

SHA-1

RSA Public Key

e24a73bd98
0e71af7c8b
6d4e48da04
406d6c6e8f

6e2903d23d
b37a9a4872
225a588c21
d2d10f1135

Compare the hashes

FIG. 3.6

Hotspot answer.

all answers are received; there is no deduction required. Emanations are energy broadcast from electronic equipment. Maintenance hooks are system maintenance backdoors left by vendors.

4. *Correct Answer and Explanation*: B. While EMI issues like crosstalk could impact all aspects listed, it most commonly impacts integrity.
   Incorrect Answers and Explanations: Answers A, C, and D are incorrect; confidentiality can be impacted (such as hearing another conversation on a voice phone call). In extreme cases, availability and authentication could be impacted, such as where crosstalk is so severe as to stop systems from functioning. These scenarios are far less common than simple integrity violation caused by EMI issues, such as crosstalk (Fig. 3.6).

ENDNOTES

1. *Three minutes with security expert Bruce Schneier.* https://www.schneier.com/news/archives/2001/09/three_minutes_with_s.html [accessed 29.04.16].
2. Schneier B. *Applied cryptography*. New York, NY: Wiley; 1996.
3. Scott R. *Bladerunner*. Warner Bros; 1982.

Domain 4: Communication and network security

INTRODUCTION

Communications and network security are fundamental to our modern life. The Internet, the World Wide Web, online banking, instant messaging, email, and many other technologies rely on network security; our modern world cannot exist without it.

Eleventh Hour CISSP®. http://dx.doi.org/10.1016/B978-0-12-811248-9.00004-8

Communications and network security focuses on the confidentiality, integrity, and availability of data in motion.

Communications and Network Security is one of the largest domains in the Common Body of Knowledge and contains more concepts than any other domain. This domain is also one of the most technically deep domains, requiring technical knowledge including *packets, segments, frames,* and their headers. The ability to understand this domain is critical for exam success.

NETWORK ARCHITECTURE AND DESIGN

Our first section is network architecture and design. We will discuss how networks should be designed and the controls they may contain, focusing on deploying defense-in-depth strategies and weighing the cost and complexity of a network control versus the benefit provided.

FUNDAMENTAL NETWORK CONCEPTS

Before we can discuss specific Communications and Network Security concepts, we need to understand the fundamental concepts behind them. Terms like *broadband* are often used informally; the exam requires a precise understanding of information security terminology.

Simplex, half-duplex, and full-duplex communication

Simplex communication is one-way, like a car radio tuned to a music station. *Half-duplex* communication sends or receives at one time only, not simultaneously, like a walkie-talkie. *Full-duplex* communications send and receive simultaneously, like two people having a face-to-face conversation.

LANs, WANs, MANs, GANs, and PANs

A *LAN* is a local-area network. A LAN is a comparatively small network, typically confined to a building or an area within a building. A *MAN* is a metropolitan area network, which is typically confined to a city, a ZIP code, a campus, or office park. A *WAN* is a wide area network, typically covering cities, states, or countries. A *GAN* is a global area network, which is a global collection of WANs.

At the other end of the spectrum, the smallest of these networks are PANs: personal area networks, with a range of 100 m or much less. Low-power wireless technologies like Bluetooth use PANs.

Internet, Intranet, and Extranet

The *Internet* is a global collection of peered networks running transmission control protocol/Internet protocol (TCP/IP), providing best effort service. An *Intranet* is a privately owned network running TCP/IP, such as a company network. An *Extranet* is a connection between private Intranets, such as connections to business partner intranets.

Circuit-switched and packet-switched networks

The original voice networks were circuit-switched, in that a circuit or channel (ie, a portion of a circuit) was dedicated between two nodes. *Circuit-switched networks* can provide dedicated bandwidth to point-to-point connections, such as a T1 connecting two offices.

One drawback of circuit-switched networks is that once a channel or circuit is connected, it is dedicated to that purpose, even if no data is being transferred. Packet-switched networks were designed to address this issue, as well as handle network failures more robustly.

Instead of using dedicated circuits, packet-switched networks break data into packets, each sent individually. If multiple routes are available between two points on a network, packet switching can choose the best route and fall back to secondary routes in case of failure. Packets may take any path across a network and are then reassembled by the receiving node. Missing packets can be retransmitted and out-of-order packets can be resequenced.

Unlike circuit-switched networks, packet-switched networks make unused bandwidth available for other connections. This can give packet-switched networks a cost advantage over circuit-switched networks.

Quality of service

Making unused bandwidth available for other applications presents a challenge: What happens when all bandwidth is consumed? Which applications "win" the required bandwidth? This is not an issue with circuit-switched networks, where applications have exclusive access to dedicated circuits or channels.

Packet-switched networks may use quality of service (QoS) to give specific traffic precedence over other traffic. For example: QoS is often applied to voice over Internet protocol (VoIP) traffic (ie, voice via packet-switched data networks) to avoid interruption of phone calls. Less time-sensitive traffic, such as simple mail transfer protocol (SMTP), a store-and-forward protocol used to exchange email between servers that often receives a lower priority. However, small delays in email exchange are less likely to be noticed as opposed to dropped phone calls.

THE OSI MODEL

The OSI (open system interconnection) reference model is a layered network model. The model is abstract; we do not directly run the OSI model in our systems (most now use the TCP/IP model). Rather, it is used as a reference point, so "Layer 1" (physical) is universally understood, whether you are running Ethernet or ATM, for example. "Layer X" in this book refers to the OSI model.

The OSI model has seven layers, as shown in Table 4.1. The layers may be listed in a top-to-bottom or bottom to top order. Using the latter, they are *Physical, Data Link, Network, Transport, Session, Presentation, and Application.*

Layer 1: Physical

Physical is layer 1 of the OSI model. This first layer describes units of data such as *bits* represented by energy (such as light, electricity, or radio waves) and the medium

Table 4.1 The OSI Model

7	Application
6	Presentation
5	Session
4	Transport
3	Network
2	Data link
1	Physical

used to carry them, such as copper or fiber optic cables. WLANs have a physical layer, even though we cannot physically touch it.

Cabling standards such as *thinnet, thicknet*, and unshielded twisted pair (UTP) exist in layer 1, among many others devices, including hubs and repeaters.

Layer 2: Data link

The data link layer handles access to the physical layer as well as LAN communication. An *Ethernet* card and its *media access control (MAC)* address are at layer 2, as are switches and bridges.

Layer 2 is divided into two sublayers: media access control (MAC) and logical link control (LLC). The MAC layer transfers data to and from the physical layer, while LLC handles LAN communications. MAC touches layer 1 and LLC touches layer 3.

Layer 3: Network

The network layer describes routing, which is moving data from a system on one LAN to a system on another. IP addresses and routers exist at layer 3, where protocols include IPv4 and IPv6, among others.

Layer 4: Transport

The transport layer handles packet sequencing, flow control, and error detection. TCP and user datagram protocol (UDP) are layer 4 protocols.

Layer 4 makes a number of features available, such as resending or resequencing packets. Taking advantage of these features is a protocol implementation decision. As we will see later, TCP takes advantage of these features, at the expense of speed. Many of these features are not implemented in UDP, which chooses speed over reliability.

Layer 5: Session

The session layer manages sessions, which provide maintenance on connections. Mounting a file share via a network requires a number of maintenance sessions, such as remote procedure calls (RPCs), which exist at the session layer. The session layer provides connections between applications and uses simplex, half-duplex, and full-duplex communication.

Layer 6: Presentation

The presentation layer presents data to the application and user in a comprehensible way. Presentation layer concepts include data conversion, characters sets such as ASCII, and image formats such as GIF (graphics interchange format), JPEG (joint photographic experts group), and TIFF (tagged image file format).

Layer 7: Application

The application-layer is where you interface with your computer application. Your web browser, word processor, and instant messaging client exist at layer 7. The protocols Telnet and FTP are application-layer protocols.

THE TCP/IP MODEL

The TCP/IP is a popular network model created by DARPA in the 1970s. TCP/IP is an informal name (named after the first two protocols created); the formal name is the Internet Protocol Suite. The TCP/IP model is simpler than the OSI model, as shown in Table 4.2.

While TCP and IP receive top billing, TCP/IP is actually a suite of protocols including UDP (user datagram protocol) and ICMP (internet control message protocol), among many others.

Network access layer

The network access layer of the TCP/IP model combines layers 1 (physical) and 2 (data link) of the OSI model. It describes layer 1 issues such as energy, bits, and the

Table 4.2 The OSI Model vs TCP/IP Model

	OSI Model	TCP/IP Model
7	Application	Application
6	Presentation	
5	Session	
4	Transport	Host-to-host transport
3	Network	Internet
2	Data link	Network access
1	Physical	

medium used to carry them (copper, fiber, wireless, etc.). It also describes layer 2 issues like converting bits into protocol units such as Ethernet frames, MAC addresses, and network interface cards (NICs).

Internet layer

The Internet layer of the TCP/IP model aligns with the layer 3 (network) layer of the OSI model. This is where IP addresses and routing live. When data is transmitted from a node on one LAN to a node on a different LAN, the Internet layer is used. IPv4, IPv6, ICMP, and routing protocols (among others) are Internet layer TCP/IP protocols.

Host-to-host transport layer

The *Host-to-Host Transport layer* is sometimes called either "Host-to-Host" or, more commonly, "Transport"; this book will use "Transport." It connects the Internet layer to the application-layer. It is where applications are addressed on a network via ports. TCP and UDP are the two transport layer protocols of TCP/IP.

Application-layer

The TCP/IP application-layer combines layers 5–7 (session, presentation, and application) of the OSI model. Most of these protocols use a client-server architecture, where a client (eg, *ssh*) connects to a listening server (called a daemon on UNIX systems), such as sshd. The clients and servers use either TCP or UDP (and sometimes both) as a transport layer protocol. TCP/IP application-layer protocols include secure shell (SSH), *Telnet,* and *FTP*, among many others.

MAC addresses

A MAC address is the unique hardware address of an Ethernet NIC, typically "burned in" at the factory. MAC addresses may be changed in software.

DID YOU KNOW?

Historically, MAC addresses are 48 bits long. They have two halves: the first 24 bits form the Organizationally Unique Identifier (OUI) and the last 24 bits form a serial number (formally called an extension identifier).

EUI-64 MAC addresses

The IEEE created the EUI-64 (extended unique identifier) standard for 64-bit MAC addresses. The OUI is still 24 bits, but the serial number is 40 bits. This allows for far more MAC addresses, compared with 48-bit addresses. *IPv6 autoconfiguration* is compatible with both types of MAC addresses.

IPv4

IPv4 is Internet protocol version 4, commonly called "IP." It is a simple protocol, designed to carry data across networks. It is so simple that it requires a "helper protocol" called ICMP (see later). IP is connectionless and unreliable; it provides "best effort" delivery of packets. If connections or reliability are required, they must be provided by a higher-level protocol carried by IP, such as TCP.

IPv4 uses 32-bit source and destination addresses, usually shown in "dotted quad" format, such as "192.168.2.4." A 32-bit address field allows 2^{32}, or nearly 4.3 billion, addresses.

IPv6

IPv6 is the successor to IPv4, featuring far larger address space (128-bit addresses compared to IPv4's 32 bits), simpler routing, and simpler address assignment. A lack of IPv4 addresses was the primary factor that led to the creation of IPv6.

DID YOU KNOW?

Most modern systems are "dual stack" and use both IPv4 and IPv6 simultaneously. Hosts may also access IPv6 networks via IPv4; this is called tunneling.

TCP

TCP is a reliable layer 4 protocol. TCP uses a three-way handshake to create reliable connections across a network. TCP can reorder segments that arrive out-of-order and retransmit missing segments.

TCP ports

TCP connects from a source port to a destination port, such as from source port 51178 to destination port 22. The TCP port field is 16 bits, allowing port numbers from 0 to 65,535.

There are two types of ports, *reserved* and *ephemeral*. A reserved port is 1023 or lower; ephemeral ports are 1024-65,535. Most operating systems require super-user privileges to open a reserved port. Any user may open an (unused) ephemeral port.

UDP

UDP is a simpler and faster cousin to TCP. UDP is commonly used for applications that are "lossy" (can handle some packet loss), such as streaming audio and video. It is also used for query-response applications, such as DNS queries.

ICMP

Internet control message protocol, or ICMP, is a helper protocol that assists layer 3. ICMP is used to troubleshoot and report error conditions; without ICMP to help, IP would fail when faced with routing loops, ports, hosts, or networks that are down, among other issues. ICMP has no concept of ports, as TCP and UDP do, but instead uses types and codes.

APPLICATION-LAYER TCP/IP PROTOCOLS AND CONCEPTS

A multitude of protocols exist at TCP/IP's application-layer, which combines the session, presentation, and application-layers of the OSI model.

Telnet

Telnet provides terminal emulation over a network. "Terminal" means text-based VT100-style terminal access. Telnet servers listen on TCP port 23. Telnet was the standard way to access an interactive command shell over a network for over 20 years.

Telnet is weak because it provides no confidentiality; all data transmitted during a Telnet session is plaintext, including the username and password used to authenticate to the system.

FTP

FTP is the file transfer protocol, used to transfer files to and from servers. Like Telnet, FTP has no confidentiality or integrity and should not be used to transfer sensitive data over insecure channels.

FTP uses two ports. The control connection, where commands are sent, is TCP port 21. "Active FTP" uses a data connection, where data is transferred, that originates from TCP port 20. Here are two socket pairs; the next two examples use arbitrary ephemeral ports:

- Client: 1025 → Server: 21 (Control Connection)
- Server: 20 → Client: 1026 (Data Connection)

Notice that the data connection originates from the server, in the opposite direction of the control channel. This breaks classic client-server data flow direction. Many firewalls will block the active FTP data connection for this reason, breaking active FTP. Passive FTP addresses this issue by keeping all communication from client to server:

- Client: 1025 → Server: 21 (Control Connection)
- Client: 1026 → Server: 1025 (Data Connection)

Passive FTP is more likely to pass through firewalls cleanly, since it flows in classic client-server direction.

SSH

Secure shell (SSH) was designed as a secure replacement for Telnet, FTP, and the UNIX "R" commands (rlogin, rshell, etc.). It provides confidentiality, integrity, and secure authentication, among other features. SSH includes SFTP (SSH FTP) and SCP (secure copy) for transferring files. SSH can also be used to securely tunnel other protocols, such as HTTP. SSH servers listen on TCP port 22 by default.

SMTP, POP, and IMAP

SMTP is the simple mail transfer protocol, which is used to transfer email between servers. SMTP servers listen on TCP port 25. *POP*v3 (post office protocol) and *IMAP* (Internet message access protocol) are used for client-server email access, which use TCP ports 110 and 143, respectively.

DNS

DNS is the domain name system, a distributed global hierarchical database that translates names to IP addresses, and vice versa. DNS uses both TCP and UDP; small responses use UDP port 53, while large responses, including zone transfers, use TCP port 53.

HTTP and HTTPS

Hypertext transfer protocol, or HTTP, transfers unencrypted web-based data. HTTPS (hypertext transfer protocol secure) transfers encrypted web-based data via SSL/*TLS* (see Section "SSL/TLS", later). HTTP uses TCP port 80, and HTTPS uses TCP port 443. HTML (hypertext markup language) is used to display web content.

LAN TECHNOLOGIES AND PROTOCOLS

LAN concepts focus on layers 1–3 technologies such as network cabling types, physical and logical network topologies, Ethernet, FDDI, and others.

Ethernet

Ethernet operates at layer 2 and is a dominant local-area networking technology that transmits network data via frames. Ethernet is baseband (ie, one channel), so it must address issues such as collisions, where two nodes attempt to transmit data simultaneously.

WAN TECHNOLOGIES AND PROTOCOLS

ISPs and other "long-haul" network providers, whose networks span from cities to countries, often use WAN technologies. Many of us have hands-on experience configuring LAN technologies such as connecting Cat5 network cabling; it is less common to have hands-on experience building WANs.

T1s, T3s, E1s, and E3s

There are a number of international circuit standards; the most prevalent are T Carriers (United States) and E Carriers (Europe).

FAST FACTS

Here is a summary of common circuits:

- A **T1** is a dedicated 1.544-megabit circuit that carries 24.64 kbit/s DS0 (Digital Signal 0) channels.
- A **T3** is 28 bundled T1s, forming a 44.736-megabit circuit.
- An **E1** is a dedicated 2.048-megabit circuit that carries 30 channels.
- An **E3** is 16 bundled E1s, forming a 34.368-megabit circuit.

Frame Relay

Frame Relay is a packet-switched layer 2 WAN protocol that provides no error recovery and focuses on speed. Higher-layer protocols carried by Frame Relay, such as TCP/IP, can be used to provide reliability.

Frame Relay multiplexes multiple logical connections over a single physical connection, which create virtual circuits. This shared bandwidth model is an alternative to dedicated circuits such as T1s. A PVC (permanent virtual circuit) is always connected and is analogous to a real dedicated circuit like a T1. A switched virtual circuit (SVC) sets up each "call," transfers data, and terminates the connection after an idle timeout.

MPLS

Multiprotocol label switching (MPLS) provides a way to forward WAN data using labels via a shared MPLS cloud network. Decisions are based on the labels, not on encapsulated header data (such as an IP header). MPLS can carry voice and data and can be used to simplify WAN routing.

CONVERGED PROTOCOLS

"Convergence" is a recent network buzzword. It means providing services such as industrial controls, storage, and voice (that were typically delivered via non-IP devices and networks) via Ethernet and TCP/IP.

DNP3

The distributed network protocol (DNP3) provides an open standard used primarily within the energy sector for interoperability between various vendors' SCADA and smart grid applications. Some protocols, such as SMTP, fit into one layer. DNP3 is a multilayer protocol and may be carried via TCP/IP (another multilayer protocol).

Recent improvements in DNP3 allow for "Secure Authentication," which addresses challenges with the original specification that could have allowed, for example, spoofing or replay attacks. DNP3 became an IEEE standard in 2010, called IEEE 1815-2010 (now deprecated). It allowed preshared keys only. IEEE 1815-2012 is the current standard; it supports public key infrastructure (PKI).

Storage protocols

Fibre Channel over Ethernet (FCoE) and Internet small computer system interface (iSCSI) are both storage area network (SAN) protocols that provide cost-effective ways to leverage existing network infrastructure technologies and protocols to interface with storage. A SAN allows block-level file access across a network, just like a directly attached hard drive.

FCoE leverages Fibre Channel, which has long been used for storage networking but dispenses with the requirement for completely different cabling and hardware. Instead, FCoE is transmitted across standard Ethernet networks. In FCoE, Fibre Channel's host bus adapters (HBAs) is able to be combined with the NIC for economies of scale. FCoE uses Ethernet, but not TCP/IP. Fibre Channel over IP (FCIP) encapsulates Fibre Channel frames via TCP/IP.

Like FCoE, iSCSI is a SAN protocol that allows for leveraging existing networking infrastructure and protocols to interface with storage. While FCoE simply uses Ethernet, iSCSI makes use of higher layers of the TCP/IP suite for communication and is routed like any IP protocol; the same is true for FCIP. By employing protocols beyond layer 2 (Ethernet), iSCSI can be transmitted beyond just the local network. iSCSI uses logical unit numbers (LUNs) to provide a way of addressing storage across the network. LUNs are also useful for basic access control for network accessible storage.

VoIP

Voice over Internet protocol (VoIP) carries voice via data networks, a fundamental change from analog POTS, or plain old telephone service, which remains in use after over 100 years. VoIP brings the advantages of packet-switched networks, such as lower cost and resiliency, to the telephone.

Common VoIP protocols include *real-time transport protocol* (RTP), designed to carry streaming audio and video. VoIP protocols such as RTP rely upon session and signaling protocols including *session initiation protocol* (SIP, a signaling protocol) and H.323. SRTP (secure real-time transport protocol) is able to provide secure VoIP, including confidentiality, integrity, and secure authentication. SRTP uses AES for confidentiality and SHA-1 for integrity.

While VoIP can provide compelling cost advantages, especially for new sites without a large legacy voice investment, there are security concerns. Many VoIP protocols, such as RTP, provide little or no security by default.

SOFTWARE-DEFINED NETWORKS

Software-defined networking (SDN) separates a router's control plane from the data (forwarding) plane. The control plane makes routing decisions. The data plane forwards data (packets) through the router. With SDN routing, decisions are made remotely instead of on each individual router.

The most well-known protocol in this space is OpenFlow, which can, among other capabilities, allow for control of switching rules to be designated or updated at a central controller. OpenFlow is a TCP protocol that uses transport layer security (TLS) encryption.

WIRELESS LOCAL-AREA NETWORKS

Wireless local-area networks (WLANs) transmit information via light or electromagnetic waves, such as radio. The most common form of wireless data networking is the 802.11 wireless standard, and the first 802.11 standard that provides reasonable security is 802.11i.

FHSS, DSSS, and OFDM

Frequency-hopping spread spectrum (FHSS) and direct-sequence spread spectrum (DSSS) are two methods for sending traffic via a radio band. Some bands, like the 2.4-GHz ISM band, experience a great amount of interference; Bluetooth, some cordless phones, some 802.11 wireless, baby monitors, and even microwaves can broadcast or interfere with this band. Both DSSS and FHSS can maximize throughput while minimizing the effects of interference.

DSSS uses the entire band at once, "spreading" the signal throughout the band. FHSS uses a number of small frequency channels throughout the band and "hops" through them in pseudorandom order.

Orthogonal frequency-division multiplexing (OFDM) is a newer multiplexing method, allowing simultaneous transmissions to use multiple independent wireless frequencies that do not interfere with each other.

802.11 abgn

802.11 wireless has many standards, using various frequencies and speeds. The original mode is simply called 802.11 (sometimes *802.11-1997*, based on the year it was created), which operated at 2 megabits per second (Mbps) using the 2.4 GHz frequency. It was quickly supplanted by *802.11b*; at 11 Mbps, *802.11g* was designed to be backwards compatible with 802.11b devices, offering speeds up to 54 Mbps using the 2.4 GHz frequency. *802.11a* offers the same top speed, using the 5 GHz frequency.

802.11n uses both 2.4 and 5 GHz frequencies and is able to use multiple antennas with multiple-input multiple-output (MIMO). This allows speeds up to 600 Mbps. Finally, 802.11ac uses the 5 GHz frequency only, offering speeds up to 1.3 Gbps. Table 4.3 summarizes the major types of 802.11 wireless.

WEP

The WEP is the wired equivalent privacy protocol was an early attempt (first ratified in 1999) to provide 802.11 wireless security. WEP has proven to be critically weak, and new attacks can break any WEP key in minutes. Due to these attacks, WEP effectively provides little integrity or confidentiality protection. In fact, many consider WEP to be broken and strongly discourage its use. The encryption algorithms

Table 4.3 Types of 802.11 Wireless

Type	Top Speed	Frequency
802.11	2 Mbps	2.4 GHz
802.11a	54 Mbps	5 GHz
802.11b	11 Mbps	2.4 GHz
802.11g	54 Mbps	2.4 GHz
802.11n	72–600 Mbps	2.4 GHz/5 GHz
802.11ac	422 Mbps–1.3 Gbps	5 GHz

specified in 802.11i and/or other encryption methods such as virtual private networks (VPNs) should be used in place of WEP.

802.11i

802.11i is the first 802.11 wireless security standard that provides reasonable security. 802.11i describes a robust security network (RSN), which allows pluggable authentication modules. RSN allows changes to cryptographic ciphers as new vulnerabilities are discovered.

CRUNCH TIME

RSN is also known as WPA2 (Wi-Fi Protected Access 2), a full implementation of 802.11i. By default, WPA2 uses AES encryption to provide confidentiality, and CCMP (counter mode CBC MAC protocol) to create a message integrity check (MIC), which provides integrity.

The less secure *WPA* (without the "2") is appropriate for access points that lack the power to implement the full 802.11i standard, providing a better security alternative to WEP. WPA uses RC4 for confidentiality and TKIP (Temporal Key Integrity Protocol) for integrity.

Bluetooth

Bluetooth, described by IEEE standard 802.15, is a PAN wireless technology, operating in the same 2.4 GHz frequency as many types of 802.11 wireless devices. Small, low-power devices such as cell phones use Bluetooth to transmit data over short distances. Bluetooth versions 2.1 and older operate at 3 Mbps or less; Versions 3 and 4 offer far faster speeds.

Sensitive devices should disable automatic discovery by other Bluetooth devices. The "security" of discovery relies on the secrecy of the 48-bit MAC address of the Bluetooth adapter. Even when disabled, Bluetooth devices are easily discovered by guessing the MAC address. The first 24 bits are the OUI, which can be easy to guess, while the last 24 bits may be determined via brute-force attack.

RFID

Radio frequency identification (RFID) is a technology used to create wirelessly readable tags for animals or objects. There are three types of RFID tags: *active, semipassive, and passive*. Active and semipassive RFID tags have a battery. An active tag broadcasts a signal, while semipassive RFID tags rely on a RFID reader's signal for power. Passive RFID tags have no battery and must rely on the RFID reader's signal for power.

SECURE NETWORK DEVICES AND PROTOCOLS

Let us look at network devices ranging from layer 1 hubs through application-layer proxy firewalls that operate up to layer 7. Many of these network devices, such as routers, have protocols dedicated to their use.

REPEATERS AND HUBS

Repeaters and hubs are layer 1 devices. A repeater receives bits on one port, and "repeats" them out the other port. The repeater has no understanding of protocols; it simply repeats bits. Repeaters can extend the length of a network.

A hub is a repeater with more than two ports. It receives bits on one port and repeats them across all other ports.

BRIDGES

Bridges and switches are layer 2 devices. A bridge has two ports and two collision domains, and it connects network segments together. Each segment typically has multiple nodes, and the bridge learns the MAC addresses of nodes on either side. Traffic sent from two nodes on the same side of the bridge will not be forwarded across the bridge. Traffic sent from a node on one side of the bridge to the other side will forward across. The bridge provides traffic isolation and makes forwarding decisions by learning the MAC addresses of connected nodes.

SWITCHES

A switch is a bridge with more than two ports. It is best practice to connect only one device per switch port. Otherwise, everything that is true about a bridge is also true about a switch.

Fig. 4.1 shows a network switch. The switch provides traffic isolation by associating the MAC address of each connected device with its port on the switch.

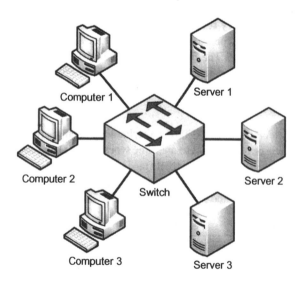

FIG. 4.1

Network switch.

A switch shrinks the collision domain to a single port. You will normally have no collisions, assuming that each port has only one connected device. Trunks connect multiple switches.

VLANs

A *VLAN* is a virtual LAN, which is like a virtual switch. Imagine you have desktops and servers connected to the same switch, and you would like to create separate desktop and server LANs. One option is to buy a second switch in order to dedicate one for desktops and one for servers. Another option is to create two VLANs, a desktop VLAN and a server VLAN, on the original switch.

One switch may support multiple VLANs, and one VLAN can span multiple switches. VLANs may also add defense-in-depth protection to networks; for example, VLANs can segment data and management network traffic.

ROUTERS

Routers are layer 3 devices that route traffic from one LAN to another. IP-based routers make routing decisions based on the source and destination IP addresses.

FIREWALLS

Firewalls filter traffic between networks. TCP/IP packet filter and stateful firewalls make decisions based on layers 3 and 4 (IP addresses and ports). Proxy firewalls can also make decisions based on layers 5–7. Firewalls are multihomed: they have multiple NICs connected to multiple different networks.

Packet filter

A *packet filter* is a simple and fast firewall. It has no concept of "state": each filtering decision is made on the basis of a single packet. There is no way to refer to past packets to make current decisions.

The packet filtering firewall shown in Fig. 4.2 allows outbound ICMP echo requests and inbound ICMP echo replies. Computer 1 can ping bank.example.com. The problem: an attacker at evil.example.com can send unsolicited echo replies, which the firewall will allow.

Stateful firewalls

Stateful firewalls have a state table that allows the firewall to compare current packets to previous ones. Stateful firewalls are slower than packet filters, but are far more secure.

Computer 1 sends an ICMP echo request to bank.example.com in Fig. 4.3. The firewall is configured to ping Internet sites, so the stateful firewall allows the traffic and adds an entry to its state table.

An echo reply is received from bank.example.com at Computer 1 in Fig. 4.3. The firewall checks to see if it allows this traffic (it does), then it checks the state table

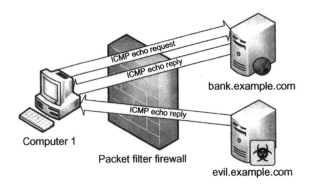

FIG. 4.2

Packet filter firewall design.

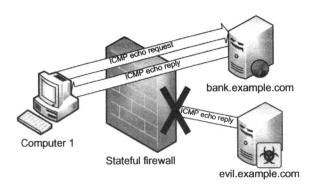

FIG. 4.3

Stateful firewall design.

for a matching echo request in the opposite direction. The firewall finds the matching entry, deletes it from the state table, and passes the traffic.

Then evil.example.com sends an unsolicited ICMP echo reply. The stateful firewall, shown in Fig. 4.3, sees no matching state table entry and denies the traffic.

Proxy firewalls

Proxies are firewalls that act as intermediary servers. Both packet filter and stateful firewalls pass traffic through or deny it; they are another hop along the route. Proxies terminate connections.

Application-layer proxy firewalls

Application-layer proxy firewalls operate up to layer 7. Unlike packet filter and stateful firewalls that make decisions based on layers 3 and 4 only, application-layer proxies can make filtering decisions based on application-layer data, such as HTTP traffic, in addition to layers 3 and 4.

MODEM

A *modem* is a modulator/demodulator. It takes binary data and modulates it into analog sound carried on phone networks designed for the human voice. The receiving modem then demodulates the analog sound back into binary data.

SECURE COMMUNICATIONS

Protecting data in motion is one of the most complex challenges we face. The Internet provides cheap global communication with little or no built-in confidentiality, integrity, or availability.

AUTHENTICATION PROTOCOLS AND FRAMEWORKS

An authentication protocol authenticates an identity claim over the network. Good security design assumes that a network eavesdropper may sniff all packets sent between the client and authentication server, so the protocol should remain secure.

802.1X and EAP

802.1X is port-based network access control (PNAC) and includes *extensible authentication protocol* (EAP). EAP is an authentication framework that describes many specific authentication protocols. EAP provides authentication at layer 2 (it is port-based, like ports on a switch) before a node receives an IP address. It is available for both wired and wireless but is more commonly deployed on WLANs. An EAP client is called a supplicant, which requests authentication to an authentication server (AS).

FAST FACTS

There are many types of EAP; we will focus on LEAP, EAP-TLS, EAP-TTLS, and PEAP:

- LEAP (*lightweight extensible authentication protocol*) is a Cisco-proprietary protocol released before 802.1X was finalized. LEAP has significant security flaws and should not be used.
- EAP-TLS (*EAP-Transport Layer Security*) uses PKI, requiring both server-side and client-side certificates. EAP-TLS establishes a secure TLS tunnel used for authentication. EAP-TLS is very secure due to the use of PKI but is complex and costly for the same reason. The other major versions of EAP attempt to create the same TLS tunnel without requiring a client-side certificate.
- EAP-TTLS (*EAP Tunneled Transport Layer Security*), developed by Funk Software and Certicom, simplifies EAP-TLS by dropping the client-side certificate requirement, allowing other authentication methods (such as passwords) for client-side authentication. EAP-TTLS is thus easier to deploy than EAP-TLS, but less secure when omitting the client-side certificate.
- PEAP (*Protected EAP*), developed by Cisco Systems, Microsoft, and RSA Security, is similar to and is a competitor of EAP-TTLS, as they both do not require client-side certificates.

VPN

Virtual private networks (VPNs secure data sent via insecure networks like the Internet. The goal is to virtually provide the privacy afforded by a circuit, such as a T1. The basic construction of VPNs involves secure authentication, cryptographic hashes such as SHA-1 to provide integrity, and ciphers such as AES to provide confidentiality.

PPP

PPP (point-to-point protocol) is a layer 2 protocol that provides confidentiality, integrity, and authentication via point-to-point links. PPP supports synchronous links, such as T1s, in addition to asynchronous links, such as modems.

IPsec

IPv4 has no built-in confidentiality; higher-layer protocols like TLS provide security. To address this lack of security at layer 3, IPsec (Internet protocol security) was designed to provide confidentiality, integrity, and authentication via encryption for IPv6. IPsec is ported to IPv4. IPsec is a suite of protocols; the major two are encapsulating security protocol (ESP) and authentication header (AH). Each has an IP protocol number; ESP is protocol 50 and AH is protocol 51.

SSL and TLS

Secure sockets layer (SSL) protects HTTP data: HTTPS uses TCP port 443. TLS is the latest version of SSL, equivalent to SSL version 3.1. The current version of TLS is 1.2.

Though initially focused on the web, SSL or TLS may be used to encrypt many types of data and can be used to tunnel other IP protocols to form VPN connections. SSL VPNs can be simpler than their IPsec equivalents: IPsec makes fundamental changes to IP networking, so installation of IPsec software changes the operating system, which requires super-user privileges. SSL client software does not require altering the operating system. Also, IPsec is difficult to firewall, while SSL is much simpler.

REMOTE ACCESS

In an age of telecommuting and the mobile workforce, secure remote access is a critical control. This includes connecting mobile users via methods such as a digital subscriber line (DSL) or cable modem, as well as newer concerns, such as instant messaging and remote meeting technology.

DSL

Digital subscriber line (DSL) has a "last mile" solution that uses existing copper pairs to provide digital service to homes and small offices.

Common types of DSL are symmetric digital subscriber line (SDSL, with matching upload and download speeds); asymmetric digital subscriber line (ADSL), featuring faster download speeds than upload speeds; and very high-rate digital subscriber line (VDSL, featuring much faster asymmetric speeds). Another option is high-data-rate DSL (HDSL), which matches SDSL speeds using two copper pairs.

Table 4.4 DSL Speed and Distances[1]

Type	Download Speed	Upload Speed	Distance from CO
ADSL	1.5–9 Mbps	16–640 Kbps	18,000 ft
SDSL	1.544 Mbps	1.544 Mbps	10,000 ft
HDSL	1.544 Mbps	1.544 Mbps	10,000 ft
VDSL	20–50+ Mbps	Up to 20 Mbps	<5000 ft

HDSL provides inexpensive T1 service. As a general rule, the closer a site is to the Central Office (CO), the faster the available service will be.

Table 4.4 summarizes the speeds and modes of DSL.

Cable modems

Cable modems are used by cable TV providers to offer Internet access via broadband cable TV. Cable TV access is not ubiquitous, but it is available in most large towns and cities in industrialized areas. Unlike DSL, cable modem bandwidth can be shared with neighbors on the same network segment.

Remote desktop console access

Two common modern protocols providing for remote access to a desktop are virtual network computing (VNC), which typically runs on TCP 5900, and remote desktop protocol (RDP), which typically runs on TCP port 3389. VNC and RDP allow for graphical access of remote systems, as opposed to the older terminal-based approach to remote access. RDP is a proprietary Microsoft protocol.

Desktop and application virtualization

Desktop virtualization is an approach that provides a centralized infrastructure that hosts a desktop image that the workforce can leverage remotely. Desktop virtualization is often referred to as VDI, which, depending on the vendor in question, stands for either virtual desktop infrastructure or virtual desktop interface.

As opposed to providing a full desktop environment, an organization can simply virtualize key applications that are centrally served. Like desktop virtualization, the centralized control associated with application virtualization allows the organization to employ strict access control and perhaps more quickly patch the application. Additionally, application virtualization can run legacy applications that would otherwise be unable to run on the systems employed by the workforce.

Screen scraping

Screen scraping presents one approach to graphical remote access to systems. Screen scraping protocols packetize and transmit information necessary to draw the accessed system's screen on the display of the system being used for remote access. VNC, a commonly used technology for accessing remote desktops, is fundamentally a screen scraping style approach to remote access. However, not all remote access protocols are screen scrapers. For example, Microsoft's popular RDP does not employ screen scraping to provide graphical remote access.

Instant messaging

Instant messaging allows two or more users to communicate with each other via real-time "chat." Chat may be one-to-one or many-to-many, as in chat groups. In addition to chatting, most modern instant messaging software allows file sharing and sometimes audio and video conferencing.

An older instant messaging protocol is IRC (Internet relay chat), a global network of chat servers and clients created in 1988 that remains very popular even today. Other chat protocols and networks include AOL instant messenger (AIM), ICQ (short for "I seek you"), and extensible messaging and presence protocol (XMPP) (formerly known as Jabber).

Chat software may be subject to various security issues, including remote exploitation, and must be patched like any other software. The file sharing capability of chat software may allow users to violate policy by distributing sensitive documents; there are similar issues with the audio and video sharing capability of many of these programs.

Remote meeting technology

Remote meeting technology is a newer technology that allows users to conduct online meetings via the Internet, including desktop sharing functionality. These technologies usually include displaying PowerPoint slides on all PCs connected to a meeting, sharing documents such as spreadsheets, and sometimes sharing audio or video.

Many of these solutions can tunnel through outbound SSL or TLS traffic, which can often pass via firewalls and any web proxies. It is important to understand and control remote meeting technologies in order to remain compliant with all applicable policy.

PDAs

Personal digital assistants (PDAs) are small networked computers that can fit in the palm of your hand. PDAs have evolved over the years, beginning with first-generation devices such as the Apple Newton (Apple coined the term PDA) and Palm Pilot. These early PDAs offered features such as a calendar and note-taking capability. PDA operating systems include Apple iOS, Windows Mobile, Blackberry, and Google's Android, among others.

Two major issues regarding PDA security are the loss of data due to theft or loss of the device, and wireless security. Sensitive data on PDAs should be encrypted, or the device itself should store minimal amount of data. A PIN should lock the device, and the device should offer *remote wipe* capability, which is the ability to remotely erase the device in case of loss or theft.

Content distribution networks

Content distribution networks (CDN, also called content delivery networks, use a series of distributed caching servers to improve performance and lower the latency of downloaded online content. They automatically determine the servers closest to end users, so users download content from the fastest and closest servers on the Internet. Examples include Akamai, Amazon CloudFront, CloudFlare, and Microsoft Azure.

SUMMARY OF EXAM OBJECTIVES

Communication and Network Security is a large and complex domain, requiring broad and sometimes deep understanding of thorny technical issues. Our modern world relies on networks, which must be secure. It is important understand why we use concepts like packet-switched networks and the OSI model, as well as how we implement those concepts.

Older Internet-connected networks often had a single dual-homed host connected to the Internet. Firewalls were created and then evolved from packet filter to stateful. Our physical design evolved from busses to stars, providing fault tolerance and hardware isolation. We have evolved from hubs to switches that provide traffic isolation, and we have deployed secure protocols such as TLS and IPsec.

We have improved our network defense-in-depth every step of the way, as well as increased the confidentiality, integrity, and availability of our network data.

TOP FIVE TOUGHEST QUESTIONS

1. Restricting Bluetooth device discovery relies on the secrecy of what?
   A. MAC address
   B. Symmetric key
   C. Private key
   D. Public key
2. What are the names of the OSI model layers in order from bottom to top?
   A. Physical, Data Link, Transport, Network, Session, Presentation, Application
   B. Physical, Network, Data Link, Transport, Session, Presentation, Application
   C. Physical, Data Link, Network, Transport, Session, Presentation, Application
   D. Physical, Data Link, Network, Transport, Presentation, Session, Application
3. What is the most secure type of EAP?
   A. EAP-TLS
   B. EAP-TTLS
   C. LEAP
   D. PEAP
4. What is the most secure type of firewall?
   A. Packet filter
   B. Stateful firewall
   C. Circuit-level proxy firewall
   D. Application-layer proxy firewall

5. Accessing an IPv6 network via an IPv4 network is called what?
   A. CIDR
   B. NAT
   C. Translation
   D. Tunneling

ANSWERS

1. Correct answer and explanation: A. Restricting Bluetooth device discovery relies on the secrecy of the 48-bit Bluetooth MAC address.
   Incorrect answers and explanations: Answers B, C, and D are incorrect. While E0 is a symmetric cipher, it not used to restrict discovery, though it is used for data encryption. Public or private keys are also not used for Bluetooth discovery.

2. Correct answer and explanation: C. The OSI model layers from bottom to top are: Physical, Data Link, Network, Transport, Session, Presentation, and Application. Remember "Please Do Not Throw Sausage Pizza Away" as a useful mnemonic to remember this.
   Incorrect answers and explanations: Answers A, B, and D are incorrect. All layers are in the wrong order.

3. Correct answer and explanation: A. EAP-TLS is the most secure (and costly) form of EAP because it requires both server and client-side certificates.
   Incorrect answers and explanations: Answers B, C, and D are incorrect. EAP-TTLS and PEAP are similar and don't require client-side certificates. LEAP is a Cisco-proprietary protocol that does not require client-side certificates; it also has fundamental security weaknesses.

4. Correct answer and explanation: D. Application-layer firewalls are the most secure, as they have the ability to filter based on OSI Layers 3–7.
   Incorrect answers and explanations: Answers A, B, and C are incorrect. All are firewalls. A packet filter is the least secure of the four, due to the lack of state. A stateful firewall is more secure than a packet filter, but its decisions are limited to Layers 3 and 4. Circuit-level proxy firewalls operate at Layer 5 and cannot filter based on application-layer data.

5. Correct answer and explanation: D. Accessing an IPv6 network via an IPv4 network is called tunneling.
   Incorrect answers and explanations: Answers A, B, and C are incorrect. CIDR is Classless Interdomain Routing, a way to create flexible subnets. NAT is network address translation, which translates one IP address for another. Translation is a distractor answer.

ENDNOTE

1. DSL and Cable Modem Networks, http://www.ciscopress.com/articles/article.asp?p=31289 (accessed 25.04.16).

Domain 5: Identity and access management (controlling access and managing identity)

5

CHAPTER OUTLINE

INTRODUCTION

Identity and access management (also known as access control) is the basis for all security disciplines, not just IT security. The purpose of access management is to allow authorized users access to appropriate data and deny access to unauthorized users.

Eleventh Hour CISSP®. http://dx.doi.org/10.1016/B978-0-12-811248-9.00005-X

AUTHENTICATION METHODS

A key concept for implementing any type of access control is the proper authentication of subjects. A subject first identifies himself or herself; however, this identification cannot be trusted alone. The subject then authenticates by providing an assurance that the claimed identity is valid. A *credential set* is the term used for the combination of both the identification and authentication of a user.

There are three basic authentication methods: *Type 1* (something you know), *Type 2* (something you have), and *Type 3* (something you are). A fourth type of authentication is some place you are.

TYPE 1 AUTHENTICATION: SOMETHING YOU KNOW

Type 1 authentication (something you know) requires testing the subject with some sort of challenge and response where the subject must respond with a knowledgeable answer. The subject is granted access on the basis of something they know, such as a password or personal identification number (PIN), which is a number-based password. This is the easiest and therefore often weakest form of authentication.

Passwords

There are four types of passwords to consider when implementing access controls: static passwords, passphrases, one-time passwords, and dynamic passwords.

Static passwords are reusable passwords that may or may not expire. They are typically user-generated and work best when combined with another authentication type, such as a smart card or biometric control.

Passphrases are long static passwords, comprised of words in a phrase or sentence. An example of a passphrase is: "I will pass the CISSP in 6 months!" Passphrases may be made stronger by using nonsense words (eg, replacing CISSP with "XYZZY" in the previous passphrase), by mixing lowercase with uppercase letters, and by using additional numbers and symbols.

One-time passwords may be used for a single authentication. They are very secure but difficult to manage. A one-time password is impossible to reuse and is valid for just a one-time use.

Dynamic passwords change at regular intervals. RSA security makes a synchronous token device called SecurID that generates a new token code every 60 seconds. The user combines their static PIN with the RSA dynamic token code to create one dynamic password that changes every time it is used. One drawback to using dynamic passwords is the expense of the tokens themselves.

Password guessing

Password guessing is an online technique that involves attempting to authenticate a particular user to the system. As we will learn in the next section, *password cracking* refers to an offline technique in which the attacker has gained access to the password hashes or database. Note that most web-based attacks on passwords are of the password guessing variety, so web applications should be designed with this in mind from a detective and preventive standpoint. Preventing successful password guessing attacks is typically done with *account lockouts*.

Password hashes and password cracking

In most cases, clear text passwords are not stored within an IT system; only the hashed outputs of those passwords are stored. *Hashing* is one-way encryption using an algorithm and no key. When a user attempts to log in, the password they type (sometimes combined with a salt, as we will discuss shortly) is hashed, and that hash is compared against the hash stored on the system. The hash function cannot be reversed; it is impossible to reverse the algorithm and produce a password from a hash. While hashes may not be reversed, an attacker may run the hash algorithm forward many times, selecting various possible passwords, and comparing the output to a desired hash, hoping to find a match (and therefore deriving the original password). This is called *password cracking*.

Dictionary attacks

A *dictionary attack* uses a word list, which is a predefined list of words, each of which is hashed. If the cracking software matches the hash output from the dictionary attack to the password hash, the attacker has successfully identified the original password.

Hybrid attacks

A *hybrid attack* appends, prepends, or changes characters in words from a dictionary before hashing in order to attempt the fastest crack of complex passwords. For example, an attacker may have a dictionary of potential system administrator passwords but also replaces each letter "o" with the number "0".

Brute-force attacks

Brute-force attacks take more time, but are more effective. The attacker calculates the hash outputs for every possible password. Just a few years ago, basic computer speed was still slow enough to make this a daunting task. However, with the advances in CPU speeds and parallel computing, the time required to execute brute-force attacks on complex passwords has been considerably reduced.

Rainbow tables

A *rainbow table* acts as a database that contains the precomputed hashed output for most or all possible passwords. Rainbow tables take a considerable amount of time to generate and are not always complete: they may not include all possible password/hash combinations. Though rainbow tables act as a database, they are more complex under the hood, relying on a time/memory tradeoff to represent and recover passwords and hashes.

Salts

A *salt* allows one password to hash multiple ways. Some systems (like modern UNIX/Linux systems) combine a salt with a password before hashing. While storing password hashes is superior to storing plaintext passwords, "The designers of the UNIX operating system improved on this method (hashing) by using a random value called a 'salt'. A salt value ensures that the same password will encrypt differently when used by different users. This method offers the advantage that an attacker must encrypt the same word multiple times (once for each salt or user) in order to mount a successful password-guessing attack."[1]

As a result, rainbow tables are far less effective, if not completely ineffective, for systems using salts. Instead of compiling one rainbow table for a system that does not uses salts, such as Microsoft LAN Manager (LM) hashes, thousands, millions, billions, or more rainbow tables would be required for systems using salts, depending on the salt length.

TYPE 2 AUTHENTICATION: SOMETHING YOU HAVE

Type 2 authentication (something you have) requires that users possess something, such as a token, which proves they are an authenticated user. A token is an object that helps prove an identity claim.

Synchronous dynamic token

Synchronous dynamic tokens use time or counters to synchronize a displayed token code with the code expected by the authentication server (AS).

Time-based synchronous dynamic tokens display dynamic token codes that change frequently, such as every 60 seconds. The dynamic code is only good during that window. The AS knows the serial number of each authorized token, as well as the user with whom it is associated and the time. It can predict the dynamic code of each token using these three pieces of information.

Counter-based synchronous dynamic tokens use a simple counter; the AS expects token code 1, and the user's token displays the same code 1. Once used, the token displays the second code, and the server also expects token code 2.

Asynchronous dynamic token

Asynchronous dynamic tokens are not synchronized with a central server. The most common variety is challenge-response tokens. Challenge-response token authentication systems produce a challenge or input for the token device. The user manually enters the information into the device along with their PIN, and the device produces an output, which is then sent to the system.

TYPE 3 AUTHENTICATION: SOMETHING YOU ARE

Type 3 authentication (something you are) is biometrics, which uses physical characteristics as a means of identification or authentication. Biometrics may be used to establish an identity or to authenticate or prove an identity claim. For example, an airport facial recognition system may be used to establish the identity of a known terrorist, and a fingerprint scanner may be used to authenticate the identity of a subject who makes the identity claim, and then swipes his/her finger to prove it.

Biometric enrollment and throughput

Enrollment describes the process of registering with a biometric system, which involves creating an account for the first time. Users typically provide their username (identity) and a password or PIN followed by biometric information, such as swiping fingerprints on a fingerprint reader or having a photograph taken of their irises. Enrollment is a one-time process that should take 2 minutes or less.

   Throughput describes the process of authenticating to a biometric system. This is also called the biometric system response time. A typical throughput is 6–10 seconds.

Accuracy of biometric systems

The accuracy of biometric systems should be considered before implementing a biometric control program. Three metrics are used to judge biometric accuracy: the *false reject rate (FRR)*, the *false accept rate (FAR)*, and the *crossover error rate (CER)*.

False reject rate

A false rejection occurs when an authorized subject is rejected by the biometric system as unauthorized. False rejections are also called a *Type I error*. False rejections cause frustration for the authorized users, reduction in work due to poor access conditions, and expenditure of resources to revalidate authorized users.

False accept rate

A false acceptance occurs when an unauthorized subject is accepted as valid. If an organization's biometric control is producing a lot of false rejections, the overall control might have to lower the accuracy of the system by lessening the amount of data it collects when authenticating subjects. When the data points are lowered, the organization risks an increase in the false acceptance rate. The organization risks an unauthorized user gaining access. This type of error is also called a *Type II error*.

CRUNCH TIME

A false accept is worse than a false reject because most organizations would prefer to reject authentic subjects to accepting impostors. FARs (Type II errors) are worse than FRRs (Type I errors). Two is greater than one, which will help you remember that FAR is Type II, which is worse than Type I (FRRs).

Crossover error rate

The CER describes the point where the FRR and FAR are equal. CER is also known as the equal error rate (EER). The CER describes the overall accuracy of a biometric system.

   As the sensitivity of a biometric system increases, FRRs will rise and FARs will drop. Conversely, as the sensitivity is lowered, FRRs will drop and FARs will rise. Fig. 5.1 shows a graph depicting the FAR versus the FRR. The CER is the intersection of both lines of the graph as shown in Fig. 5.1, based on the 2007 *ISACA Biometric Auditing Guide*, #G36.[2]

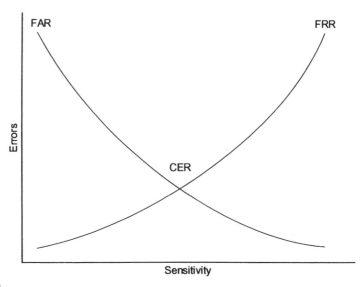

FIG. 5.1

Crossover error rate.

Types of biometric controls

There are a number of biometric controls used today. Below are the major implementations and their specific pros and cons with regards to access control security.

Fingerprints

Fingerprints are the most widely used biometric control available today. Smartcards can carry fingerprint information. Many US government office buildings rely on fingerprint authentication for physical access to the facility. Examples include smart keyboards, which require users to present a fingerprint to unlock the computer's screen saver.

The data used for storing each person's fingerprint must be of a small enough size to be used for authentication. This data is a mathematical representation of fingerprint *minutiae*, which include specific details of fingerprint friction ridges like whorls, ridges, and bifurcation, among others. Fig. 5.2 shows minutiae types (from left) bifurcation, ridge ending, core, and delta.[3]

Retina scan

A *retina scan* is a laser scan of the capillaries that feed the retina of the back of the eye. This can seem personally intrusive because the light beam must directly enter the pupil, and the user usually needs to press their eye up to a laser scanner eyecup. The laser scan maps the blood vessels of the retina. Health information of the user can be gained through a retina scan. Conditions such as pregnancy and diabetes can be determined, which may raise legitimate privacy issues. Because of the need for

FIG. 5.2

Fingerprint minutiae.[3]

close proximity of the scanner in a retina scan, exchange of bodily fluids is possible when using retina scanning as a means of access control.

EXAM WARNING

Retina scans are rarely used because of health risks and privacy issues. Alternatives should be considered for biometric controls that risk exchange of bodily fluid or raise legitimate privacy concerns.

Iris scan

An *iris scan* is a passive biometric control. A camera takes a picture of the iris, the colored portion of the eye, and then compares photos within the authentication database. This scan is able to work even if the individual is wearing contact lenses or glasses. Each person's irises are unique, including twins' irises. Benefits of iris scans include high-accuracy and passive scanning, which may be accomplished without the subject's knowledge. There is no exchange of bodily fluids with iris scans.

Hand geometry

In *hand geometry* biometric control, measurements are taken from specific points on the subject's hand: "The devices use a simple concept of measuring and recording the length, width, thickness, and surface area of an individual's hand while guided on a plate."[5] Hand geometry devices are fairly simple and can store information using as few as 9 bytes.

Keyboard dynamics

Keyboard dynamics refer to how hard a person presses each key and the rhythm in which the keys are pressed. Surprisingly, this type of access control is cheap to implement and can be effective. As people learn how to type and use a computer keyboard, they develop specific habits that are difficult to impersonate, although not impossible.

Dynamic signature

Dynamic signatures measure the process by which someone signs his/her name. This process is similar to keyboard dynamics, except that this method measures the handwriting of the subjects while they sign their name. Measuring time, pressure, loops in the signature, and beginning and ending points all help to ensure the user is authentic.

Voiceprint

A *voiceprint* measures the subject's tone of voice while stating a specific sentence or phrase. This type of access control is vulnerable to replay attacks (replaying a recorded voice), so other access controls must be implemented along with the voiceprint. One such control requires subjects to state random words, which protects against an attacker playing prerecorded specific phrases. Another issue is that people's voices may substantially change due to illness, resulting in a false rejection.

Facial scan

Facial scan technology has greatly improved over the last few years. Facial scanning (also called facial recognition) is the process of passively taking a picture of a subject's face and comparing that picture to a list stored in a database. Although not frequently used for biometric authentication control due to the high cost, law enforcement, and security agencies use facial recognition and scanning technologies for biometric identification to improve security of high-valued, publicly accessible targets.

SOMEPLACE YOU ARE

Someplace you are describes location-based access control using technologies such as the global positioning system (GPS), IP address-based geolocation, or the physical location for a point-of-sale purchase. These controls can deny access if the subject is in the incorrect location.

ACCESS CONTROL TECHNOLOGIES

There are several technologies used for the implementation of access controls. As each technology is presented, it is important to identify what is unique about each technical solution.

CENTRALIZED ACCESS CONTROL

Centralized access control concentrates access control in one logical point for a system or organization. Instead of using local access control databases, systems authenticate via third-party ASs. Centralized access control can be used to provide single sign-on (SSO), where a subject may authenticate once, then access multiple systems. Centralized access control can centrally provide the three As of access control: authentication, authorization, and accountability.

- *Authentication*: proving an identity claim.
- *Authorization*: actions-authenticated subjects are allowed to perform on a system.
- *Accountability*: the ability to audit a system and demonstrate the actions of subjects.

DECENTRALIZED ACCESS CONTROL

Decentralized access control allows IT administration to occur closer to the mission and operations of the organization. In decentralized access control, an organization spans multiple locations, and the local sites support and maintain independent systems, access control databases, and data. Decentralized access control is also called distributed access control.

This model provides more local power because each site has control over its data. This is empowering, but it also carries risks. Different sites may employ different access control models, different policies, and different levels of security, leading to an inconsistent view. Even organizations with a uniform policy may find that adherence varies per site. An attacker is likely to attack the weakest link in the chain; for example, a small office with a lesser-trained staff makes a more tempting target than a central data center with a more experienced staff.

SINGLE SIGN-ON

Single sign-on (SSO) allows multiple systems to use a central AS. This allows users to authenticate once and have access to multiple different systems. It also allows security administrators to add, change, or revoke user privileges on one central system.

The primary disadvantage to SSO is that it may allow an attacker to gain access to multiple resources after compromising one authentication method, such as a password. SSO should always be used with multifactor authentication for this reason.

USER ENTITLEMENT, ACCESS REVIEW, AND AUDIT

Access aggregation occurs as individual users gain more access to more systems. This can happen intentionally, as a function of SSO. It can also happen unintentionally, because users often gain new entitlements, also called access rights, as they take on new roles or duties. This can result in *authorization creep*, in which users gain more entitlements without shedding the old ones. The power of these entitlements can compound over time, defeating controls such as least privilege and separation of duties. User entitlements must be routinely reviewed and audited. Processes should be developed that reduce or eliminate old entitlements as new ones are granted.

FEDERATED IDENTITY MANAGEMENT

Federated identity management (FIdM) applies SSO at a much wider scale: ranging from cross-organization to Internet scale. It is sometimes simply called identity management (IdM).

According to EDUCAUSE, "Identity management refers to the policies, processes, and technologies that establish user identities and enforce rules about access to digital resources. In a campus setting, many information systems—such as email, learning management systems, library databases, and grid computing applications—require users to authenticate themselves (typically with a username and password). An authorization process then determines which systems an authenticated user is permitted to access. With an enterprise identity management system, rather than having separate credentials for each system, a user can employ a single digital identity to access all resources to which the user is entitled. FIdM permits extending this approach above the enterprise level, creating a trusted authority for digital identities across multiple organizations. In a federated system, participating institutions share identity attributes based on agreed-upon standards, facilitating authentication from other members of the federation and granting appropriate access to online resources. This approach streamlines access to digital assets while protecting restricted resources."[6]

SAML

FIdM may use OpenID or SAML (security association markup language). SAML is an XML-based framework for exchanging security information, including authentication data. As discussed in Chapter 3, Domain 3: Security Engineering, extensible markup language (XML) is a markup language designed as a standard way to encode documents and data. One goal of SAML is to enable web SSO at an Internet scale. Other forms of SSO also use SAML to exchange data.

IDENTITY AS A SERVICE

With identity being a required precondition to effectively manage confidentiality, integrity, and availability, it is evident that identity plays a key role in security. Identity as a service (IDaaS), or cloud identity, allows organizations to leverage cloud service for IdM. The idea of leveraging public cloud services for IdM can be disconcerting. However, as with all matters of security, there are elements of cloud identity that can increase or decrease risk.

One of the most significant justifications for leveraging IDaaS stems from organizations' continued adoption and integration of cloud-hosted applications and other public facing third-party applications. Many of the IDaaS vendors can directly integrate with these services to allow for more streamlined IdM and SSO. Microsoft Accounts, formerly Live ID, are an example of cloud identity increasingly found within many enterprises.

LDAP

Lightweight directory access protocol (LDAP) provides a common open protocol for interfacing and querying directory service information provided by network operating systems. LDAP is widely used for the overwhelming majority of internal identity services including, most notably, Active Directory. Directory services play a key role in many applications by exposing key user, computer, services, and other objects to be queried via LDAP.

LDAP is an application layer protocol that uses port 389 via TCP or user datagram protocol (UDP). LDAP queries can be transmitted in cleartext and, depending upon configuration, can allow for some or all data to be queried anonymously. Naturally, LDAP does support authenticated connections and also secure communication channels leveraging TLS.

KERBEROS

Kerberos is a third-party authentication service that may be used to support SSO. Kerberos, also called Cerberus, (http://www.kerberos.org/) was the name of the three-headed dog that guarded the entrance to Hades in Greek mythology.

Kerberos uses symmetric encryption and provides mutual authentication of both clients and servers. It protects against network sniffing and replay attacks. The current version of Kerberos is Version 5, described by RFC 4120 (http://www.ietf.org/rfc/rfc4120.txt).

FAST FACTS

Kerberos has the following components:

- *Principal*: Client (user) or service.
- *Realm*: A logical Kerberos network.
- *Ticket*: Data that authenticates a principal's identity.
- *Credentials*: A ticket and a service key.
- *KDC*: Key Distribution Center, which authenticates principals.
- *TGS*: Ticket Granting Service.
- *TGT*: Ticket Granting Ticket.
- *C/S*: Client Server, regarding communications between the two.

Kerberos operational steps

For example, a Kerberos principal, a client run by user Alice, wishes to access a printer. Alice may print after taking these five (simplified) steps: Stopped here.

1. Kerberos Principal Alice contacts the Key Distribution Center (KDC), which acts as an AS, requesting authentication.
2. The KDC sends Alice a session key, encrypted with Alice's secret key. The KDC also sends a TGT (Ticket Granting Ticket), encrypted with the Ticket Granting Service's (TGS) secret key.
3. Alice decrypts the session key and uses it to request permission to print from the TGS.
4. Seeing Alice has a valid session key (and therefore has proven her identity claim), the TGS sends Alice a C/S session key (second session key) to use for printing. The TGS also sends a service ticket, encrypted with the printer's key.
5. Alice connects to the printer. The printer, seeing a valid C/S session key, knows Alice has permission to print and also knows that Alice herself is authentic.

This process is summarized in Fig. 5.3.

The session key in Step 2 of Fig. 5.3 is encrypted with Alice's key, which is represented as {Session Key}Key^{Alice}. Also note that the TGT is encrypted with the TGS's key; this means that Alice cannot decrypt the TGT (only the TGS can), so she simply sends it to the TGS. The TGT contains a number of items, including a copy of Alice's session key. This is how the TGS knows that Alice has a valid session key, which proves Alice is authenticated.

SESAME

SESAME stands for secure European system for applications in a multivendor environment, an SSO system that supports heterogeneous environments. SESAME can be thought of as a sequel of sorts to Kerberos, "SESAME adds to Kerberos: heterogeneity, sophisticated access control features, scalability of public key systems, better manageability, audit and delegation."[7] Of those improvements, the most compelling is the addition of public key (asymmetric) encryption. It addresses one of the biggest weaknesses in Kerberos: the plaintext storage of symmetric keys.

SESAME uses privilege attribute certificates (PACs) in place of Kerberos' tickets. More information on SESAME is available at: https://www.cosic.esat.kuleuven.be/sesame/.

ACCESS CONTROL PROTOCOLS AND FRAMEWORKS

Both centralized and decentralized models may support remote users authenticating to local systems. A number of protocols and frameworks may be used to support this need, including RADIUS, Diameter, TACACS/TACACS+, PAP, and CHAP, which we will discuss now.

RADIUS

The remote authentication dial in user service (RADIUS) protocol is a third-party authentication system. RADIUS is described in RFCs 2865 and 2866, and it uses the UDP ports 1812 (authentication) and 1813 (accounting). RADIUS formerly used the

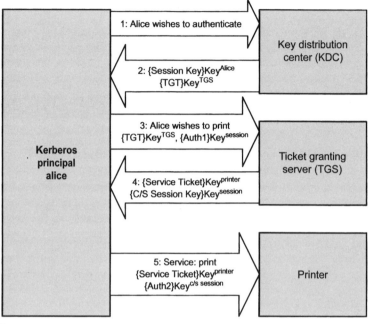

FIG. 5.3

Kerberos steps.

unofficially assigned ports of 1645 and 1646 for the same respective purposes, and some implementations continue to use those ports.

RADIUS is considered an AAA system comprised of three components: authentication, authorization, and accounting. It authenticates a subject's credentials against an authentication database. It authorizes users by allowing specific users to access specific data objects. It accounts for each data session by creating a log entry for each RADIUS connection made.

Diameter

Diameter is RADIUS' successor, designed to provide an improved AAA framework. RADIUS provides limited accountability and has problems with flexibility, scalability, reliability, and security; therefore, Diameter is more flexible.

TACACS and TACACS+

The *terminal access controller access control system (TACACS)* is a centralized access control system that requires users to send an ID and static (reusable) password for authentication. TACACS uses UDP port 49 and may also use TCP. However, reusable passwords are a vulnerability; the improved *TACACS+* provides better password protection by allowing a two-factor strong authentication.

TACACS+ is not backwards compatible with TACACS. TACACS+ uses TCP port 49 for authentication with the TACACS+ server.

PAP and CHAP

The *password authentication protocol (PAP)* is insecure: a user enters a password and it is sent across the network in clear text. When received by the PAP server, it is authenticated and validated. Sniffing the network may disclose the plaintext passwords.

The *challenge-handshake authentication protocol (CHAP)* provides protection against playback attacks. It uses a central location that challenges remote users. As stated in the RFC, "CHAP depends upon a 'secret' known only to the authenticator and the peer. The secret is not sent over the link. Although the authentication is only one-way, by negotiating CHAP in both directions the same secret set may easily be used for mutual authentication."[8]

ACCESS CONTROL MODELS

Now that we have reviewed the cornerstone access control concepts, we can discuss the different access control models: the primary models are discretionary access control (DAC), mandatory access control (MAC), and nondiscretionary access control.

DISCRETIONARY ACCESS CONTROLS

DAC gives subjects full control of objects they have created or have been given access to, including sharing the objects with other subjects. Subjects are empowered and control their data. Standard UNIX and Windows operating systems use DAC for file systems; subjects can grant other subjects access to their files, change their attributes, alter them, or delete them.

MANDATORY ACCESS CONTROLS

MAC is system-enforced access control based on a subject's clearance and an object's labels. Subjects and objects have clearances and labels, respectively, such as confidential, secret, and top-secret. A subject may access an object only if the subject's clearance is equal to or greater than the object's label. Subjects cannot share objects with other subjects who lack the proper clearance, or "write down" objects to a lower classification level (such as from top-secret to secret). MAC systems are usually focused on preserving the confidentiality of data.

NONDISCRETIONARY ACCESS CONTROL

Role-based access control (RBAC) defines how information is accessed on a system based on the role of the subject. A role could be a nurse, a backup administrator, a help desk technician, etc. Subjects are grouped into roles, and each defined role has access permissions based upon the role, not the individual.

RBAC is a type of *nondiscretionary access control* because users do not have discretion regarding the groups of objects they are allowed to access and are unable to transfer objects to other subjects.

Task-based access control is another nondiscretionary access control model related to RBAC. Task-based access control is based on the tasks each subject must perform, such as writing prescriptions, restoring data from a backup tape, or opening a help desk ticket. It attempts to solve the same problem that RBAC solves, except it focuses on specific tasks instead of roles.

RULE-BASED ACCESS CONTROLS

As one would expect, a *rule-based access control* system uses a series of defined rules, restrictions, and filters for accessing objects within a system. The rules are in the form of "if/then" statements. An example of a rule-based access control device is a proxy firewall that allows users to surf the web with predefined approved content only. The statement may read, "If the user is authorized to surf the web and the site is on the approved list, then allow access." Other sites are prohibited, and this rule is enforced across all authenticated users.

CONTENT-DEPENDENT AND CONTEXT-DEPENDENT ACCESS CONTROLS

Content-dependent and context-dependent access controls are not full-fledged access control methods in their own right as MAC and DAC are, but they typically play a defense-in-depth supporting role. They may be added as an additional control, typically to DAC systems.

Content-dependent access control adds additional criteria beyond identification and authentication; that is, the actual content the subject is attempting to access. All employees of an organization may have access to the HR database to view their accrued sick time and vacation time. Should an employee attempt to access the content of the CIO's HR record, access is denied.

Context-dependent access control applies additional context before granting access. A commonly used context is time. After identification and authentication, a help desk worker who works Monday through Friday from 09:00 am to 05.00 pm will be granted access at noon on a Tuesday. A context-dependent access control system could deny access on Sunday at 01:00 am, which is the wrong time and therefore the wrong context.

SUMMARY OF EXAM OBJECTIVES

If one thinks of the castle analogy for security, then access control would be the moat and castle walls. Identity and access management ensures that the border protection mechanisms, in both a logical and physical viewpoint, are secured. The purpose of access control is to allow authorized users access to appropriate data and deny access to unauthorized users; this is also known as limiting subjects' access to objects. Even though this task is a complex and involved one, it is possible to implement a strong access control program without overburdening the users who rely on access to the system.

Protecting the CIA triad is another key aspect to implementing access controls. Maintaining confidentiality, integrity, and availability is of utmost importance. Securing the CIA of a system means enacting specific procedures for data access. These procedures will change depending on the functionality the users require and the sensitivity of the data stored on the system.

TOP FIVE TOUGHEST QUESTIONS

(1) What access control method weighs additional factors, such as time of attempted access, before granting access?
   (a) Content-dependent access control
   (b) Context-dependent access control
   (c) Role-based access control
   (d) Task-based access control

(2) What service is known as cloud identity, which allows organizations to leverage cloud service for identity management?
   (a) IaaS
   (b) IDaaS
   (c) PaaS
   (d) SaaS

(3) What is an XML-based framework for exchanging security information, including authentication data?
   (a) Kerberos
   (b) OpenID
   (c) SAML
   (d) SESAME

(4) What protocol is a common open protocol for interfacing and querying directory service information provided by network operating systems using port 389 via TCP or UDP?
   (a) CHAP
   (b) LDAP
   (c) PAP
   (d) RADIUS

(5) What technique would raise the false accept rate (FAR) and lower the false reject rate (FRR) in a fingerprint scanning system?
   (a) Decrease the amount of minutiae that is verified
   (b) Increase the amount of minutiae that is verified
   (c) Lengthen the enrollment time
   (d) Lower the throughput time

ANSWERS

(1) Correct answer and explanation: B. Context-dependent access control adds additional factors beyond username and password, such as the time of attempted access.
Incorrect Answers and Explanations: Answers A, C, and D are incorrect. Content-dependent access control uses the content, such as file contents, as an additional factor. Role-based control is based on the subject's role, while task-based access control is based on the tasks the subject needs to perform.

(2) Correct answer and explanation: B. Identity as a service, also called cloud identity, allows organizations to leverage cloud service for identity management.
Incorrect answers and explanations: Answers *A*, *C*, and *D* are incorrect. IaaS (infrastructure as a service) provides an entire virtualized operating system, which the customer configures from the OS on up. PaaS (platform as a service) provides a preconfigured operating system, and the customer configures the applications. SaaS (software as a service) is completely configured, from the operating system to applications, and the customer simply uses the application.

(3) Correct answer and explanation: C. SAML is an XML-based framework for exchanging security information, including authentication data.
Incorrect answers and explanations: Answers A, B, and D are incorrect. Kerberos is a third-party authentication service that may be used to support single sign-on. OpenID is a framework for exchanging authentication data, but it is not XML-based. SESAME stands for secure European system for applications in a multivendor environment, a single sign-on system that supports heterogeneous environments.

(4) Correct answer and explanation: B. Lightweight directory access protocol is an open protocol for interfacing and querying directory service information from network operating systems using port 389 TCP or UDP.
Incorrect answers and explanations: Answers A, C, and D are incorrect. CHAP, PAP, and RADIUS do not provide directory service information provided by network operating systems using port 389 TCP or UDP.

(5) Correct answer and explanation: A. Decreasing the amount of minutiae will make the accuracy of the system lower, which lower false rejects but raises false accepts.
Incorrect answers and explanations: Answers B, C, and D are incorrect. Increasing the amount of minutiae will make the system more accurate, increasing the FRR and lowering the FAR. Enrollment and throughput time are not directly connected to FAR and FRR.

ENDNOTES

1. *Password Protection for Modern Operating systems.* http://static.usenix.org/publications/login/2004-06/pdfs/alexander.pdf [accessed 25.04.16].

2. ISACA. *IT standards, guidelines, and tools and techniques for audit and assurance and control professionals.* http://www.isaca.org/knowledge-center/standards/documents/it-audit-assurance-guidance-1march2010.pdf; 2010 [accessed 25.04.16].
3. *NIST Tech Beat March 16, 2006.* http://www.nist.gov/public_affairs/techbeat/tb2006_0316.htm [accessed 25.04.16].
4. *Hand Geometry.* https://www.fbi.gov/about-us/cjis/fingerprints_biometrics/biometric-center-of-excellence/files/hand-geometry.pdf [accessed 25.04.16].
5. *Things you should know about federated identity management.* http://net.educause.edu/ir/library/pdf/EST0903.pdf [accessed 25.04.16].
6. *Sesame in a nutshell.* https://www.cosic.esat.kuleuven.be/sesame/html/sesame_what.html [accessed 25.04.16].
7. *RFC 1994 CHAP.* http://www.faqs.org/rfcs/rfc1994.html [accessed 25.04.16].

Domain 6: Security assessment and testing

6

CHAPTER OUTLINE

INTRODUCTION

Security assessment and testing are critical components of any information security program. Organizations must accurately assess their real-world security, focus on the most critical components, and make necessary changes to improve.

In this domain, we will discuss two major components of assessment and testing: overall security assessments, including vulnerability scanning, penetration testing, and security audits; and testing software via static and dynamic methods.

Eleventh Hour CISSP®. http://dx.doi.org/10.1016/B978-0-12-811248-9.00006-1

ASSESSING ACCESS CONTROL

A number of processes exist to assess the effectiveness of access control. Tests with a narrower scope include penetration tests, vulnerability assessments, and security audits. A security assessment is a broader test that may include narrower tests, such as penetration tests, as subsections.

PENETRATION TESTING

A penetration tester is a white hat hacker who receives authorization to attempt to break into an organization's physical or electronic perimeter (sometimes both). *Penetration tests* (called "pen tests" for short) are designed to determine whether black hat hackers could do the same. They are a narrow but often useful test, especially if the penetration tester is successful.

Penetration tests may include the following tests:

- Network (Internet)
- Network (internal or DMZ)
- War dialing
- Wireless
- Physical (attempt to gain entrance into a facility or room)

Network attacks may leverage client-side attacks, server-side attacks, or Web application attacks. *War dialing*, which gets its name from the 1983 movie *WarGames*, uses a modem to dial a series of phone numbers, looking for an answering modem carrier tone. The penetration tester then attempts to access the answering system.

Social engineering is a no-tech or low-tech method that uses the human mind to bypass security controls. Social engineering may be used in combination with many types of attacks, especially client-side attacks or physical tests. An example of a social engineering attack combined with a client-side attack is emailing malware with a subject line of "Category 5 Hurricane is about to hit Florida!"

A *zero-knowledge* test, also called black-box test, is "blind"; the penetration tester begins with no external or trusted information and begins the attack with public information only. A *full-knowledge test* (also called *crystal-box test*) provides internal information to the penetration tester, including network diagrams, policies and procedures, and sometimes reports from previous penetration testers. *Partial-knowledge* tests are in between zero and full knowledge; the penetration tester receives some limited trusted information.

Penetration testing tools and methodology

Penetration testers often use penetration testing tools, which include the open-source Metasploit (http://www.metasploit.org), and closed-source Core Impact (http://www.coresecurity.com), and Immunity Canvas (http://www.immunitysec.com). Pen testers also use custom tools, as well as malware samples and code posted to the Internet.

Penetration testers use the following methodology:

- Planning
- Reconnaissance
- Scanning (also called enumeration)
- Vulnerability assessment
- Exploitation
- Reporting

Black hat hackers typically follow a similar methodology although they may perform less planning and obviously omit reporting. Black hats will also cover their tracks by erasing logs and other signs of intrusion, and they frequently violate system integrity by installing back doors in order to maintain access. A penetration tester should always protect data and system integrity.

Assuring confidentiality, data integrity, and system integrity

Penetration testers must ensure the confidentiality of any sensitive data that is accessed during the test. If the target of a penetration test is a credit card database, the penetration tester may have no legal right to view or download the credit cards. Testers will often request that a dummy file containing no regulated or sensitive data be placed in the same area of the system as the credit card data and protected with the same permissions. If the tester can read and/or write to that file, then they prove they could have done the same to the credit card data.

Penetration testers must ensure the system integrity and data integrity of their client's systems. Any active attack, as opposed to a passive read-only attack, against a system could potentially cause damage; this can be true even for an experienced penetration tester. This risk must be clearly understood by all parties, and tests are often performed during change maintenance windows for this reason.

One potential issue that should be discussed before the penetration test commences is the risk of encountering signs of a previous or current successful malicious attack. Penetration testers sometimes discover that they are not the first attacker to compromise a system and that someone has beaten them to it. Attackers will often become more malicious if they believe they have been discovered, sometimes violating data and system integrity. The integrity of the system is at risk in this case, and the penetration tester should end the penetration test and immediately escalate the issue.

Finally, the final penetration test report should be protected at a very high level, as it contains a roadmap to attack the organization.

VULNERABILITY TESTING

Vulnerability scanning or vulnerability-testing scans a network or system for a list of predefined vulnerabilities such as system misconfiguration, outdated software, or a lack of patching. A vulnerability-testing tool such as Nessus (http://www.tenable.com/products/nessus-vulnerability-scanner) or OpenVAS (http://www.openvas.org) may be used to identify the vulnerabilities.

SECURITY AUDITS

A *security audit* is a test against a published standard. Organizations may be audited for Payment Card Industry Data Security Standard (PCI DSS) compliance (discussed in Chapter 3), for example. PCI DSS includes many required controls, such as firewalls, specific access control models, and wireless encryption. An auditor then verifies that a site or organization meets the published standard.

SECURITY ASSESSMENTS

Security assessments are a holistic approach to assessing the effectiveness of access control. Instead of looking narrowly at penetration tests or vulnerability assessments, security assessments have a broader scope.

Security assessments view many controls across multiple domains and may include the following:

- Policies, procedures, and other administrative controls
- Assessing the real world-effectiveness of administrative controls
- Change management
- Architectural review
- Penetration tests
- Vulnerability assessments
- Security audits

As the above list shows, a security assessment may include other distinct tests, such as a penetration test. The goal is to broadly cover many other specific tests to ensure that all aspects of access control are considered.

LOG REVIEWS

Reviewing security audit logs within an IT system is one of the easiest ways to verify that access control mechanisms are performing adequately. Reviewing audit logs is primarily a detective control.

The intelligence gained from proactive audit log management and monitoring can be very beneficial; the collected antivirus logs of thousands of systems can give a very accurate picture of the current state of malware. Antivirus alerts combined with a spike in failed authentication alerts from authentication servers or a spike in outbound firewall denials may indicate that a password-guessing worm is attempting to spread across a network.

SOFTWARE TESTING METHODS

There is a variety of software testing methods. In addition to testing the features and stability of the software, testing increasingly focuses on discovering specific programmer errors leading to vulnerabilities that risk system compromise, including a lack of bounds checking. Two general approaches to automated code review exist: static and dynamic testing.

STATIC AND DYNAMIC TESTING

Static testing tests the code passively; the code is not running. This includes walk-throughs, syntax checking, and code reviews. Static analysis tools review the raw source code itself looking for evidence of known insecure practices, functions, libraries, or other characteristics used in the source code. The Unix lint program performs static testing for C programs.

Dynamic testing tests the code while executing it. With dynamic testing, security checks are performed while actually running or executing the code or application under review.

Both approaches are appropriate and complement each other. Static analysis tools might uncover flaws in code that have not even yet been fully implemented in a way that would expose the flaw to dynamic testing. However, dynamic analysis might uncover flaws that exist in the particular implementation and interaction of code that static analysis missed.

White-box software testing gives the tester access to program source code, data structures, variables, etc. *Black-box testing* gives the tester no internal details; the software is treated as a black box that receives inputs.

TRACEABILITY MATRIX

A *traceability matrix*, sometimes called a requirements traceability matrix (RTM), can be used to map customers' requirements to the software testing plan; it traces the requirements and ensures that they are being met. It does this by mapping customer usage to test cases. Fig. 6.1 shows a sample RTM.

Requirement ID	Requirements tested	Use case 1.1	Use case 1.2	Use case 1.3	Use case 1.4	...
Test cases	34	2	4	7	5	
TC1.1.1	2	X		X		
TC1.1.2	1				X	
TC1.2.1	3	X		X	X	
TC1.2.2	1		X			
TC1.2.3	2			X	X	
...						

FIG. 6.1

Sample requirements traceability matrix.[1]

SYNTHETIC TRANSACTIONS

Synthetic transactions, or synthetic monitoring, involve building scripts or tools that simulate activities normally performed in an application. The typical goal of using synthetic transactions/monitoring is to establish expected norms for the performance of these transactions. These synthetic transactions can be automated to run on a periodic basis to ensure the application is still performing as expected. These types of transactions can also be useful for testing application updates prior to deployment to ensure that functionality and performance will not be negatively impacted. This type of testing or monitoring is most commonly associated with custom-developed web applications.

SOFTWARE TESTING LEVELS

It is usually helpful to approach the challenge of testing software from multiple angles, addressing various testing levels from low to high. The software testing levels designed to accomplish that goal are unit testing, installation testing, integration testing, regression testing, and acceptance testing.

FAST FACTS

- *Unit testing*: Low-level tests of software components, such as functions, procedures, or objects.
- *Installation testing*: Testing software as it is installed and first operated.
- *Integration testing*: Testing multiple software components as they are combined into a working system. Subsets may be tested, or *Big Bang* integration testing is used for all integrated software components.
- *Regression testing*: Testing software after updates, modifications, or patches.
- *Acceptance testing*: Testing to ensure that the software meets the customer's operational requirements. When this testing is done directly by the customer, it is called user acceptance testing.

FUZZING

Fuzzing (also called *fuzz testing*) is a type of black-box testing that submits random, malformed data as inputs into software programs to determine if they will crash. A program that crashes when receiving malformed or unexpected input is likely to suffer from a boundary-checking issue and may be vulnerable to a buffer overflow attack.

Fuzzing is typically automated, repeatedly presenting random input strings as command line switches, environment variables, and program inputs. Any program that crashes or hangs has failed the fuzz test.

COMBINATORIAL SOFTWARE TESTING

Combinatorial software testing is a black-box testing method that seeks to identify and test all unique combinations of software inputs. An example of combinatorial software testing is *pairwise testing*, also called *all-pairs testing*.

MISUSE CASE TESTING

Misuse case testing leverages use cases for applications, which spell out how various functionalities will be leveraged within an application. Formal use cases are typically built as a flow diagram written in UML (Unified Modeling Language) and are created to help model expected behavior and functionality.

Misuse case testing models how a security impact could be realized by an adversary abusing the application. This can be seen simply as a different type of use case, but the reason for calling out misuse case testing specifically is to highlight the general lack of attacks against the application.

TEST COVERAGE ANALYSIS

Test or code coverage analysis attempts to identify the degree to which code testing applies to the entire application. The goal is to ensure that there are no significant gaps where a lack of testing could allow for bugs or security issues to be present that otherwise should have been discovered.

INTERFACE TESTING

Interface testing is primarily concerned with appropriate functionality being exposed across all the ways users can interact with the application. From a security-oriented vantage point, the goal is to ensure that security is uniformly applied across the various interfaces. This type of testing exercises the various attack vectors an adversary could leverage.

SUMMARY OF EXAM OBJECTIVES

In this domain, we have learned about various methods to test real-world security of an organization, including vulnerability scanning, penetration testing, security assessments, and audits. Vulnerability scanning determines one half of the $Risk = Threat \times Vulnerability$ equation. Penetration tests seek to match those vulnerabilities with threats in order to demonstrate real-world risk. Assessments provide a broader view of the security picture, and audits demonstrate compliance with a published specification, such as PCI DSS.

We discussed testing code security, including static methods such as source code analysis, walkthroughs, and syntax checking. We discussed dynamic methods used on running code, including fuzzing and various forms of black-box testing. We also discussed synthetic transactions, which attempt to emulate real-world use of an application through the use of scripts or tools that simulate activities normally performed in an application.

TOP FIVE TOUGHEST QUESTIONS

1. What can be used to ensure that software meets the customer's operational requirements?
   a. Integration testing
   b. Installation testing
   c. Acceptance testing
   d. Unit testing
2. What term describes a black-box testing method that seeks to identify and test all unique combinations of software inputs?
   a. Combinatorial software testing
   b. Dynamic testing
   c. Misuse case testing
   d. Static testing
   Use the following scenario to answer questions 3–5:
   You are the CISO (chief information security officer) of a large bank and have hired a company to provide an overall security assessment, as well as complete a penetration test of your organization. Your goal is to determine overall information security effectiveness. You are specifically interested in determining if theft of financial data is possible.
   Your bank has recently deployed a custom-developed, three-tier web application that allows customers to check balances, make transfers, and deposit checks by taking a photo with their smartphone and then uploading the check image. In addition to a traditional browser interface, your company has developed a smartphone app for both Apple iOS and Android devices.
   The contract has been signed, and both scope and rules of engagement have been agreed upon. A 24/7 operational IT contact at the bank has been made available in case of any unexpected developments during the penetration test, including potential accidental disruption of services.
3. Assuming the penetration test is successful, what is the best way for the penetration testing firm to demonstrate the risk of theft of financial data?
   a. Instruct the penetration testing team to conduct a thorough vulnerability assessment of the server containing financial data.
   b. Instruct the penetration testing team to download financial data, redact it, and report accordingly.
   c. Instruct the penetration testing team that they may only download financial data via an encrypted and authenticated channel.
   d. Place a harmless "flag" file in the same location as the financial data, and inform the penetration testing team to download the flag.
4. You would like to have the security firm test the new web application, but have decided not to share the underlying source code. What type of test could be used to help determine the security of the custom web application?
   a. Secure compiler warnings

    b. Fuzzing

    c. Static testing

    d. White-box testing

5. During the course of the penetration test, the testers discover signs of an active compromise of the new custom-developed, three-tier web application. What is the best course of action?

    a. Attempt to contain and eradicate the malicious activity.

    b. Continue the test.

    c. Quietly end the test, immediately call the operational IT contact, and escalate the issue.

    d. Shut the server down.

ANSWERS

1. Correct answer and explanation: C. Acceptance testing is designed to ensure the software meets the customer's operational requirements.
Incorrect answers and explanations: Answers A, B, and D are incorrect. Integration testing examines multiple software components as they are combined into a working system. Installation testing examines software as it is installed and first operated. Unit testing is a low-level test of software components, such as functions, procedures, or objects.

2. Correct answer and explanation: A. Combinatorial software testing is a black-box testing method that seeks to identify and test all unique combinations of software inputs.
Incorrect answers and explanations: Answers B, C, and D are incorrect. Dynamic testing examines code while executing it. Misuse case testing formally models how security would be impacted by an adversary abusing the application. Static testing examines the code passively; the code is not running. This form of testing includes walkthroughs, syntax checking, and code reviews.

3. Correct answer and explanation: D. A flag is a dummy file containing no regulated or sensitive data. It is placed in the same area of the system as the credit card data and protected with the same permissions. If the tester can read and/or write to that file, then they prove they could have done the same to the credit card data.
Incorrect answers and explanations: Answers A, B, and C are incorrect. Answer A is a vulnerability assessment, not a penetration test. Answers B and C are dangerous and could involve unauthorized access of regulated data, such as health care records.

4. Correct answer and explanation: B. Fuzzing is a black-box testing method that does not require access to source code.
Incorrect answers and explanations: Answers A, C, and D are incorrect. All are static methods that require access to source code.

5. Correct answer and explanation: C. Attackers will often act more maliciously if they believe they have been discovered, sometimes violating data and system integrity. The integrity of the system is at risk in this case, and the penetration tester should end the penetration test and immediately escalate the issue. Incorrect answers and explanations: Answers A, B, and D are incorrect. The client must be notified immediately, as incident handling is not the penetration tester's responsibility.

ENDNOTE

1. *Combinatorial software testing.* http://csrc.nist.gov/groups/SNS/acts/documents/kuhn-kacker-lei-hunter09.pdf [accessed 25.04.16].

Domain 7: Security operations

7

Eleventh Hour CISSP®. http://dx.doi.org/10.1016/B978-0-12-811248-9.00007-3

INTRODUCTION

Security operations is concerned with threats to a production-operating environment. Threat agents can be internal or external actors, and operations security must account for both of these threat sources in order to be effective. Security operations is about people, data, media, and hardware, as well as the threats associated with each of these in a production environment.

ADMINISTRATIVE SECURITY

All organizations contain people, data, and the means for people to use the data. A fundamental aspect of operations security is ensuring that controls are in place to inhibit people either inadvertently or intentionally compromising the confidentiality, integrity, or availability of data or the systems and media holding that data. Administrative security provides the means to control people's operational access to data.

ADMINISTRATIVE PERSONNEL CONTROLS

Administrative personnel controls represent important operations security concepts that should be mastered by the CISSP candidate. These are fundamental concepts within information security that permeate multiple domains.

Least privilege or minimum necessary access

One of the most important concepts in all of information security is that of the *principle of least privilege*. The principle of least privilege dictates that persons have no more than the access that is strictly required for the performance of their duties. The principle of least privilege may also be referred to as the principle of minimum necessary access. Regardless of name, adherence to this principle is a fundamental tenet of security and should serve as a starting point for administrative security controls.

Need to know

In organizations with extremely sensitive information that leverage mandatory access control (MAC), a basic determination of access is enforced by the system. The access determination is based upon clearance levels of subjects and classification levels of objects. Though the vetting process for someone accessing highly sensitive information is stringent, clearance level alone is insufficient when dealing with the most sensitive of information. An extension to the principle of least privilege in MAC environments is the concept of compartmentalization.

Compartmentalization, a method for enforcing *need to know*, goes beyond the mere reliance upon clearance level and necessitates simply that someone requires access to information. Compartmentalization is best understood by considering a highly sensitive military operation; while there may be a large number of individuals, some of whom might be of high rank, only a subset will "need to know" specific information. The others have no "need to know," and therefore will not be granted access.

Separation of duties

Separation of duties prescribes that multiple people are required to complete critical or sensitive transactions. The goal of separation of duties is to ensure that in order for someone to abuse their access to sensitive data or transactions, they must convince another party to act in concert. *Collusion* is the term used for the two parties conspiring to undermine the security of the transaction. The classic action movie example of separation of duties involves two keys, a nuclear sub, and a rogue captain.

Rotation of duties/job rotation

Rotation of duties, also known as job rotation or rotation of responsibilities, provides an organization with a means to help mitigate the risk associated with any one individual having too many privileges. Rotation of duties simply requires that one person does not perform critical functions or responsibilities for an extended period of time. There are multiple issues that rotation of duties can help to begin to address. One issue addressed by job rotation is the "hit by a bus" scenario. Imagine, morbid as it is, that one individual in the organization is hit by a bus on his/her way to work. If the operational impact of the loss of an individual would be too great, then perhaps one way to assuage this impact would be to ensure that there is additional depth of coverage for this individual's responsibilities.

Mandatory leave/forced vacation

An additional operational control that is closely related to rotation of duties is that of *mandatory leave*, also known as forced vacation. Though there are various justifications for requiring employees to be away from work, the primary security considerations are similar to that addressed by rotation of duties: reducing or detecting personnel single points of failure, and detecting and deterring fraud.

Nondisclosure agreement

A *nondisclosure agreement* (NDA) is a work-related contractual agreement ensuring that, prior to being given access to sensitive information or data, an individual or organization appreciates their legal responsibility to maintain the confidentiality of that sensitive information. Job candidates, consultants, or contractors often sign NDAs before they are hired. NDAs are largely a directive control.

Background checks

Background checks (also known as background investigations or preemployment screening) are an additional administrative control commonly employed by many organizations. The majority of background investigations are performed as part of a preemployment screening process. Some organizations perform cursory background investigations that include a criminal record check. Others perform more in-depth checks, such as verifying employment history, obtaining credit reports, and, in some cases, requiring the submission of a drug screening.

FORENSICS

Digital forensics provides a formal approach to dealing with investigations and evidence with special consideration of the legal aspects of this process. The forensic process must preserve the "crime scene" and the evidence in order to prevent the unintentional violation of the integrity of either the data or the data's environment. A primary goal of forensics is to prevent unintentional modification of the system. *Live forensics* includes taking a bit-by-bit image or *binary image* of physical memory, gathering details about running processes, and gathering network connection data.

FORENSIC MEDIA ANALYSIS

In addition to the valuable data gathered during the live forensic capture, the main source of forensic data typically comes from binary images of secondary storage and portable storage devices such as hard disk drives, USB flash drives, CDs, DVDs, and possibly associated cellular (mobile) phones and mp3 players.

FAST FACTS

Here are the four basic types of disk-based forensic data:

- *Allocated space*: portions of a disk partition that are marked as actively containing data.
- *Unallocated space*: portions of a disk partition that do not contain active data. This includes portions that have never been allocated, as well as previously allocated portions that have been marked unallocated. If a file is deleted, the portions of the disk that held the deleted file are marked as unallocated and made available for use.
- *Slack space*: data is stored in specific-sized chunks known as clusters, which are sometimes referred to as sectors or blocks. A cluster is the minimum size that can be allocated by a file system. If a particular file, or final portion of a file, does not require the use of the entire cluster, then some extra space will exist within the cluster. This leftover space is known as slack space; it may contain old data, or it can be used intentionally by attackers to hide information.
- *"Bad" blocks/clusters/sectors*: hard disks routinely end up with sectors that cannot be read due to some physical defect. The sectors marked as bad will be ignored by the operating system since no data could be read in those defective portions. Attackers could intentionally mark sectors or clusters as being bad in order to hide data within this portion of the disk.

NETWORK FORENSICS

Network forensics is the study of data in motion, with a special focus on gathering evidence via a process that will support admission into a court of law. This means the integrity of the data is paramount, as is the legality of the collection process. Network forensics is closely related to network intrusion detection; the difference is the former focuses on legalities, while the later focuses on operations.

EMBEDDED DEVICE FORENSICS

One of the greatest challenges facing the field of digital forensics is the proliferation of consumer-grade electronic hardware and embedded devices. While forensic investigators have had decades to understand and develop tools and techniques to analyze magnetic disks, newer technologies such as solid-state drives lack both forensic understanding and forensic tools capable of analysis.

ELECTRONIC DISCOVERY (eDISCOVERY)

Electronic discovery, or eDiscovery, pertains to legal counsel gaining access to pertinent electronic information during the pretrial discovery phase of civil legal proceedings. The general purpose of discovery is to gather potential evidence that will allow for building a case. Electronic discovery differs from traditional discovery simply in that eDiscovery seeks ESI, or electronically stored information, which is typically acquired via a forensic investigation. While the difference between traditional discovery and eDiscovery might seem miniscule, given the potentially vast quantities of electronic data stored by organizations, eDiscovery can become logistically and financially cumbersome.

Some of the challenges associated with eDiscovery stem from the seemingly innocuous backup policies of organizations. While long-term storage of computer information has generally been thought to be a sound practice, this data is discoverable. Discovery does not take into account whether ESI is conveniently accessible or transferable.

Appropriate data retention policies, in addition to software and systems designed to facilitate eDiscovery, can greatly reduce the burden on the organization when required to provide ESI for discovery. When considering data retention policies, consider not only how long information should be kept, but also how long the information needs to be accessible to the organization. Any data for which there is no longer a need should be appropriately purged according to the data retention policy.

INCIDENT RESPONSE MANAGEMENT

All organizations will experience security incidents. Because of the certainty of security incidents eventually impacting organizations, there is a great need to be equipped with a regimented and tested methodology for identifying and responding to these incidents.

METHODOLOGY

Different books and organizations may use different terms and phases associated with the incident response process; this section will mirror the terms associated with the examination. Many incident-handling methodologies treat containment, eradication, and recovery as three distinct steps, as we will in this book. Other names for each step are sometimes used; the current exam lists a seven-step lifecycle but curiously omits the first step in most incident handling methodologies: preparation. Perhaps preparation is implied, like the identification portion of AAA systems. We will therefore cover eight steps, mapped to the current exam:

1. Preparation
2. Detection (identification)
3. Response (containment)
4. Mitigation (eradication)
5. Reporting
6. Recovery
7. Remediation
8. Lessons learned (postincident activity, postmortem, or reporting)

Preparation

The preparation phase includes steps taken before an incident occurs. These include training, writing incident response policies and procedures, and providing tools such as laptops with sniffing software, crossover cables, original OS media, removable

	Action	Completed
	Detection and Analysis	
1.	Determine whether an incident has occurred	
1.1	Analyze the precursors and indicators	
1.2	Look for correlating information	
1.3	Perform research (eg, search engines, knowledge base)	
1.4	As soon as the handler believes an incident has occurred, begin documenting the investigation and gathering evidence	
2.	Prioritize handling the incident based on the relevant factors (functional impact, information impact, recoverability effort, etc.)	
3.	Report the incident to the appropriate internal personnel and external organizations	
	Containment, Eradication, and Recovery	
4.	Acquire, preserve, secure, and document evidence	
5.	Contain the incident	
6.	Eradicate the incident	
6.1	Identify and mitigate all vulnerabilities that were exploited	
6.2	Remove malware, inappropriate materials, and other components	
6.3	If more affected hosts are discovered (eg, new malware infections), repeat the Detection and Analysis steps (1.1, 1.2) to identify all other affected hosts, then contain (5) and eradicate (6) the incident for them	
7.	Recover from the incident	
7.1	Return affected systems to an operationally ready state	
7.2	Confirm that the affected systems are functioning normally	
7.3	If necessary, implement additional monitoring to look for future related activity	
	Post-Incident Activity	
8.	Create a follow-up report	
9.	Hold a lessons learned meeting (mandatory for major incidents, optional otherwise)	

FIG. 7.1

Incident handling checklist.[1]

drives, etc. Preparation should include anything that may be required to handle an incident or that will make incident response faster and more effective. One preparation step is preparing an incident handling checklist. Fig. 7.1 is an incident handling checklist from NIST Special Publication 800-61r2.

Detection (identification)

One of the most important steps in the incident response process is the *detection phase*. Detection, also called identification, is the phase in which events are analyzed in order to determine whether these events might comprise a security incident. Without strong detective capabilities built into the information systems, the organization has little hope of being able to effectively respond to information security incidents in a timely fashion.

Response (containment)

The *response phase*, or containment, of incident response is the point at which the incident response team begins interacting with affected systems and attempts to keep further damage from occurring as a result of the incident. Responses might include taking a system off the network, isolating traffic, powering off the system, or other items to control both the scope and severity of the incident. This phase is also typically where a binary (bit-by-bit) forensic backup is made of systems involved in the incident. An important trend to understand is that most organizations will now capture volatile data before pulling the power plug on a system.

Mitigation (eradication)

The *mitigation phase*, or eradication, involves the process of understanding the cause of the incident so that the system can be reliably cleaned and ultimately restored to operational status later in the recovery phase. In order for an organization to recover from an incident, the cause of the incident must be determined. The cause must be known so that the systems in question can be returned to a known good state without significant risk of the compromise persisting or reoccurring. A common occurrence is for organizations to remove the most obvious piece of malware affecting a system and think that is sufficient; when in reality, the obvious malware may only be a symptom and the cause may still be undiscovered.

Once the cause and symptoms are determined, the system needs to be restored to a good state and should not be vulnerable to further impact. This will typically involve either rebuilding the system from scratch or restoring from a known good backup.

Reporting

The reporting phase of incident handling occurs throughout the process, beginning with detection. Reporting must begin immediately upon detection of malicious activity. Reporting contains two primary areas of focus: technical and nontechnical reporting. The incident handling teams must report the technical details of the incident as they begin the incident handling process, while maintaining sufficient bandwidth to also notify management of serious incidents. A common mistake is forgoing the latter while focusing on the technical details of the incident itself, but this is a mistake. Nontechnical stake holders including business and mission owners must be notified immediately of any serious incident and kept up to date as the incident-handing process progresses.

Recovery

The *recovery phase* involves cautiously restoring the system or systems to operational status. Typically, the business unit responsible for the system will dictate when the system will go back online. Remember to be cognizant of the possibility that the infection, attacker, or other threat agent might have persisted through the eradication phase. For this reason, close monitoring of the system after it returns to production is necessary. Further, to make the security monitoring of this system easier, strong preference is given to the restoration of operations occurring during off-peak production hours.

Remediation

Remediation steps occur during the mitigation phase, where vulnerabilities within the impacted system or systems are mitigated. Remediation continues after that phase and becomes broader. For example, if the root-cause analysis determines that a password was stolen and reused, local mitigation steps could include changing the compromised password and placing the system back online. Broader remediation steps could include requiring dual-factor authentication for all systems accessing sensitive data. We will discuss root-cause analysis shortly.

Lessons learned

The goal of this phase is to provide a final report on the incident, which will be delivered to management. Important considerations for this phase should include detailing ways in which the compromise could have been identified sooner, how the response could have been quicker or more effective, which organizational shortcomings might have contributed to the incident, and what other elements might have room for improvement. Feedback from this phase feeds directly into continued preparation, where the lessons learned are applied to improving preparation for the handling of future incidents.

ROOT-CAUSE ANALYSIS

To effectively manage security incidents, root-cause analysis must be performed. Root-cause analysis attempts to determine the underlying weakness or vulnerability that allowed the incident to be realized. Without successful root-cause analysis, the victim organization could recover systems in a way that still includes the particular weaknesses exploited by the adversary causing the incident. In addition to potentially recovering systems with exploitable flaws, another possibility includes reconstituting systems from backups or snapshots that have already been compromised.

OPERATIONAL PREVENTIVE AND DETECTIVE CONTROLS

Many preventive and detective controls require higher operational support and are a focus of daily operations security. For example, routers and switches tend to have comparatively low operational expenses (OPEX). Other controls, such as NIDS and NIPS, antivirus, and application whitelisting have comparatively higher OPEX and are a focus in this domain.

INTRUSION DETECTION SYSTEMS AND INTRUSION PREVENTION SYSTEMS

An intrusion detection system (IDS) detects malicious actions, including violations of policy. An intrusion prevention system (IPS) also prevents malicious actions. There are two basic types of IDSs and IPSs: network based and host based.

IDS and IPS event types

There are four types of IDS events: true positive, true negative, false positive, and false negative. We will use two streams of traffic, a worm and a user surfing the Web, to illustrate these events.

- True positive: A worm is spreading on a trusted network; NIDS alerts
- True negative: User surfs the Web to an allowed site; NIDS is silent
- False positive: User surfs the Web to an allowed site; NIDS alerts
- False negative: A worm is spreading on a trusted network; NIDS is silent

The goal is to have only true positives and true negatives, but most IDSs have false positives and false negatives as well. False positives waste time and resources, as monitoring staff spends time investigating nonmalicious events. A false negative is arguably the worst-case scenario because malicious network traffic is neither prevented nor detected.

NIDS and NIPS

A network-based intrusion detection system (NIDS) detects malicious traffic on a network. NIDS usually require promiscuous network access in order to analyze all traffic, including all unicast traffic. NIDS are passive devices that do not interfere with the traffic they monitor; Fig. 7.2 shows a typical NIDS architecture. The NIDS sniffs the internal interface of the firewall in read-only mode and sends alerts to a NIDS Management server via a different (ie, read/write) network interface.

The difference between a NIDS and a *NIPS* is that the NIPS alters the flow of network traffic. There are two types of NIPS: active response and inline. Architecturally, an active response NIPS is like the NIDS in Fig. 7.2; the difference is that the monitoring interface is read/write. The active response NIPS may "shoot down" malicious traffic via a variety of methods, including forging TCP RST segments to source or destination (or both), or sending ICMP port, host, or network unreachable to source.

An inline NIPS is "in line" with traffic, acting as a Layer 3–7 firewall by passing or allowing traffic, as shown in Fig. 7.3.

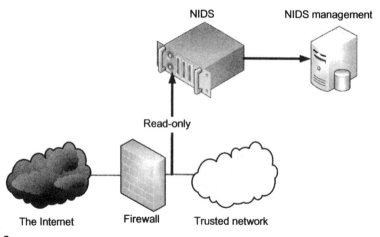

FIG. 7.2

NIDS architecture.

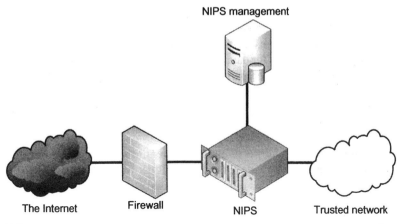

FIG. 7.3

Inline NIPS architecture.

Note that a NIPS provides defense-in-depth protection in addition to a firewall; it is not typically used as a replacement. Also, a false positive by a NIPS is more damaging than one by a NIDS because legitimate traffic is denied, which may cause production problems. A NIPS usually has a smaller set of rules compared to a NIDS for this reason, and only the most trustworthy rules are used. A NIPS is not a replacement for a NIDS; many networks use both a NIDS and a NIPS.

HIDS and HIPS
Host-based intrusion detection systems (HIDS) and host-based intrusion prevention systems (HIPS) are host-based cousins to NIDS and NIPS. They process information within the host and may process network traffic as it enters the host, but the exam's focus is usually on files and processes.

SECURITY INFORMATION AND EVENT MANAGEMENT
Correlation of security-relevant data is the primary utility provided by Security Information and Event Management (SIEM). The goal of data correlation is to better understand the context so as to arrive at a greater understanding of risk within the organization due to activities that are noted across various security platforms. While SIEMs typically come with some built-in alerts that look for particular correlated data, custom correlation rules are typically created to augment the built-in capabilities.

DATA LOSS PREVENTION
As prominent and high-volume data breaches continue unabated, the desire for solutions designed to address data loss has grown. Data loss prevention (DLP) is a class of solutions that are tasked specifically with trying to detect or preferably prevent data

from leaving an organization in an unauthorized manner. The approaches to DLP vary greatly. One common approach employs network-oriented tools that attempt to detect and/or prevent sensitive data being exfiltrated in cleartext. This approach does little to address the potential for data exfiltration over an encrypted channel. Dealing with the potential for encrypted exfiltration typically requires endpoint solutions to provide visibility prior to encryption.

ENDPOINT SECURITY

Because endpoints are the targets of attacks, preventive and detective capabilities on the endpoints themselves provide a layer beyond network-centric security devices. Modern endpoint security suites often encompass a variety of products beyond simple antivirus software. These suites can increase the depth of security countermeasures well beyond the gateway or network perimeter.

An additional benefit offered by endpoint security products is their ability to provide preventive and detective control even when communications are encrypted all the way to the endpoint in question. Typical challenges associated with endpoint security are associated with volume considerations; vast number of products/systems must be managed, while significant amounts of data must be analyzed and potentially retained.

Antivirus

The most commonly deployed endpoint security product is antivirus software. Antivirus is one of many layers of endpoint defense-in-depth security. Although antivirus vendors often employ heuristic or statistical methods for malware detection, the predominant means of detecting malware is still signature based.

Application whitelisting

Application whitelisting is a more recent addition to endpoint security suites. The primary focus of application whitelisting is to determine in advance which binaries are considered safe to execute on a given system. Once this baseline has been established, any binary attempting to run that is not on the list of "known-good" binaries is prevented from doing so. A weakness of this approach is when a "known-good" binary is exploited by an attacker and used maliciously.

Removable media controls

The need for better control of removable media has been felt on two fronts in particular. First, malware-infected removable media inserted into an organization's computers has been a method for compromising otherwise reasonably secure organizations. Second, the volume of storage that can be contained in something the size of a fingernail is astoundingly large and has been used to surreptitiously exfiltrate sensitive data.

Disk encryption

Another endpoint security product found with increasing regularity is disk encryption software.

Full disk encryption, also called whole disk encryption, encrypts an entire disk. This is superior to partially encrypted solutions, such as encrypted volumes, directories, folders, or files. The problem with the latter approach is the risk of leaving sensitive data on an unencrypted area of the disk.

ASSET MANAGEMENT

A holistic approach to operational information security requires organizations to focus on systems as well as the people, data, and media. Systems security is another vital component to operational security, and there are specific controls that can greatly help system security throughout the system's lifecycle.

CONFIGURATION MANAGEMENT

Basic *configuration management* practices associated with system security will involve tasks such as disabling unnecessary services; removing extraneous programs; enabling security capabilities such as firewalls, antivirus, and intrusion detection or prevention systems; and configuring security and audit logs.

Baselining

Security *baselining* is the process of capturing a snapshot of the current system security configuration. Establishing an easy means for capturing the current system security configuration can be extremely helpful in responding to a potential security incident.

Vulnerability management

Vulnerability scanning is a way to discover poor configurations and missing patches in an environment. The term *vulnerability management* is used rather than just vulnerability scanning in order to emphasize the need for management of the vulnerability information. The remediation or mitigation of vulnerabilities should be prioritized based on both risk to the organization and ease of remediation procedures.

Zero-day vulnerabilities and zero-day exploits

A zero-day vulnerability is a vulnerability that is known before the existence of a patch. *Zero-day vulnerabilities*, also commonly written 0-day, are becoming increasingly important as attackers are becoming more skilled in discovery and disclosure of zero-day vulnerabilities is being monetized. A *zero-day exploit*, rather than vulnerability, refers to the existence of exploit code for a vulnerability that has yet to be patched.

CHANGE MANAGEMENT

In order to maintain consistent and known operational security, a regimented *change management* or change control process needs to be followed. The purpose of the change control process is to understand, communicate, and document any changes with the primary goal of being able to understand, control, and avoid direct or indirect negative impact that the change might impose.

FAST FACTS

Because of the variability of the change management process, specifically named phases have not been offered in this section. However, the general flow of the change management process includes:

- Identifying a change
- Proposing a change
- Assessing the risk associated with the change
- Testing the change
- Scheduling the change
- Notifying impacted parties of the change
- Implementing the change
- Reporting results of the change implementation

All changes must be closely tracked and auditable; a detailed change record should be kept. Some changes can destabilize systems or cause other problems; change management auditing allows operations staff to investigate recent changes in the event of an outage or problem. Audit records also allow auditors to verify that change management policies and procedures have been followed.

CONTINUITY OF OPERATIONS

Continuity of operations is principally concerned with the availability portion of the confidentiality, integrity, and availability triad.

SERVICE LEVEL AGREEMENTS

A *service level agreement* (SLA) stipulates all expectations regarding the behavior of the department or organization that is responsible for providing services and the quality of those services. SLAs will often dictate what is considered acceptable regarding things such as bandwidth, time to delivery, response times, etc.

FAULT TOLERANCE

In order for systems and solutions within an organization to be able to continually provide operational availability, they must be implemented with fault tolerance in mind. Availability is not solely focused on system uptime requirements; it requires that data be accessible in a timely fashion as well.

Redundant array of inexpensive disks

Even if only one full backup tape is needed for recovery of a system due to a hard disk failure, the time to recover a large amount of data can easily exceed the recovery time dictated by the organization. The goal of a *redundant array of inexpensive disks (RAID)* is to help mitigate the risk associated with hard disk failures. There are various RAID levels that consist of different approaches to disk array configurations.

FAST FACTS

Three critical RAID terms are mirroring, striping, and parity.

- *Mirroring* achieves full data redundancy by writing the same data to multiple hard disks.
- *Striping* focuses on increasing read and write performance by spreading data across multiple hard disks. Writes can be performed in parallel across multiple disks rather than serially on one disk. This parallelization increases performance and does not contribute to data redundancy.
- *Parity* achieves data redundancy without incurring the same degree of cost as that of mirroring in terms of disk usage and write performance.

RAID 0: Striped set

RAID 0 employs striping to increase the performance of read and writes. Striping offers no data redundancy, so RAID 0 is a poor choice if recovery of data is critical. Fig. 7.4 shows RAID 0.

RAID 1: Mirrored set

RAID 1 creates/writes an exact duplicate of all data to an additional disk. Fig. 7.5 shows RAID 1.

RAID 2: Hamming code

RAID 2 is a legacy technology that requires either 14 or 39 hard disks and a specially designed hardware controller, which makes RAID 2 cost prohibitive. RAID 2 stripes at the bit level.

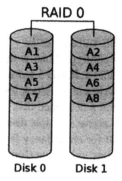

FIG. 7.4

RAID 0—striped set.

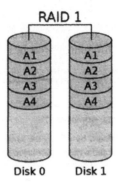

FIG. 7.5

RAID 1—mirrored set.

RAID 3: Striped set with dedicated parity (byte level)

Striping is desirable due to the performance gains associated with spreading data across multiple disks. However, striping alone is not as desirable due to the lack of redundancy. With *RAID 3*, data at the byte level is striped across multiple disks, but an additional disk is leveraged for storage of parity information, which is used for recovery in the event of a failure.

RAID 4: Striped set with dedicated parity (block level)

RAID 4 provides the same functionality as RAID 3, but stripes data at the block level rather than byte level. Like RAID 3, RAID 4 employs a dedicated parity drive rather than having parity data distributed amongst all disks, as in RAID 5.

RAID 5: Striped set with distributed parity

One of the most popular RAID configurations is that of *RAID 5*, striped set with distributed parity. Like RAIDs 3 and 4, RAID 5 writes parity information that is used for recovery purposes. RAID 5 writes at the block level, like RAID 4. However, unlike RAIDs 3 and 4, which require a dedicated disk for parity information, RAID 5 distributes the parity information across multiple disks. One of the reasons for RAID 5's popularity is that the disk cost for redundancy is potentially lower than that of a mirrored set, while at the same time gaining performance improvements associated with RAID 0. RAID 5 allows for data recovery in the event that any one disk fails. Fig. 7.6 shows RAID 5.

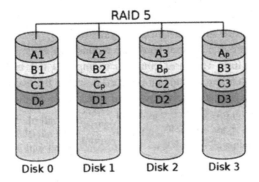

FIG. 7.6

RAID 5—striped set with distributed parity.

RAID 6: Striped set with dual-distributed parity

While RAID 5 accommodates the loss of any one drive in the array, *RAID 6* can allow for the failure of two drives and still function. This redundancy is achieved by writing the same parity information to two different disks.

RAID 1+0 or RAID 10

RAID 1+0 or RAID 10 is an example of what is known as nested RAID or multi-RAID, which simply means that one standard RAID level is encapsulated within another. With RAID 10, which is also commonly written as RAID 1+0 to explicitly indicate the nesting, the configuration is that of a striped set of mirrors.

CRUNCH TIME

Table 7.1 provides a brief description of the various RAID levels that are most commonly used.

Table 7.1 RAID Levels

RAID Level	Description
RAID 0	Block-level striped set
RAID 1	Mirrored set
RAID 3	Byte-level striping with dedicated parity
RAID 4	Block-level striping with dedicated parity
RAID 5	Block-level striping with distributed parity
RAID 6	Block-level striping with double distributed parity

System redundancy

Redundant hardware and redundant systems

Many systems can provide internal hardware redundancy of components that are extremely prone to failure. The most common example of this built-in redundancy is systems or devices that have redundant onboard power in the event of a power supply failure. Sometimes systems simply have field replaceable modular versions of commonly failing components. Though physically replacing a power supply might increase downtime, having an inventory of spare modules to service all of the datacenter's servers would be less expensive than having all servers configured with an installed redundant power supply.

Redundant systems (ie, alternative systems) make entire systems available in case of failure of the primary system.

High availability clusters

A *high-availability cluster*, also called a *failover cluster*, uses multiple systems that are already installed, configured, and plugged in, so that if a failure causes one of the systems to fail, another can be seamlessly leveraged to maintain the availability of the service or application being provided.

Each member of an *active-active* HA cluster actively processes data in advance of a failure. This is commonly referred to as load balancing. Having systems in an active-active or load-balancing configuration is typically more costly than having the systems in an *active-passive* or hot standby configuration, in which the backup systems only begin processing when a failure is detected.

BCP AND DRP OVERVIEW AND PROCESS

The terms and concepts associated with Business Continuity and Disaster Recovery Planning are very often misunderstood. Clear understanding of what is meant by both Business Continuity and Disaster Recovery Planning, as well as what they entail, is critical for the CISSP candidate.

BUSINESS CONTINUITY PLANNING

Though many organizations will simply use the phrases *Business Continuity Planning* (BCP) or *Disaster Recovery Planning* (DRP) interchangeably, they are two distinct disciplines. Though both types of planning are essential to the effective management of disasters and other disruptive events, their goals are different. The overarching goal of BCP is to ensure that the business will continue to operate before, throughout, and after a disaster event is experienced. The focus of BCP is on the business as a whole, ensuring that those critical services or functions the business provides or performs can still be carried out both in the wake of a disruption and after the disruption has been weathered.

DISASTER RECOVERY PLANNING

The Disaster Recovery Plan (DRP) provides a short-term plan for dealing with specific IT-oriented disruptions. Mitigating a malware infection that shows risk of spreading to other systems is an example of a specific IT-oriented disruption that a DRP would address. The DRP focuses on efficiently attempting to mitigate the impact of a disaster by preparing the immediate response and recovery of critical IT systems. DRP is considered tactical rather than strategic and provides a means for immediate response to disasters.

RELATIONSHIP BETWEEN BCP AND DRP

The BCP is an umbrella plan that includes multiple specific plans, most importantly the DRP. DRP serves as a subset of the overall BCP, which would be doomed to fail if it did not contain a tactical method for immediately dealing with disruption of information systems. Fig. 7.7, taken from *NIST Special Publication 800-34*, provides a visual means for understanding the interrelatedness of BCP and DRP, as well as *Continuity of Operations Plan (COOP)*, *Occupant Emergency Plan (OEP)*, and others.

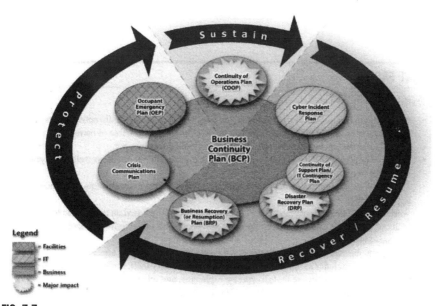

FIG. 7.7

BCP and related plans.[2]

DISASTERS OR DISRUPTIVE EVENTS

Given that BCP and DRP are created because of the potential of disasters impacting operations, it is vital that organizations understand the nature of disasters and disruptive events.

FAST FACTS

The three common ways of categorizing the causes for disasters are derived from whether the threat agent is natural, human, or environmental in nature.[2]

- Natural—This category includes threats such as earthquakes, hurricanes, tornadoes, floods, and some types of fires. Historically, natural disasters have provided some of the most devastating disasters to which an organization must respond.
- Human—The human category of threats represents the most common source of disasters. Human threats can be further classified by whether they constitute an intentional or unintentional threat.
- Environmental—Threats focused on information systems or datacenter environments; includes items such as power issues (blackout, brownout, surge, spike, etc.), system component or other equipment failures, and application or software flaws.

The analysis of threats and the determination of the associated likelihood of those threats are important parts of the BCP and DRP process. Table 7.2 provides a quick summary of some of the disaster events and what type of disaster they constitute.

FAST FACTS

Types of disruptive events include:

- Errors and omissions: typically considered the most common source of disruptive events. This type of threat is caused by humans who unintentionally serve as a source of harm.
- Natural disasters: include earthquakes, hurricanes, floods, tsunamis, etc.
- Electrical or power problems: loss of power may cause availability issues, as well as integrity issues due to corrupted data.
- Temperature and humidity failures: may damage equipment due to overheating, corrosion, or static electricity.
- Warfare, terrorism, and sabotage: threats can vary dramatically based on geographic location, industry, and brand value, as well as the interrelatedness with other high-value target organizations.
- Financially motivated attackers: attackers who seek to make money by attacking victim organizations, includes exfiltration of cardholder data, identity theft, pump-and-dump stock schemes, bogus antimalware tools, corporate espionage, and others.
- Personnel shortages: may be caused by strikes, pandemics, or transportation issues. A lack of staff may lead to operational disruption.

Table 7.2 Examples of Disruptive Events

Disruptive Event	Type
Earthquake/tornado/hurricane/etc.	Natural
Strike	Human (intentional)
Cyber terrorism	Human (intentional/technical)
Malware	Human (intentional/technical)
Denial of service	Human (intentional/technical)
Errors and omissions	Human (unintentional)
Electrical fire	Environmental
Equipment failure	Environmental

THE DISASTER RECOVERY PROCESS

Having discussed the importance of BCP and DRP as well as examples of threats that justify this degree of planning, we will now focus on the fundamental steps involved in recovering from a disaster.

Respond

In order to begin the disaster recovery process, there must be an initial response that begins the process of assessing the damage. Speed is essential during this initial assessment, which will determine if the event in question constitutes a disaster.

Activate team

If a disaster is declared, then the recovery team needs to be activated. Depending on the scope of the disaster, this communication could prove extremely difficult. The use of calling trees, which will be discussed in the "Call Trees" section later in this chapter, can help to facilitate this process to ensure that members can be activated as smoothly as possible.

Communicate

One of the most difficult aspects of disaster recovery is ensuring that consistent timely status updates are communicated back to the central team managing the response and recovery process. This communication often must occur out-of-band, meaning that the typical communication method of leveraging an office phone will quite often not be a viable option. In addition to communication of internal status regarding the recovery activities, the organization must be prepared to provide external communications, which involves disseminating details regarding the organization's recovery status with the public.

Assess

Though an initial assessment was carried out during the initial response portion of the disaster recovery process, a more detailed and thorough assessment will be performed by the disaster recovery team. The team will proceed to assessing the extent of the damage to determine the proper steps necessary to ensure the organization's ability to meet its mission.

Reconstitution

The primary goal of the reconstitution phase is to successfully recover critical business operations at either a primary or secondary site. If an alternate site is leveraged, adequate safety and security controls must be in place in order to maintain the expected degree of security the organization typically employs. The use of an alternate computing facility for recovery should not expose the organization to further security incidents. In addition to the recovery team's efforts in reconstituting critical business functions at an alternate location, a salvage team will be employed to begin the recovery process at the primary facility that experienced the disaster. Ultimately, the expectation is that unless it is wholly unwarranted given the circumstances, the primary site will be recovered and that the alternate facility's operations will "fail back" or be transferred again to the primary center of operations.

DEVELOPING A BCP/DRP

Developing BCP/DRP is vital for an organization's ability to respond and recover from an interruption in normal business functions or catastrophic event. In order to ensure that all planning has been considered, the BCP/DRP has a specific set of requirements to review and implement. Below are listed these high-level steps, according to NIST SP800-34, to achieving a sound, logical BCP/DRP. NIST SP800-34 is the National Institute of Standards and Technologies Contingency Planning Guide for Federal Information Systems.

- Project Initiation
- Scope of the Project
- Business Impact Analysis (BIA)
- Identify Preventive Controls
- Recovery Strategy
- Plan Design and Development
- Implementation, Training, and Testing
- BCP/DRP Maintenance[2]

PROJECT INITIATION

In order to develop the BCP/DRP, the scope of the project must be determined and agreed upon.

FAST FACTS

Project Initiation involves seven distinct milestones,[2] as listed below:

- *Develop the contingency planning policy statement*: A formal department or agency policy provides the authority and guidance necessary to develop an effective contingency plan.
- *Conduct the BIA*: The BIA helps identify and prioritize critical IT systems and components. A template for developing the BIA is also provided to assist the user.
- *Identify preventive controls*: Measures taken to reduce the effects of system disruptions can increase system availability and reduce contingency life-cycle costs.
- *Develop recovery strategies*: Thorough recovery strategies ensure that the system may be recovered quickly and effectively following a disruption.
- *Develop an IT contingency plan*: The contingency plan should contain detailed guidance and procedures for restoring a damaged system.
- *Plan testing, training, and exercises*: Testing the plan identifies planning gaps, whereas training prepares recovery personnel for plan activation; both activities improve plan effectiveness and overall agency preparedness.
- *Plan maintenance*: The plan should be a living document that is updated regularly to remain current with system enhancements.[2]

ASSESSING THE CRITICAL STATE

Assessing the critical state can be difficult because determining which pieces of the IT infrastructure are critical depends solely on the how it supports the users within the organization. For example, without consulting all of the users, a simple mapping program may not seem to be a critical asset for an organization. However, if there is a user group that drives trucks and makes deliveries for business purposes, this mapping software may be critical for them to schedule pickups and deliveries.

CONDUCT BIA

BIA is the formal method for determining how a disruption to the IT system(s) of an organization will impact the organization's requirements, processes, and interdependencies with respect to the business mission.[2] It is an analysis to identify and prioritize critical IT systems and components. It enables the BCP/DRP project manager to fully characterize the IT contingency requirements and priorities.[2] The objective is to correlate the IT system components with the critical service it supports. It also aims to quantify the consequence of a disruption to the system component and how that will affect the organization. The primary goal of the BIA is to determine the Maximum Tolerable Downtime (MTD) for a specific IT asset. This will directly impact what disaster recovery solution is chosen.

Identify critical assets

The critical asset list is a list of those IT assets that are deemed business-essential by the organization. These systems' DRP/BCP must have the best available recovery capabilities assigned to them.

Conduct BCP/DRP-focused risk assessment

The BCP/DRP-focused risk assessment determines what risks are inherent to which IT assets. A vulnerability analysis is also conducted for each IT system and major application. This is done because most traditional BCP/DRP evaluations focus on physical security threats, both natural and human.

Determine MTD

The primary goal of the BIA is to determine the *MTD*, which describes the total time a system can be inoperable before an organization is severely impacted. MTD is comprised of two metrics: the *Recovery Time Objective (RTO)*, and the *Work Recovery Time (WRT)* (see later).

Alternate terms for MTD

Depending on the business continuity framework that is used, other terms may be substituted for MTD. These include *Maximum Allowable Downtime*, Maximum Tolerable Outage, and Maximum Acceptable Outage.

Failure and recovery metrics

A number of metrics are used to quantify how frequently systems fail, how long a system may exist in a failed state, and the maximum time to recover from failure. These metrics include the *Recovery Point Objective (RPO)*, RTO, WRT, Mean Time Between Failures (MTBF), Mean Time to Repair (MTTR), and *Minimum Operating Requirements (MOR)*.

Recovery point objective

The RPO is the amount of data loss or system inaccessibility (measured in time) that an organization can withstand. "If you perform weekly backups, someone made a decision that your company could tolerate the loss of a week's worth of data. If back-ups are performed on Saturday evenings and a system fails on Saturday afternoon, you have lost the entire week's worth of data. This is the RPO. In this case, the RPO is 1 week."[3]

The RPO represents the maximum acceptable amount of data/work loss for a given process because of a disaster or disruptive event.

Recovery time objective and work recovery time

The RTO describes the maximum time allowed to recover business or IT systems. RTO is also called the systems recovery time. This is one part of MTD; once the system is physically running, it must be configured.

CRUNCH TIME

WRT describes the time required to configure a recovered system. "Downtime consists of two elements, the systems recovery time and the WRT. Therefore, MTD = RTO + WRT."[3]

Mean time between failures

MTBF quantifies how long a new or repaired system will run before failing. It is typically generated by a component vendor and is largely applicable to hardware as opposed to applications and software.

Mean time to repair

The MTTR describes how long it will take to recover a specific failed system. It is the best estimate for reconstituting the IT system so that business continuity may occur.

Minimum operating requirements

MOR describe the minimum environmental and connectivity requirements in order to operate computer equipment. It is important to determine and document what the MOR is for each IT-critical asset because in the event of a disruptive event or disaster, proper analysis can be conducted quickly to determine if the IT assets will be able to function in the emergency environment.

IDENTIFY PREVENTIVE CONTROLS

Preventive controls can prevent disruptive events from having an impact. For example, as stated in Chapter 3, HVAC systems are designed to prevent computer equipment from overheating and failing.

DID YOU KNOW?

The BIA will identify some risks that may be mitigated immediately. This is another advantage of performing BCP/DRP, including the BIA: it improves your security, even if no disaster occurs.

RECOVERY STRATEGY

Once the BIA is complete, the BCP team knows the MTD. This metric, as well as others including the RPO and RTO, is used to determine the recovery strategy. A cold site cannot be used if the MTD is 12 h, for example. As a general rule, the shorter the MTD, the more expensive the recovery solution will be.

Redundant site

A *redundant site* is an exact production duplicate of a system that has the capability to seamlessly operate all necessary IT operations without loss of services to the end user of the system. A redundant site receives data backups in real time so that in the event of a disaster, the users of the system have no loss of data. It is a building configured exactly like the primary site and is the most expensive recovery option because it effectively more than doubles the cost of IT operations. To be fully redundant, a site must have real-time data backups to the redundant system and the end user should not notice any difference in IT services or operations in the event of a disruptive event.

Hot site

A *hot site* is a location that an organization may relocate to following a major disruption or disaster. It is a datacenter with a raised floor, power, utilities, computer peripherals, and fully configured computers. The hot site will have all necessary hardware and critical applications data mirrored in real time. A hot site will have the capability to allow the organization to resume critical operations within a very short period of time, sometimes in less than an hour.

It is important to note the difference between a hot site and a redundant site. Hot sites can quickly recover critical IT functionality; it may even be measured in minutes instead of hours. However, a redundant site will appear as operating normally to the end user no matter what the state of operations is for the IT program. A hot site has all the same physical, technical, and administrative controls implemented of the production site.

Warm site

A *warm site* has some aspects of a hot site; for example, readily accessible hardware and connectivity, but it will have to rely upon backup data in order to reconstitute a system after a disruption. It is a datacenter with a raised floor, power, utilities, computer peripherals, and fully configured computers.

Cold site

A *cold site* is the least expensive recovery solution to implement. It does not include backup copies of data, nor does it contain any immediately available hardware. After a disruptive event, a cold site will take the longest amount of time of all recovery solutions to implement and restore critical IT services for the organization. Especially in a disaster area, it could take weeks to get vendor hardware shipments in place, so organizations using a cold site recovery solution will have to be able to withstand a significantly long MTD measured in weeks, not days. A cold site is typically a datacenter with a raised floor, power, utilities, and physical security, but not much beyond that.

Reciprocal agreement

Reciprocal agreements are a bidirectional agreement between two organizations in which one organization promises another organization that it can move in and share space if it experiences a disaster. It is documented in the form of a contract written to gain support from outside organizations in the event of a disaster. They are also referred to as mutual aid agreements and they are structured so that each organization will assist the other in the event of an emergency.

Mobile site

Mobile sites are veritable datacenters on wheels in that they are towable trailers that contain racks of computer equipment, as well as HVAC, fire suppression, and physical security. They are a good fit for disasters such as a datacenter flood, where the datacenter is damaged but the rest of the facility and surrounding property are intact. They may be towed onsite, supplied with power and a network, and brought online.

RELATED PLANS

As discussed previously, the BCP is an umbrella plan that contains other plans. In addition to the DRP, other plans include the *COOP, the Business Resumption/Recovery Plan (BRP), Continuity of Support Plan, Cyberincident Response Plan, OEP, and the Crisis Management Plan (CMP)*. Table 7.3, from NIST Special Publication 800-34, summarizes these plans.

Table 7.3 Summary of BCP Plans From NIST SP 800-34[2]

Plan	Purpose	Scope
Business Continuity Plan (BCP)	Provide procedures for sustaining essential business operations while recovering from a significant disruption	Addresses business processes; IT addressed based only on its support for business process
Business Recovery (or Resumption) Plan (BRP)	Provide procedures for recovering business operations immediately following a disaster	Addresses business processes; not IT-focused; IT addressed based only on its support for business process
Continuity of Operations Plan (COOP)	Provide procedures and capabilities to sustain an organization's essential, strategic functions at an alternate site for up to 30 days	Addresses the subset of an organization's missions that are deemed most critical; usually written at headquarters level; not IT-focused
Continuity of Support Plan/IT Contingency Plan	Provide procedures and capabilities for recovering a major application or general support system	Same as IT contingency plan; addresses IT system disruptions; not business process-focused
Crisis Communications Plan	Provides procedures for disseminating status reports to personnel and the public	Addresses communications with personnel and the public; not IT-focused
Cyberincident Response Plan	Provide strategies to detect, respond to, and limit consequences of malicious cyber incident	Focuses on information security responses to incidents affecting systems and/or networks
Disaster Recovery Plan (DRP)	Provide detailed procedures to facilitate recovery of capabilities at an alternate site	Often IT-focused; limited to major disruptions with long-term effects
Occupant Emergency Plan (OEP)	Provide coordinated procedures for minimizing loss of life or injury and protecting property damage in response to a physical threat	Focuses on personnel and property particular to the specific facility; not business process or IT system functionality based

Continuity of operations plan

The COOP describes the procedures required to maintain operations during a disaster. This includes transfer of personnel to an alternate disaster recovery site and operations of that site.

Business recovery plan

The BRP, also known as the Business Resumption Plan, details the steps required to restore normal business operations after recovering from a disruptive event. This may include switching operations from an alternate site back to a repaired primary site.

The BRP picks up when the COOP is complete. This plan is narrow and focused: the BRP is sometimes included as an appendix to the BCP.

Continuity of support plan

The Continuity of Support Plan focuses narrowly on support of specific IT systems and applications. It is also called the IT Contingency Plan, emphasizing IT over general business support.

Cyberincident response plan

The Cyberincident Response Plan is designed to respond to disruptive cyberevents, including network-based attacks, worms, computer viruses, Trojan horses, etc. For example, self-propagating malicious code such as a worm has the potential to disrupt networks. Loss of network connectivity alone may constitute a disaster for many organizations.

Occupant emergency plan

The OEP provides the "response procedures for occupants of a facility in the event of a situation posing a potential threat to the health and safety of personnel, the environment, or property. Such events would include a fire, hurricane, criminal attack, or a medical emergency."[2] This plan is facilities-focused, as opposed to business- or IT-focused.

The OEP is focused on safety and evacuation, and should describe specific safety drills, including evacuation or fire drills. Specific safety roles should be described, including safety warden and meeting point leader, as described in Chapter 3.

Crisis management plan

The *CMP* is designed to provide effective coordination among the managers of the organization in the event of an emergency or disruptive event. The CMP details the actions management must take to ensure that life and safety of personnel and property are immediately protected in case of a disaster.

Crisis communications plan

A critical component of the CMP is the Crisis Communications Plan, which is sometimes simply called the communications plan. This is a plan for communicating to staff and the public in the event of a disruptive event. Instructions for notifying the affected members of the organization are an integral part to any BCP/DRP.

It is often said that bad news travels fast. Also, in the event of a postdisaster information vacuum, bad information will often fill the void. Public relations professionals understand this risk and know to consistently give the organization's "official story," even when there is little to say. All communication with the public should be channeled via senior management or the public relations team.

CALL TREES

A key tool leveraged for staff communication by the Crisis Communications Plan is the Call Tree, which is used to quickly communicate news throughout an organization without overburdening any specific person. The call tree works by assigning each employee a small number of other employees they are responsible for calling in an emergency event. For example, the organization's president may notify his board of directors of an emergency situation and they, in turn, will notify their top-tier managers. The top-tier managers will then call the people they have been assigned to call. The call tree continues until all affected personnel have been contacted.

The call tree is most effective when there is a two-way reporting of successful communication. For example, each member of the board of directors would report back to the president when each of their assigned call tree recipients had been contacted and had made contact with their subordinate personnel. Remember that cell phones and landlines may become congested or unusable during a disaster; the call tree should contain alternate contact methods in case the primary methods are unavailable.

EMERGENCY OPERATIONS CENTER

The Emergency Operations Center (EOC) is the command post established during or just after an emergency event. Placement of the EOC will depend on resources that are available. For larger organizations, the EOC may be a long distance away from the physical emergency; however, protection of life and personnel safety is always of the utmost importance.

BACKUPS AND AVAILABILITY

Though many organizations are diligent in going through the process of creating backups, verification of recoverability from those backup methods is at least as important and is often overlooked. When the detailed recovery process for a given backup solution is thoroughly reviewed, some specific requirements will become obvious. One of the most important points to make when discussing backup with respect to disaster recovery and business continuity is to ensure that critical backup media is stored offsite. Further, that offsite location should be situated such that, during a disaster event, the organization can efficiently access the media with the purpose of taking it to a primary or secondary recovery location.

HARDCOPY DATA

In the event that there is a disruptive event, such as a natural disaster that disables the local power grid, and power dependency is problematic, there is the potential to operate the organization's most critical functions using only hardcopy data. *Hardcopy data* is any data that are accessed through reading or writing on paper rather than processing through a computer system.

ELECTRONIC BACKUPS

Electronic backups are archives that are stored electronically and can be retrieved in case of a disruptive event or disaster. Choosing the correct data backup strategy is dependent upon how users store data, the availability of resources and connectivity, and what the ultimate recovery goal is for the organization.

Preventative restoration is a recommended control; an organization can restore data to test the validity of the backup process. If a reliable system, such as a mainframe, copies data to tape every day for years, what assurance does the organization have that the process is working? Do the tapes and the data they contain have integrity?

Full backups

A full system backup means that every piece of data is copied and stored on the backup repository. Conducting a full backup is time consuming and a strain on bandwidth and resources. However, full backups will ensure that any and all necessary data is protected.

Incremental backups

Incremental backups archive data that have changed since the last full or incremental backup. For example, a site performs a full backup every Sunday, with daily incremental backups from Monday through Saturday. If data is lost after the Wednesday incremental backup, four tapes are required for restoration: the Sunday full backup, as well as the Monday, Tuesday, and Wednesday incremental backups.

Differential backups

Differential backups operate in a similar manner as the incremental backups except for one key difference: differential backups archive data that have changed since the last full backup.

For example, the same site in our previous example switches to differential backups. They lose data after the Wednesday differential backup. Now only two tapes are required for restoration: the Sunday full backup and the Wednesday differential backup.

Tape rotation methods

A common tape rotation method is called *FIFO* (First In, First Out). Assume you are performing full daily backups and have 14 rewritable tapes total. FIFO (also called round robin) means you will use each tape in order and cycle back to the first tape after the 14th is used. This ensures 14 days of data is archived. The downside of this plan is you only maintain 14 days of data; this schedule is not helpful if you seek to restore a file that was accidentally deleted 3 weeks ago.

Grandfather-Father-Son (GFS) addresses this problem. There are 3 sets of tapes: 7 daily tapes (the son), 4 weekly tapes (the father), and 12 monthly tapes (the grandfather). Once per week, a son tape graduates to father. Once every 5 weeks a father tape graduates to grandfather. After running for a year, this method ensures there are backup tapes available for the past 7 days, weekly tapes for the past 4 weeks, and monthly tapes for the past 12 months.

Electronic vaulting

Electronic vaulting is the batch process of electronically transmitting data that is to be backed up on a routine, regularly scheduled time interval. It is used to transfer bulk information to an offsite facility. There are a number of commercially available tools and services that can perform electronic vaulting for an organization. Electronic vaulting is a good tool for data that need to be backed up on a daily or possibly even hourly rate. It solves two problems at the same time: it stores sensitive data offsite and it can perform the backup at very short intervals to ensure that the most recent data is backed up.

Remote journaling

A database journal contains a log of all database transactions. Journals may be used to recover from a database failure. Assume a database checkpoint (snapshot) is saved every hour. If the database loses integrity 20 min after a checkpoint, it may be recovered by reverting to the checkpoint and then applying all subsequent transactions described by the database journal.

Remote journaling saves the database checkpoints and database journal to a remote site. In the event of failure at the primary site, the database may be recovered.

Database shadowing

Database shadowing uses two or more identical databases that are updated simultaneously. The shadow database(s) can exist locally, but it is best practice to host one shadow database offsite. The goal of database shadowing is to greatly reduce the recovery time for a database implementation. Database shadowing allows faster recovery when compared with remote journaling.

HA options

Increasingly, systems are being required to have effectively zero downtime, or an MTD of zero. Recovery of data on tape is certainly ill equipped to meet these availability demands. The immediate availability of alternate systems is required should a failure or disaster occur. A common way to achieve this level of uptime requirement is to employ a high availability cluster.

The goal of a high availability cluster is to decrease the recovery time of a system or network device so that the availability of the service is less affected than it would be by having to rebuild, reconfigure, or otherwise stand up a replacement system.

FAST FACTS
_____

Two typical deployment approaches exist:

- *Active-active cluster* involves multiple systems, all of which are online and actively processing traffic or data. This configuration is also commonly referred to as load balancing and is especially common with public facing systems, such as Web server farms.
- *Active-passive cluster* involves devices or systems that are already in place, configured, powered on, and ready to begin processing network traffic should a failure occur on the primary system. Active-passive clusters are often designed such that any configuration changes made on the primary system or device are replicated to the standby system. Also, to expedite the recovery of the service, many failover cluster devices will automatically begin to process services on the secondary system should a disruption impact the primary device. It can also be referred to as a hot spare, standby, or failover cluster configuration.

DRP TESTING, TRAINING, AND AWARENESS

Testing, training, and awareness must be performed for the "disaster" portion of a BCP/ DRP. Skipping these steps is one of the most common BCP/DRP mistakes. Some organizations "complete" their DRP, consider the matter resolved, and put the big DRP binder on a shelf to collect dust. This thought process is wrong on numerous levels.

First, a DRP is never complete but is rather a continually amended method for ensuring the ability for the organization to recover in an acceptable manner. Second, while well-meaning individuals carry out the creation and update of a DRP, even the most diligent of administrators will make mistakes. To find and correct these issues prior to their hindering recovery in an actual disaster, testing must be carried out on a regular basis. Third, any DRP that will be effective will have some inherent complex operations and maneuvers to be performed by administrators. There will always be unexpected occurrences during disasters, but each member of the DRP should be exceedingly familiar with the particulars of their role in a DRP, which is a call for training on the process.

Finally, it is important to be aware of the general user's role in the DRP, as well as the organization's emphasis on ensuring the safety of personnel and business operations in the event of a disaster. This section will provide details on steps to effectively test, train, and build awareness for the organization's DRP.

DRP TESTING

In order to ensure that a DRP represents a viable plan for recovery, thorough testing is needed. Given the DRP's detailed tactical subject matter, it should come as no surprise that routine infrastructure, hardware, software, and configuration changes will alter the way the DRP needs to be carried out. Organizations' information systems are in a constant state of flux, but unfortunately, much of these changes do not readily make their way into an updated DRP. To ensure both the initial and continued efficacy of the DRP as a feasible recovery methodology, testing needs to be performed.

DRP review

The DRP Review is the most basic form of initial DRP testing and is focused on simply reading the DRP in its entirety to ensure completeness of coverage. This review is typically performed by the team that developed the plan and will involve team members reading the plan in its entirety to quickly review the overall plan for any obvious flaws. The DRP Review is primarily just a sanity check to ensure that there are no glaring omissions in coverage or fundamental shortcomings in the approach.

Read-through

Read-through (also known as *checklist* or *consistency*) testing lists all necessary components required for successful recovery and ensures that they are or will be readily available should a disaster occur. For example, if the disaster recovery plan calls for the reconstitution of systems from tape backups at an alternate computing facility, the site in question should have an adequate number of tape drives on hand to carry out the recovery in the indicated window of time. The read-through test is often performed concurrently with the structured walkthrough or tabletop testing as a solid first-testing threshold. The read-through test is focused on ensuring that the organization has or can acquire in a timely fashion sufficient levels of resources upon which successful recovery is dependent.

Walkthrough/tabletop

Another test that is commonly completed at the same time as the checklist test is that of the *walkthrough*, which is also often referred to as a *structured walkthrough* or *tabletop exercise*. During this type of DRP test, which is usually performed prior to more in-depth testing, the goal is to allow individuals who are knowledgeable about the systems and services targeted for recovery to thoroughly review the overall approach. The term structured walkthrough is illustrative, as the group will discuss the proposed recovery procedures in a structured manner to determine whether there are any noticeable omissions, gaps, erroneous assumptions, or simply technical missteps that would hinder the recovery process from successfully occurring.

Simulation test/walkthrough drill

A *simulation test*, also called a *walkthrough drill* (not to be confused with the discussion-based structured walkthrough), goes beyond talking about the process and actually has teams to carry out the recovery process. A simulated disaster to which the team must respond as they are directed to by the DRP. As smaller disaster simulations are successfully managed, the scope of simulations will vary significantly and tend to grow more complicated and involve more systems.

Parallel processing

Another type of DRP test is *parallel processing*. This type of test is common in environments where transactional data is a key component of the critical business processing. Typically, this test will involve recovery of critical processing components at an alternate computing facility and then restore data from a previous backup. Note that regular production systems are not interrupted.

The transactions from the day after the backup are then run against the newly restored data, and the same results achieved during normal operations for the date in question should be mirrored by the recovery system's results. Organizations that are highly dependent upon mainframe and midrange systems will often employ this type of test.

Partial and complete business interruption

Arguably, the highest fidelity of all DRP tests involves *business interruption testing*. However, this type of test can actually be the cause of a disaster, so extreme caution should be exercised before attempting an actual interruption test. As the name implies, the business interruption style of testing will have the organization actually stop processing normal business at the primary location and will instead leverage the alternate computing facility. These types of tests are more common in organizations where fully redundant, often load-balanced operations already exist.

FAST FACTS

Each DRP testing method varies in complexity and cost, and simpler tests are less expensive. Here are the plans, ranked in order of cost and complexity, from low to high:

- DRP Review
- Read-Through/Checklist/Consistency
- Structured Walkthrough/Tabletop
- Simulation Test/Walkthrough Drill
- Parallel Processing
- Partial Interruption
- Complete Business Interruption

CONTINUED BCP/DRP MAINTENANCE

Once the initial BCP/DRP plan is completed, tested, trained, and implemented, it must be kept up to date. Business and IT systems change quickly, and IT professionals are accustomed to adapting to that change. BCP/DRP plans must keep pace with all critical business and IT changes.

CHANGE MANAGEMENT

Change management includes tracking and documenting all planned changes, including formal approval for substantial changes and documentation of the results of the completed change. All changes must be auditable.

CRUNCH TIME

The change control board manages this process. The BCP team should be a member of the change control board and attend all meetings. The goal of the BCP team's involvement on the change control board is to identify any changes that must be addressed by the BCP/DRP plan.

BCP/DRP MISTAKES

BCP and DRP are a business' last line of defense against failure. If other controls have failed, BCP/DRP is the final control. If it fails, the business may fail.

The success of BCP/DRP is critical, but many plans fail. The BCP team should consider the failure of other organizations' plans and view their own procedures under intense scrutiny. They should ask themselves this question: "Have we made mistakes that threaten the success of our plan?"

FAST FACTS

Common BCP/DRP mistakes include:

- Lack of management support
- Lack of business unit involvement
- Lack of prioritization among critical staff
- Improper (often overly narrow) scope
- Inadequate telecommunications management
- Inadequate supply chain management
- Incomplete or inadequate CMP
- Lack of testing
- Lack of training and awareness
- Failure to keep the BCP/DRP plan up to date

SPECIFIC BCP/DRP FRAMEWORKS

Given the patchwork of overlapping terms and processes used by various BCP/DRP frameworks, this chapter focused on universal best practices without attempting to map to a number of different (and sometimes inconsistent) terms and processes described by various BCP/DRP frameworks.

A handful of specific frameworks are worth discussing, including NIST SP 800-34, ISO/IEC-27031, and BCI.

NIST SP 800-34

The National Institute of Standards and Technology (NIST) Special Publication 800-34 Rev. 1 "Contingency Planning Guide for Federal Information Systems" may be downloaded at http://csrc.nist.gov/publications/nistpubs/800-34-rev1/sp800-34-rev1_errata-Nov11-2010.pdf. The document is of high quality and is in the public domain. Plans can sometimes be significantly improved by referencing SP 800-34 when writing or updating a BCP/DRP.

ISO/IEC-27031

ISO/IEC-27031 is a new guideline that is part of the ISO 27000 series, which also includes ISO 27001 and ISO 27002 (discussed in Chapter 2). ISO/IEC 27031 focuses on BCP (DRP is handled by another framework; see below).

FAST FACTS

According to http://www.iso27001security.com/html/27031.html, ISO/IEC 27031 is designed to:

- "Provide a framework (methods and processes) for any organization—private, governmental, and nongovernmental
- Identify and specify all relevant aspects including performance criteria, design, and implementation details for improving ICT readiness as part of the organization's ISMS, helping to ensure business continuity
- Enable an organization to measure its continuity, security and hence readiness to survive a disaster in a consistent and recognized manner."[4]

Terms and acronyms used by ISO/IEC 27031 include:

- ICT—Information and Communications Technology
- ISMS—Information Security Management System

A separate ISO plan for disaster recovery is ISO/IEC 24762:2008, "Information technology—Security techniques—Guidelines for information and communications technology disaster recovery services." More information is available at http://www.iso.org/iso/catalogue_detail.htm?csnumber=41532

BS-25999 AND ISO 22301

British Standards Institution (BSI, http://www.bsigroup.co.uk/) released BS-25999, which is in two parts:

- "Part 1, the Code of Practice, provides business continuity management best practice recommendations. Please note that this is a guidance document only.
- Part 2, the Specification, provides the requirements for a Business Continuity Management System (BCMS) based on BCM best practice. This is the part of the standard that you can use to demonstrate compliance via an auditing and certification process."[5]

BS-25999-2 has been replaced with ISO 22301:2012 Societal security—Business continuity management systems—Requirements. "ISO 22301 will supersede the original British standard, BS 25999-2 and builds on the success and fundamentals of this standard. BS ISO 22301 specifies the requirements for setting up and managing an effective BCMS for any organization, regardless of type or size. BSI recommends that every business has a system in place to avoid excessive downtime and reduced productivity in the event of an interruption."[6]

BCI

The Business Continuity Institute (BCI, http://www.thebci.org/) published a six-step Good Practice Guidelines (GPG), most recently updated in 2013: "The Good Practice Guidelines (GPG) are the independent body of knowledge for good Business Continuity practice worldwide. They represent current global thinking in good Business

Continuity (BC) practice and now include terminology from ISO 22301:2012, the International Standard for Business Continuity management systems."[7]

FAST FACTS

GPG 2013 describes six Professional Practices (PP).

- Management Practices
  - PP1 Policy and Program Management
  - PP2 Embedding Business Continuity
- Technical Practices
  - PP3 Analysis
  - PP4 Design
  - PP5 Implementation
  - PP6 Validation[8]

SUMMARY OF EXAM OBJECTIVES

In this chapter, we have discussed operational security. Operations security concerns the security of systems and data while being actively used in a production environment. Ultimately, operations security is about people, data, media, and hardware, all of which are elements that need to be considered from a security perspective. The best technical security infrastructure in the world will be rendered moot if an individual with privileged access decides to turn against the organization and there are no preventive or detective controls in place within the organization.

We also discussed Business Continuity and Disaster Recovery Planning, which serve as an organization's last control to prevent failure. Of all controls, a failed BCP or DRP can be most devastating, potentially resulting in organizational failure, injury, or loss of life.

TOP FIVE TOUGHEST QUESTIONS

1. Which plan details the steps required to restore normal business operations after recovering from a disruptive event?
   A. Business Continuity Plan (BCP)
   B. Business Resumption Plan (BRP)
   C. Continuity of Operations Plan (COOP)
   D. Occupant Emergency Plan (OEP)
2. What metric describes how long it will take to recover a failed system?
   A. Minimum Operating Requirements (MOR)
   B. Mean Time Between Failures (MTBF)
   C. The Mean Time to Repair (MTTR)
   D. Recovery Point Objective (RPO)

3. What metric describes the moment in time in which data must be recovered and made available to users in order to resume business operations?
   A. Mean Time Between Failures (MTBF)
   B. The Mean Time to Repair (MTTR)
   C. Recovery Point Objective (RPO)
   D. Recovery Time Objective (RTO)
4. Maximum Tolerable Downtime (MTD) is comprised of which two metrics?
   A. Recovery Point Objective (RPO) and Work Recovery Time (WRT)
   B. Recovery Point Objective (RPO) and Mean Time to Repair (MTTR)
   C. Recovery Time Objective (RTO) and Work Recovery Time (WRT)
   D. Recovery Time Objective (RTO) and Mean Time to Repair (MTTR)
5. Which level of RAID does NOT provide additional reliability?
   A. RAID 1
   B. RAID 5
   C. RAID 0
   D. RAID 3

ANSWERS

1. Correct answer and explanation: B. Business Resumption Planning details the steps required to restore normal business operations after a recovering from a disruptive event.
   Incorrect answers and explanations: Answers A, C, and D are incorrect. Business Continuity Planning develops a long-term plan to ensure the continuity of business operations. The Continuity of Operations Plan describes the procedures required to maintain operations during a disaster. The Occupant Emergency Plan provides the response procedures for occupants of a facility in the event a situation poses a threat to the health and safety of personnel, the environment, or property.
2. Correct answer and explanation: C. The Mean Time to Repair (MTTR) describes how long it will take to recover a failed system. It is the best estimate for reconstituting the IT system so that business continuity may occur.
   Incorrect answers and explanations: A, B, and D. Answers A, B, and D are incorrect. Minimum Operating Requirements describe the minimum environmental and connectivity requirements in order to operate computer equipment. Mean Time Between Failures quantifies how long a new or repaired system will run before failing. The Recovery Point Objective (RPO) is the moment in time in which data must be recovered and made available to users in order to resume business operations.
3. Correct Answer and Explanation: C. The Recovery Point Objective (RPO) is the moment in time in which data must be recovered and made available to users in order to resume business operations.

Incorrect answers and explanations: Answers A, B, and D are incorrect. Mean Time Between Failures quantifies how long a new or repaired system will run before failing. Mean Time to Repair describes how long it will take to recover a failed system. Recovery Time Objective describes the maximum time allowed to recover business or IT systems.

4. Correct answer and explanation: C. The Recovery Time Objective (RTO, the time it takes bring a failed system back online) and Work Recovery Time (WRT, the time required to configure a failed system) are used to calculate the Maximum Tolerable Downtime. $RTO + WRT = MTD$.
   Incorrect answers and explanations: Answers A, B, and D are incorrect. Maximum Tolerable Downtime does not directly use Recovery Point Objective or Mean Time to Repair as metrics.

5. Correct answer and explanation: C. RAID 0 provides only striping and is used simply for performance purposes. It offers no additional data redundancy or resiliency.
   Incorrect answers and explanations: Answers A, B, and D are incorrect. RAIDs 1, 3, and 5 all provide reliability gains through either mirroring or parity measures.

ENDNOTES

1. *NIST special publication 800–61: computer security incident handling guide.* http://nvlpubs.nist.gov/nistpubs/SpecialPublications/NIST.SP.800-61r2.pdf [accessed 26.04.16].
2. Swanson M, Wohl A, Pope L, Grance T, Hash J, Thomas R. *NIST SP 800-34 contingency planning guide for information technology systems.* https://www.fismacenter.com/sp800-34.pdf [accessed 26.04.16].
3. *Understanding security risk management: recovery time requirements.* http://searchsecuritychannel.techtarget.com/generic/0,295582,sid97_gci1268749,00.html [accessed 26.04.16].
4. *ISO/IEC 27031:2011 Information technology—security techniques—guidelines for information and communications technology readiness for business continuity.* http://www.iso27001security.com/html/27031.html [accessed 26.04.16].
5. *ISO 22301 business continuity standard in IT.* http://eradar.eu/business-continuity/ [accessed 26.04.16].
6. *Moving from BS 25999-2 to ISO 22301.* http://www.bsigroup.com/Documents/iso-22301/resources/BSI-BS25999-to-ISO22301-Transition-UK-EN.pdf [accessed 26.04.16].
7. *The good practice guidelines.* http://www.thebci.org/index.php/resources/the-good-practice-guidelines [accessed 26.04.16].
8. *Good practice guidelines 2013 global edition.* http://www.thebci.org/index.php/the-gpg-lite [accessed 26.04.16].

Domain 8: Software development security

8

CHAPTER OUTLINE

Eleventh Hour CISSP®. http://dx.doi.org/10.1016/B978-0-12-811248-9.00008-5

INTRODUCTION

Software is everywhere. It is not only in our computers but also in our houses, our cars, and our medical devices. The problem is that all software programmers make mistakes. As software has grown in complexity, the number of mistakes has grown along with it, and the potential impact of a software crash has also grown. Many cars are now connected to the Internet and use "fly-by-wire" systems to control the vehicle. In those cases, the gearshift is no longer directly mechanically connected to the transmission; instead, it serves as an electronic input device, like a keyboard. What if a software crash interrupts I/O? What if someone remotely hacks into the car and takes control of it, as demonstrated by Charlie Miller and Chris Valasek?[1]

Developing software that is robust and secure is critical, and this chapter will show how to do that. We will cover programming fundamentals such as compiled versus interpreted languages, as well as procedural and object-oriented programming (OOP) languages. We will discuss application development models such as the *waterfall model*, *spiral model*, and *extreme programming* (XP), among others. We will also discuss newer concepts such as *DevOps*, added in the 2015 exam update. We will describe common software vulnerabilities, ways to test for them, and maturity frameworks that can be used to assess the maturity of the programming process and provide ways to improve it.

PROGRAMMING CONCEPTS

Let us begin by understanding some cornerstone programming concepts. As computers have become more powerful and ubiquitous, the process and methods used to create computer software has grown and changed.

MACHINE CODE, SOURCE CODE, AND ASSEMBLERS

Machine code, also called machine language, is software that is executed directly by the central processing unit (CPU). Machine code is CPU dependent; it is a series of 1s and 0s that translate to instructions that are understood by the CPU. *Source code* is computer programming language instructions that are written in text that must be translated into machine code before execution by the CPU. High-level languages contain English-like instructions such as "printf" (print formatted).

Assembly language is a low-level computer programming language. Assembly language instructions are short mnemonics, such as "ADD," "SUB" (subtract), and "JMP" (jump), that match to machine language instructions. An assembler converts assembly language into machine language. A *disassembler* attempts to convert machine language into assembly.

COMPILERS, INTERPRETERS, AND BYTECODE

Compilers take source code, such as C or Basic, and compile it into machine code. *Interpreted languages* differ from compiled languages; for example, interpreted code, such as shell code, is compiled on the fly each time the program is run. *Bytecode*, such as Java bytecode, is also interpreted code. Bytecode exists as an intermediary form that is converted from source code, but still must be converted into machine code before it can run on the CPU. Java Bytecode is platform-independent code that is converted into machine code by the Java virtual machine.

COMPUTER-AIDED SOFTWARE ENGINEERING

Computer-aided software engineering (CASE) uses programs to assist in the creation and maintenance of other computer programs. Programming has historically been performed by (human) programmers or teams, and CASE adds software to the programming "team."

There are three types of CASE software:

1. "Tools: support only specific task in the software-production process.
2. Workbenches: support one or a few software process activities by integrating several tools in a single application.
3. Environments: support all or at least part of the software-production process with a collection of Tools and Workbenches."[2]

Fourth-generation computer languages, object-oriented languages, and GUIs are often used as components of CASE.

TYPES OF PUBLICLY RELEASED SOFTWARE

Once programmed, publicly released software may come in different forms, such as with or without the accompanying source code, and released under a variety of licenses.

Open-source and closed-source software

Closed-source software is software that is typically released in executable form, though the source code is kept confidential. Examples include Oracle and Microsoft Windows 10. *Open-source* software publishes source code publicly; examples include Ubuntu Linux and the Apache web server. Proprietary software is software that is subject to intellectual property protections, such as patents or copyrights.

Free software, shareware, and crippleware

Free software is a controversial term that is defined differently by different groups. "Free" may mean it is free of charge (sometimes called "free as in beer"), or "free" may mean the user is free to use the software in any way they would like, including modifying it (sometimes called "free as in liberty"). The two types are called gratis and libre, respectively.

Freeware is "free as in beer" (gratis) software, which is free of charge to use. *Shareware* is fully functional proprietary software that may be initially used free of charge. If the user continues to use the Shareware for a specific period of time specified by the license, such as 30 days, the Shareware license typically requires payment. *Crippleware* is partially functioning proprietary software, often with key features disabled. The user is typically required to make a payment to unlock the full functionality.

APPLICATION DEVELOPMENT METHODS

As software has grown in complexity, software programming has increasingly become a team effort. Team-based projects require project management, including providing a project framework with deliverables and milestones; divvying up tasks; team communication; progress evaluation and reporting; and, hopefully, a final delivered product.

WATERFALL MODEL

The *waterfall model* is a linear application development model that uses rigid phases; when one phase ends, the next begins. Steps occur in sequence, and the unmodified waterfall model does not allow developers to go back to previous steps. It is called the waterfall because it simulates water falling; once water falls, it cannot go back up. A modified waterfall model allows a return to a previous phase for verification or validation, ideally confined to connecting steps.

SASHIMI MODEL

The *sashimi model* has highly overlapping steps; it can be thought of as a real-world successor to the waterfall model and is sometimes called the sashimi waterfall model. It is named after the Japanese delicacy sashimi, which has overlapping layers of fish (and also a hint for the exam). The model is based on the hardware design model used by Fuji-Xerox: "Business scholars and practitioners were asking such questions as 'What are the key factors to the Japanese manufacturers' remarkable successes?' and 'What are the sources of their competitive advantage?' The sashimi system seems to give answers to these questions."[3]

Peter DeGrace described the sashimi model in relation to software development in his book *Wicked problems, righteous solutions: A catalog of modern software*. Sashimi's steps are similar to those of the waterfall model in that the difference is the explicit overlapping, shown in Fig. 8.1.

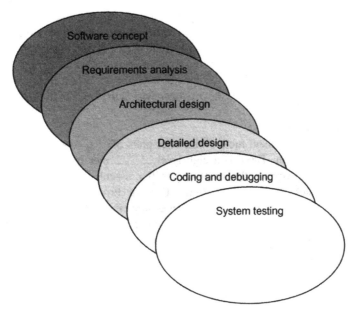

FIG. 8.1

The Sashimi model.[4]

AGILE SOFTWARE DEVELOPMENT

Agile software development evolved as a reaction to rigid software development models such as the waterfall model. Agile methods include *scrum* and XP. The Agile Manifesto (http://agilemanifesto.org/) states:

"We are uncovering better ways of developing software by doing it and helping others do it. Through this work we have come to value:

- Individuals and interactions over processes and tools
- Working software over comprehensive documentation
- Customer collaboration over contract negotiation
- Responding to change over following a plan"[5]

Agile embodies many modern development concepts, including more flexibility, fast turnaround with smaller milestones, strong communication within the team, and more customer involvement.

Scrum

The Scrum development model (named after a scrum in the sport of rugby) is an Agile model first described in *The New New Product Development Game* by Hirotaka Takeuchi and Ikujiro Nonaka. In relation to product development, they said, "Stop running the relay race and take up rugby."[6] The "relay race" is the waterfall, where teams hand work off to other teams as steps are completed. Takeuchi and Nonaka suggested,

"Instead, a holistic or 'rugby' approach—where a team tries to go the distance as a unit, passing the ball back and forth—may better serve today's competitive requirements."[6]

Peter DeGrace (of sashimi fame) described and named Scrum in relation to software development. Scrums contain small teams of developers, called the *Scrum Team*. The *Scrum Master*, a senior member of the organization who acts like a coach for the team, supports the Scrum Team. Finally, the *product owner* is the voice of the business unit.

Extreme programming

XP is an Agile development method that uses pairs of programmers who work off a detailed specification. There is a high level of customer involvement. "Extreme Programming improves a software project in five essential ways; communication, simplicity, feedback, respect, and courage. Extreme Programmers constantly communicate with their customers and fellow programmers. They keep their design simple and clean. They get feedback by testing their software starting on day one. They deliver the system to the customers as early as possible and implement changes as suggested."[7]. XP core practices include:

- Planning: specifies the desired features, which are called the user stories. They are used to determine the iteration (timeline) and drive the detailed specifications.
- Paired programming: programmers work in teams.
- Forty-hour workweek: the forecasted iterations should be accurate enough to forecast how many hours will be required to complete the project. If programmers must put in additional overtime, the iteration must be flawed.
- Total customer involvement: the customer is always available and carefully monitors the project.
- Detailed test procedures: these are called unit tests.[7]

SPIRAL

The spiral model is a software development model designed to control risk. The spiral model repeats steps of a project, starting with modest goals, and expanding outwards in ever-wider spirals called rounds. Each round of the spiral constitutes a project, and each round may follow a traditional software development methodology, such as modified waterfall. A risk analysis is performed each round. Fundamental flaws in the project or process are more likely to be discovered in the earlier phases, resulting in simpler fixes. This lowers the overall risk of the project; large risks should be identified and mitigated.

RAPID APPLICATION DEVELOPMENT

Rapid application development (RAD) rapidly develops software via the use of prototypes, "dummy" GUIs, back-end databases, and more. The goal of RAD is quickly meeting the business need of the system, while technical concerns are secondary. The customer is heavily involved in the process.

SDLC

The *systems development life cycle* (*SDLC*, also called the *software development life cycle* or simply the *system life cycle*) is a system development model. SDLC is used across the IT industry, but SDLC focuses on security when used in context of the exam. Think of "our" SDLC as the *secure* systems development life cycle; the security is implied.

FAST FACTS

The following overview is summarized from NIST SP 800-14:

- *Prepare a security plan*: Ensure that security is considered during all phases of the IT system life cycle and that security activities are accomplished during each of the phases.
- *Initiation*: The need for a system is expressed and the purpose of the system is documented.
  - *Conduct a sensitivity assessment*: Look at the security sensitivity of the system and the information to be processed.
- *Development/acquisition*: The system is designed, purchased, programmed, or developed.
  - *Determine security requirements*: Determine technical features, like access controls; assurances, like background checks for system developers; or operational practices, like awareness and training.
  - *Incorporate security requirements in specifications*: Ensure that the previously gathered information is incorporated in the project plan.
  - *Obtain the system and related security activities*: May include developing the system's security features, monitoring the development process itself for security problems, responding to changes, and monitoring threats.
- *Implementation*: The system is tested and installed.
  - *Install/turn-on controls*: A system often comes with security features disabled. These need to be enabled and configured.
  - *Security testing*: Used to certify a system; may include testing security management, physical facilities, personnel, procedures, the use of commercial or in-house services such as networking services, and contingency planning.
  - *Accreditation*: The formal authorization by the accrediting (management) official for system operation and an explicit acceptance of risk.
- *Operation/maintenance*: The system is modified by the addition of hardware and software and by other events.
  - *Security operations and administration*: Examples include backups, training, managing cryptographic keys, user administration, and patching.
  - *Operational assurance*: Examines whether a system is operated according to its current security requirements.
  - *Audits and monitoring*: A system audit is a one-time or periodic event to evaluate security. Monitoring refers to an ongoing activity that examines either the system or the users.
- *Disposal*: The secure decommission of a system.
  - *Information*: Information may be moved to another system, or it could also be archived, discarded, or destroyed.
  - *Media sanitization*: There are three general methods of purging media: overwriting, degaussing (for magnetic media only), and destruction.[8]

INTEGRATED PRODUCT TEAMS

An integrated product team (IPT) is a customer-focused group that focuses on the entire lifecycle of a project:

> *An Integrated Product Team (IPT) is a multidisciplinary group of people who are collectively responsible for delivering a defined product or process. The IPT is composed of people who plan, execute, and implement life cycle decisions for the system being acquired. It includes empowered representatives (stakeholders) from all of the functional areas involved with the product—all who have a stake in the success of the program, such as design, manufacturing, test and evaluation (T&E), and logistics personnel, and, especially, the customer.*[9]

IPTs are more agile methods than traditional hierarchical teams; they "…move away from a pattern of hierarchical decision-making to a process where decisions are made across organizational structures by integrated product teams. It means we are breaking down institutional barriers. It also means that our senior acquisition staffs are in a receive mode—not just a transmit mode. The objective is to be receptive to ideas from the field to obtain buy-in and lasting change."[10]

SOFTWARE ESCROW

Software escrow describes the process of having a third-party store an archive of computer software. This is often negotiated as part of a contract with a proprietary software vendor. The vendor may wish to keep the software source code secret, but the customer may be concerned that the vendor could go out of business and potentially orphan the software. Orphaned software with no available source code will not receive future improvements or patches.

CODE REPOSITORY SECURITY

The security of private/internal code repositories largely falls under other corporate security controls discussed previously: defense in depth, secure authentication, firewalls, version control, etc.

Public code third-party repositories such as GitHub (http://www.github.com) raise additional security concerns. They provide the following list of security controls:

- System security
- Operational security
- Software security
- Secure communications
- File system and backups
- Employee access
- Maintaining security
- Credit card safety[11]

SECURITY OF APPLICATION PROGRAMMING INTERFACES

An application programming interface (API) allows an application to communicate with another application or an operating system, database, network, etc. For example, the Google Maps API allows an application to integrate third-party content, such as restaurants overlaid on a Google Map.

FAST FACTS

The OWASP enterprise security API toolkits project includes these critical API controls:

- Authentication
- Access control
- Input validation
- Output encoding/escaping
- Cryptography
- Error handling and logging
- Communication security
- HTTP security
- Security configuration[12]

SOFTWARE CHANGE AND CONFIGURATION MANAGEMENT

Software change and configuration management provide a framework for managing changes to software as it is developed, maintained, and eventually retired. Some organizations treat this as one discipline; the exam treats configuration management and change management as separate but related disciplines.

In regard to the Software Development Security domain, configuration management tracks changes to a specific piece of software; for example, tracking changes to a content management system, including specific settings within the software. Change management is broader in that it tracks changes across an entire software development program. In both cases, both configuration and change management are designed to ensure that changes occur in an orderly fashion and do not harm information security; ideally, it would be improved.

DEVOPS

Traditional software development was performed with strict separation of duties between the developers, quality assurance teams, and production teams. Developers had hardware that mirrored production models and test data. They would hand code off to the quality assurance teams, who also had hardware that mirrored production models, as well as test data. The quality assurance teams would then hand tested code over to production, who had production hardware and real data.

In the old, less model, developers had no direct contact with production and in fact were strictly walled off from production via separation of duties.

DevOps is a more agile development and support model, echoing the Agile programming methods we learned about previously in this chapter, including Sashimi and Scrum. DevOps is "the practice of operations and development engineers participating together in the entire service lifecycle, from design through the development process to production support."[13]

DATABASES

A *database* is a structured collection of related data. Databases allow queries (searches), insertions (updates), deletions, and many other functions. The database is managed by the *database management system* (DBMS), which controls all access to the database and enforces the database security. Databases are managed by *database administrators*. Databases may be searched with a database *query language*, such as the *structured query language* (SQL). Typical database security issues include the confidentiality and integrity of the stored data. Integrity is a primary concern when replicated databases are updated.

RELATIONAL DATABASES

The most common modern database is the *relational database*, which contain two-dimensional *tables*, or relations, of related data. Tables have rows and columns; a row is a database record, called a *tuple*, and a column is called an *attribute*. A single cell (ie, intersection of a row and column) in a database is called a value. Relational databases require a unique value called the *primary key* in each tuple in a table. Table 8.1 shows a relational database employee table, sorted by the primary key, which is the social security number (SSN).

Table 8.1 attributes are SSN, name, and title. Tuples include each row: 133-73-1337, 343-53-4334, etc. "Gaff" is an example of a value (cell). *Candidate keys* are any attribute (column) in the table with unique values; candidate keys in the previous table include SSN and name. SSN was selected as the primary key because it is truly unique; two employees might have the same name, but not the same SSN. The primary key may join two tables in a relational database.

Table 8.1 Relational Database Employee Table

SSN	Name	Title
133-73-1337	J.F. Sebastian	Designer
343-53-4334	Eldon Tyrell	Doctor
425-22-8422	Gaff	Detective
737-54-2268	Rick Deckard	Detective
990-69-4771	Hannibal Chew	Engineer

Table 8.2 HR Database Table

SSN	Vacation Time	Sick Time
133-73-1337	15 days	20 days
343-53-4334	60 days	90 days
425-22-8422	10 days	15 days
737-54-2268	3 days	1 day
990-69-4771	15 days	5 days

Foreign keys

A *foreign key* is a key in a related database table that matches a primary key in a parent database table. Note that the foreign key is the local table's primary key; it is called the foreign key when referring to a parent table. Table 8.2 is the HR database table that lists employee's vacation time (in days) and sick time (also in days); it has a foreign key of SSN. The HR database table may be joined to the parent (employee) database table by connecting the foreign key of the HR table to the primary key of the employee table.

Referential, semantic, and entity integrity

Databases must ensure the integrity of the data in the tables; this is called data integrity, discussed in the "Database Integrity" section below. There are three additional specific integrity issues that must be addressed beyond the correctness of the data itself: referential, semantic, and entity integrity. These are tied closely to the logical operations of the DBMS.

CRUNCH TIME

Referential integrity means that every foreign key in a secondary table matches a primary key in the parent table; if this is not true, referential integrity has been broken. *Semantic integrity* means that each attribute (column) value is consistent with the attribute data type. *Entity integrity* means each tuple has a unique primary key that is not null.

The HR database table shown in Table 8.2, seen previously, has referential, semantic, and entity integrity. Table 8.3, on the other hand, has multiple problems: one tuple violates referential integrity, another tuple violates semantic integrity, and the last two tuples violate entity integrity.

Table 8.3 Database Table Lacking Integrity

SSN	Vacation Time	Sick Time
467-51-9732	7 days	14 days
737-54-2268	3 days	Nexus 6
133-73-1337	16 days	22 days
133-73-1337	15 days	20 days

The tuple with the foreign key 467-51-9732 has no matching entry in the employee database table. This breaks referential integrity, as there is no way to link this entry to a name or title. Cell "Nexus 6" violates semantic integrity; the sick time attribute requires values of days, and "Nexus 6" is not a valid amount of sick days. Finally, the last two tuples both have the same primary key; this breaks entity integrity.

DATABASE NORMALIZATION

Database *normalization* seeks to make the data in a database table logically concise, organized, and consistent. Normalization removes redundant data and improves the integrity and availability of the database.

DATABASE VIEWS

Database tables may be queried; the results of a query are called a *database view*. Views may be used to provide a *constrained user interface*; for example, nonmanagement employees can be shown their individual records only via database views. Table 8.4 shows the database view resulting from querying the employee table "Title" attribute with a string of "Detective." While employees of the HR department may be able to view the entire employee table, this view may be authorized for the captain of the detectives, for example.

DATABASE QUERY LANGUAGES

Database query languages allow the creation of database tables, read/write access to those tables, and many other functions. Database query languages have at least two subsets of commands: *data definition language* (DDL) and *data manipulation language* (DML). DDL is used to create, modify, and delete tables, while DML is used to query and update data stored in the tables.

HIERARCHICAL DATABASES

Hierarchical databases form a tree: the global domain name service (DNS) servers form a global tree. The root name servers are at the "root zone" at the base of the tree, while individual DNS entries form the leaves. The DNS name www.syngress. com points to the syngress.com DNS database, which is part of the dot com (.com)

Table 8.4 Employee Table Database View "Detective"

SSN	Name	Titie
425-22-8422	Gaff	Detective
737-54-2268	Rick Deckard	Detective

top level domain (TLD), which is part of the global DNS (root zone). From the root, you may go back down another branch, to the dot gov (.gov) TLD, to the nist.gov (National Institute of Standards and Technologies) domain, to www.nist.gov.

OBJECT-ORIENTED DATABASES

While databases traditionally contain passive data, object-oriented databases combine data with functions (code) in an object-oriented framework. OOP is used to manipulate the objects and their data, which is managed by an object database management system.

DATABASE INTEGRITY

In addition to the previously discussed relational database integrity issues of semantic, referential, and entity integrity, databases must also ensure data integrity; that is, the integrity of the entries in the database tables. This treats integrity as a more general issue by mitigating unauthorized modifications of data. The primary challenge associated with data integrity within a database is simultaneous attempted modifications of data. A database server typically runs multiple threads (ie, lightweight processes), each capable of altering data. What happens if two threads attempt to alter the same record?

DBMSs may attempt to *commit* updates, which will make the pending changes permanent. If the commit is unsuccessful, the DBMSs can *rollback* (also called abort) and restore from a *savepoint* (clean snapshot of the database tables).

A *database journal* is a log of all database transactions. Should a database become corrupted, the database can be reverted to a back-up copy and then subsequent transactions can be "replayed" from the journal, restoring database integrity.

DATABASE REPLICATION AND SHADOWING

Databases may be highly available, replicated with multiple servers containing multiple copies of tables. Integrity is the primary concern with replicated databases.

Database replication mirrors a live database, allowing simultaneous reads and writes to multiple replicated databases by clients. Replicated databases pose additional integrity challenges. A two-phase (or multiphase) commit can be used to assure integrity.

A *shadow database* is similar to a replicated database with one key difference: a shadow database mirrors all changes made to a primary database, but clients do not access the shadow. Unlike replicated databases, the shadow database is one way.

DATA WAREHOUSING AND DATA MINING

As the name implies, a *data warehouse* is a large collection of data. Modern data warehouses may store many terabytes (1024 gigabytes) or even petabytes (1024 terabytes) of data. This requires large, scalable storage solutions. The storage must be of a high performance level and allow analysis and searches of the data.

Once data is collected in a warehouse, *data mining* is used to search for patterns. Commonly sought patterns include signs of fraud. Credit card companies manage some of the world's largest data warehouses, tracking billions of transactions per year. Fraudulent transactions are a primary concern of credit card companies that lead to millions of dollars in lost revenue. No human could possibly monitor all of those transactions, so the credit card companies use data mining to separate the signal from noise. A common data mining fraud rule monitors multiple purchases on one card in different states or countries in a short period of time. A violation record can be produced when this occurs, leading to suspension of the card or a phone call to the card owner's home.

OBJECT-ORIENTED PROGRAMMING

OOP uses an object metaphor to design and write computer programs. An object is a "black box" that is able to perform functions, like sending and receiving messages. Objects contain data and *methods* (the functions they perform). The object provides *encapsulation* (also called *data hiding*), which means that we do not know, from the outside, how the object performs its function. This provides security benefits, so users should not be exposed to unnecessary details.

CORNERSTONE OBJECT-ORIENTED PROGRAMMING CONCEPTS

Cornerstone OOP concepts include objects, methods, messages, inheritance, delegation, polymorphism, and polyinstantiation. We will use an example object called "Addy" to illustrate the cornerstone concepts. Addy is an object that adds two integers; it is an extremely simple object but has enough complexity to explain core OOP concepts. Addy *inherits* an understanding of numbers and math from his *parent class*, which is called mathematical operators. A specific object is called an *instance*. Note that objects may inherit from other objects, in addition to classes.

In our case, the programmer simply needs to program Addy to support the method of addition (inheritance takes care of everything else Addy must know). Fig. 8.2 shows Addy adding two numbers.

$1+2$ is the input message and 3 is the output message. Addy also supports delegation; if he does not know how to perform a requested function, he can delegate that request to another object (ie, "Subby" in Fig. 8.3).

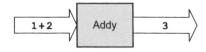

FIG. 8.2

The "Addy" object.

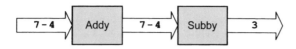

FIG. 8.3

Delegation.

Addy also supports polymorphism, a word (based on the Greek roots "poly" and "morph," meaning many and forms, respectively). Addy has the ability to overload his plus (+) operator, performing different methods depending on the context of the input message. For example, Addy adds when the input message contains "number+number"; polymorphism allows Addy to concatenate two strings when the input message contains "string+string," as shown in Fig. 8.4.

Finally, polyinstantiation means "many instances," such as two instances or specific objects with the same names that contain different data. This may be used in multilevel secure environments to keep top-secret and secret data separate, for example. (See Domain 3: Security Engineering for more information about polyinstantiation.) Fig. 8.5 shows two polyinstantiated Addy objects with the same name but different data; note that these are two separate objects. Also, to a secret-cleared subject, the Addy object with secret data is the only known Addy object.

FIG. 8.4

Polymorphism.

FAST FACTS

Here is a summary of OOP concepts illustrated by Addy:

- Object: Addy
- Class: Mathematical operators
- Method: Addition
- Inheritance: Addy inherits an understanding of numbers and math from his parent class mathematical operators. The programmer simply needs to program Addy to support the method of addition
- Example input message: 1+2
- Example output message: 3
- Polymorphism: Addy can change behavior based on the context of the input, overloading the + to perform addition, or concatenation, depending on the context
- Polyinstantiation: Two Addy objects (secret and top-secret), with different data

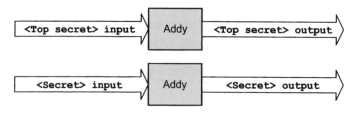

FIG. 8.5

Polyinstantiation.

OBJECT REQUEST BROKERS

As we have seen previously, mature objects are designed to be reused, as they lower risk and development costs. *Object request brokers* (ORBs) can be used to locate objects because they act as object search engines. ORBs are *middleware*, which connects programs to programs. Common object brokers included COM, DCOM, and CORBA.

ASSESSING THE EFFECTIVENESS OF SOFTWARE SECURITY

Once the project is underway and software has been programmed, the next steps include testing the software, focusing on the confidentiality, integrity, and availability of the system, as well as the application and the data processed by the application. Special care must be given to the discovery of software vulnerabilities that could lead to data or system compromise. Finally, organizations need to be able to gauge the effectiveness of their software creation process and identify ways to improve it.

SOFTWARE VULNERABILITIES

Programmers make mistakes; this has been true since the advent of computer programming. The number of average defects per line of software code can often be reduced, though not eliminated, by implementing mature software development practices.

Types of software vulnerabilities

This section will briefly describe common application vulnerabilities. An additional source of up-to-date vulnerabilities can be found in the list "CWE/SANS Top 25 Most Dangerous Programming Errors," available at http://cwe.mitre.org/top25/; the following summary is based on this list. CWE refers to Common Weakness Enumeration, a dictionary of software vulnerabilities by MITRE (see http://cwe.mitre.org/). SANS is the SANS Institute; see http://www.sans.org.

- Hard-coded credentials: Backdoor username/passwords left by programmers in production code
- Buffer overflow: Occurs when a programmer does not perform variable bounds checking
- SQL injection: manipulation of a back-end SQL server via a front-end web server
- *Directory Path Traversal*: escaping from the root of a web server (such as/var/ www) into the regular file system by referencing directories such as "../.."
- PHP *Remote File Inclusion* (RFI): altering normal PHP URLs and variables such as "http://good.example.com?file=readme.txt" to include and execute remote content, such as http://good.example.com?file=http://evil.example.com/bad.php[14]

Buffer overflows
Buffer overflows can occur when a programmer fails to perform bounds checking. This technique can be used to insert and run shellcode (machine code language that executes a shell, such as Microsoft Windows cmd.exe or a UNIX/Linux shell).

Buffer overflows are mitigated by secure application development, including bounds checking.

TOC/TOU race conditions
Time of check/Time of use (TOC/TOU) attacks are also called *race conditions*. This means that an attacker attempts to alter a condition after it has been checked by the operating system, but before it is used. TOC/TOU is an example of a state attack, where the attacker capitalizes on a change in operating system state.

Cross-site scripting and cross-site request forgery
Cross-site scripting (XSS) leverages the third-party execution of web scripting languages such as JavaScript within the security context of a trusted site. Cross-site request forgery (CSRF, or sometimes XSRF) leverages a third-party redirect of static content within the security context of a trusted site. XSS and CSRF are often confused because they both are web attacks; the difference is XSS executes a script in a trusted context:

```
<script>alert("XSS Test!");</script>
```

The previous code would pop up a harmless "XSS Test!" alert. A real attack would include more JavaScript, often stealing cookies or authentication credentials.

CSRF often tricks a user into processing a URL, sometimes by embedding the URL in an HTML image tag, that performs a malicious act; for example, tricking a white hat into rendering the following image tag:

```
<img  src="https://bank.example.com/transfer-money?from=WHITEHAT&
to=BLACKHAT">
```

Privilege escalation
Privilege escalation vulnerabilities allow an attacker with typically limited access to be able to access additional resources. Improper software configurations and poor coding and testing practices often lead to privilege escalation vulnerabilities.

Backdoors

Backdoors are shortcuts in a system that allow a user to bypass security checks, such as username/password authentication. Attackers will often install a backdoor after compromising a system.

DISCLOSURE

Disclosure describes the actions taken by a security researcher after discovering a software vulnerability. *Full disclosure* is the controversial practice of releasing vulnerability details publicly. *Responsible disclosure* is the practice of privately sharing vulnerability information with a vendor and withholding public release until a patch is available.

SOFTWARE CAPABILITY MATURITY MODEL

The Software *Capability Maturity Model* (CMM) is a maturity framework for evaluating and improving the software development process. Carnegie Mellon University's (CMU) Software Engineering Institute (SEI) developed the model. It is now managed by the CMMI Institute, "a 100%-controlled subsidiary of Carnegie Innovations, Carnegie Mellon University's technology commercialization enterprise."[15] The goal of CMM is to develop a methodical framework for creating quality software that allows measurable and repeatable results.

FAST FACTS

The five levels of CMM are described in (see: http://www.sei.cmu.edu/reports/93tr024.pdf):

1. *Initial*: The software process is characterized as ad hoc and occasionally even chaotic. Few processes are defined, and success depends on individual effort.
2. *Repeatable*: Basic project management processes are established to track cost, schedule, and functionality. The necessary process discipline is in place to repeat earlier successes on projects with similar applications.
3. *Defined*: The software process for both management and engineering activities is documented, standardized, and integrated into a standard software process for the organization. Projects use an approved, tailored version of the organization's standard software process for developing and maintaining software.
4. *Managed*: Detailed measures of the software process and product quality are collected, analyzed, and used to control the process. Both the software process and products are quantitatively understood and controlled.
5. *Optimizing*: Continual process improvement is enabled by quantitative feedback from the process and from piloting innovative ideas and technologies.[15]

ACCEPTANCE TESTING

Acceptance testing examines whether software meets various end-state requirements, whether from a user or customer, contract, or compliance perspective. The International Software Testing Qualifications Board (ISTQB) defines acceptance testing as "a formal testing with respect to user needs, requirements, and business processes conducted to determine whether or not a system satisfies the acceptance criteria and to enable the user, customers or other authorized entity to determine whether or not to accept the system."[16]

FAST FACTS

The ISTQB also lists four levels of acceptance testing:

- "The User Acceptance test: focuses mainly on the functionality, thereby validating the fitness-for-use of the system by the business user. The user acceptance test is performed by the users and application managers.
- The Operational Acceptance test: also known as Production Acceptance test validates whether the system meets the requirements for operation. In most of the organization, the operational acceptance test is performed by the system administration before the system is released. The operational acceptance test may include testing of backup/restore, disaster recovery, maintenance tasks, and periodic check of security vulnerabilities.
- Contract Acceptance testing: performed against the contract's acceptance criteria for producing custom-developed software. Acceptance should be formally defined when the contract is agreed.
- Compliance acceptance testing: also known as regulation acceptance testing, which is performed against the regulations that must be followed, such as governmental, legal, or safety regulations."[17]

COMMERCIAL OFF-THE-SHELF SOFTWARE

Vendor claims are more readily verifiable for Commercial Off-the-Shelf (COTS) Software. When considering purchasing COTS, perform a bake-off to compare products that already meet requirements. Don't rely on product roadmaps to become reality. A particularly important security requirement is to look for integration with existing infrastructure and security products. While best-of-breed point products might be the organization's general preference, recognize that an additional administrative console with additional user provisioning will add to the operational costs of the products; consider the TCO of the product not just the capital expense and annual maintenance costs.

CUSTOM-DEVELOPED THIRD-PARTY PRODUCTS

An alternative to COTS is to employ custom-developed applications. These custom developed third-party applications provide both additional risks and potential benefits beyond COTS. Contractual language and service-level agreements (SLA) are vital when dealing with third-party development shops. Never assume that security will be a consideration in the development of the product unless they are contractually obligated to provide security capabilities.

Basic security requirements should be discussed in advance of signing the contracts and crafting the SLAs to ensure that the vendor will be able to deliver those capabilities. Much like COTS, key questions include What happens if the vendor goes out of business? What happens if a critical feature is missing? How easy is it to find in-house or third-party support for the vendor's products?

SUMMARY OF EXAM OBJECTIVES

We live in an increasingly computerized world, and software is everywhere. The confidentiality, integrity, and availability of data processed by software are critical, as is the normal functionality (availability) of the software itself. This domain has shown how software works, and the challenges programmers face while trying to write error-free code that is able to protect data and itself in the face of attacks.

Best practices include following a formal methodology for developing software, followed by a rigorous testing regimen. We have seen that following a software development maturity model such as the CMM can dramatically lower the number of errors programmers make.

TOP FIVE TOUGHEST QUESTIONS

1. What describes a more agile development and support model, where developers directly support operations?
   A. DevOps
   B. Sashimi
   C. Spiral
   D. Waterfall
2. Two objects with the same name have different data. What OOP concept does this illustrate?
   A. Delegation
   B. Inheritance
   C. Polyinstantiation
   D. Polymorphism
3. What type of testing determines whether software meets various end-state requirements from a user or customer, contract, or compliance perspective?
   A. Acceptance testing
   B. Integration testing
   C. Regression testing
   D. Unit testing
4. A database contains an entry with an empty primary key. What database concept has been violated?
   A. Entity integrity
   B. Normalization
   C. Referential integrity
   D. Semantic integrity
5. Which vulnerability allows a third party to redirect static content within the security context of a trusted site?
   A. Cross-site request forgery (CSRF)
   B. Cross-site ccripting (XSS)
   C. PHP remote file inclusion (RFI)
   D. SQL injection

ANSWERS

1. Correct answer and explanation: A. DevOps is a more agile development and support model, where developers directly support operations.
   Incorrect answers and explanations: Answers B, C, and D are incorrect. Sashimi, spiral, and waterfall are software development methodologies that do not describe a model for developers directly supporting operations.

2. Correct answer and explanation: C. Polyinstantiation means "many instances," such as two objects with the same names that have different data.
   Incorrect answers and explanations: Answers A, B, and D are incorrect. Delegation allows objects to delegate messages to other objects. Inheritance means an object inherits capabilities from its parent class. Polymorphism allows the ability to overload operators, performing different methods depending on the context of the input message.

3. Correct answer and explanation: Answer A is correct; acceptance testing determines whether software meets various end-state requirements from a user or customer, contract, or compliance perspective.
   Incorrect answers and explanations: Answers B, C, and D are incorrect. Integration testing tests multiple software components as they are combined into a working system. Regression testing tests software after updates, modifications, or patches. Unit testing consists of low-level tests of software components, such as functions, procedures, or objects.

4. Correct answer and explanation: A. *Entity integrity* means each tuple has a unique primary key that is not null.
   Incorrect answers and explanations: Answers B, C, and D are incorrect. Normalization seeks to make the data in a database table logically concise, organized, and consistent. Referential integrity means that every foreign key in a secondary table matches a primary key in the parent table; if this is not true, referential integrity has been broken. Semantic integrity means each attribute (column) value is consistent with the attribute data type.

5. Correct answer and explanation: A. Cross-site request forgery (CSRF) allows a third party to redirect static content within the security context of a trusted site.
   Incorrect answers and explanations: Answers B, C, and D are incorrect. XSS is a third-party execution of web scripting languages, such as Javascript, within the security context of a trusted site. XSS is similar to CSRF; the difference is XSS uses active code. PHP RFI alters normal PHP variables to reference remote content, which can lead to execution of malicious PHP code. SQL injection manipulates a back-end SQL server via a front-end web server.

ENDNOTES

1. *Hackers remotely kill a jeep on the highway—with me in it.* http://www.wired.com/2015/07/hackers-remotely-kill-jeep-highway/ [accessed 25.04.16].
2. *Empirical analysis of CASE tool effects on software development effort.* http://csse.usc.edu/csse/TECHRPTS/2000/usccse2000-504/usccse2000-504.pdf [accessed 25.04.16].

3. *From Sashimi to Zen-in: the evolution of concurrent engineering at Fuji xerox.* http://www.jaist.ac.jp/ks/labs/umemoto/Fuji-Xerox.pdf [accessed 25.04.16].

4. *Software process models.* http://www.thomasalspaugh.org/pub/fnd/softwareProcess.html [accessed 25.04.16].

5. *Manifesto for Agile software development.* http://agilemanifesto.org/ [accessed 25.04.16].

6. *The new new product development game.* http://agilix.nl/resources/TheNewNewProduct DevelopmentGame.pdf [accessed 25.04.16].

7. *The rules of extreme programming.* http://www.extremeprogramming.org/rules.html [accessed 25.04.16].

8. *Generally accepted principles and practices for securing information technology systems.* http://csrc.nist.gov/publications/nistpubs/800-14/800-14.pdf [accessed 25.04.16].

9. *DoD integrated product and process development handbook.* http://www.acq.osd.mil/se/docs/DoD-IPPD-Handbook-Aug98.pdf [accessed 25.04.16].

10. *The use of integrated product teams in DOD acquisition.* http://www.navair.navy.mil/nawctsd/Resources/Library/Acqguide/teams.htm [accessed 25.04.16].

11. *GitHub Security.* https://help.github.com/articles/github-security/ [accessed 25.04.16].

12. *OWASP enterprise security API toolkits.* https://www.owasp.org/images/8/81/Esapi-datasheet.pdf [accessed 25.04.16].

13. *What is DevOps?* http://theagileadmin.com/what-is-devops/ [accessed 25.04.16].

14. *2011 CWE/SANS top 25 most dangerous software errors.* http://cwe.mitre.org/top25/ [accessed 25.04.16].

15. *Capability maturity model^{sm} for software, version 1.1.* http://www.sei.cmu.edu/reports/93tr024.pdf [accessed 25.04.16].

16. *ISTQB Glossary.* http://astqb.org/glossary/search/acceptance%20testing [accessed 25.04.16].

17. *What is acceptance testing?* http://istqbexamcertification.com/what-is-acceptance-testing/ [accessed 25.04.16].

Index

Note: Page numbers followed by *b* indicates boxes, *f* indicates figures and *t* indicates tables.

30365920R00133

Made in the USA
San Bernardino, CA
24 March 2019